Ma

This book is due for return on or before the last date shown below.

FOR MARGARET AND GERRY

Management

A Sociological Introduction

KEITH GRINT

Polity Press

First published in 1995 by Polity Press
in association with Blackwell Publishers Ltd.

2 4 6 8 10 7 5 3 1

Editorial office:
Polity Press
65 Bridge Street
Cambridge CB2 1UR, UK

Marketing and production:
Blackwell Publishers Ltd
108 Cowley Road
Oxford OX4 1JF, UK

Blackwell Publishers Inc.
238 Main Street
Cambridge, MA 02142, USA

ISBN 0–7456–1148–6
ISBN 0–7456–1149–4 (pbk)

A CIP catalogue record for this book is available from the British Library and from the Library of Congress.

Typeset in Times on 10/11½ by CentraCet Ltd, Cambridge
Printed in Great Britain by T J Press Ltd, Padstow, Cornwall

This book is printed on acid-free paper.

Contents

Acknowledgements

One version of chapter 5 first appeared in *Organization*, vol. 1, no. 1, pp. 179–202, and another, 'Utopian Management', was written with Eileen Hogan and appeared in the Templeton College Management Research Paper series. A version of chapter 4 first appeared in *Human Resource Management Journal*, vol. 3, no. 3, pp. 61–77. Chapter 8 was originally written with Steve Woolgar and one version appeared in *Science, Technology and Human Values*, vol. 20, no. 3; another version appeared in K. Grint and R. Gill (eds) (1995), *The Gender–Technology Relation* (London: Taylor and Francis).

This book was originally suggested by David Held and I would like to thank him and all his colleagues at Polity Press for their continuing support and encouragement, and Fiona Sewell for her editing skills. At Templeton College, Val Martin managed to keep the world at bay and I would like to take this opportunity to thank her. Many other people at Templeton also enabled me to write this but I would especially like to mention Chong Choi and Ian Kessler for their efforts in furthering the cause of cross-cultural research across Europe; and David Perrow, Gill Powell, Juanita Broadhurst, Judith Button, Jenny Roberts, Lyn Winkworth and Marlene Simpson for helping me track down those all too elusive references. I should also like to mention my long-suffering doctoral students: Tima Bansal, Martin Dumas, Rebekka Greminger, Mihaela Kelemen, Kate O'Donovan, Robert Padulo and Mark Stein, for helping me sort out my own thoughts on management and sociology. Beyond Templeton, I would like to thank Steve Woolgar for his help with chapter 8 and for making sense (relatively), and Marianne de Laet for her comments on the same chapter. I would also like to thank Eileen Hogan for helping with chapter 6, for bringing Utopia back in from the cold, and for personally demonstrating its value. At home Kris has manifested a spirit of perfectionism that I can learn from but not match; Beki (AKA Burnard) has confirmed my assumption that identity is seldom fixed and usually amusing; and Katy has graciously taken it easy with me at karate so that I could continue writing. Finally, I would like to thank Sandra for opening the door to literary theory, for demonstrating that it is possible to have four jobs simultaneously and, most of all, for being there.

1

Into the Heart of Darkness: A Short Theoretical Journey

> Theory is when you know everything and nothing works;
> Practice is when everything works and nobody knows why;
> Here we combine Theory with Practice:
> Nothing works and nobody knows why.
>
> (Anonymous)

Introduction

In Joseph Conrad's *Heart of Darkness*, Marlow, the narrator, tells the story of his journey up the river Congo in search of the mysterious Kurtz, an idealized figure of the company who, as Marlow approaches, takes on the appearance of increasing irrationality. When Marlow eventually reaches this European icon of morality he discovers a world of evil far darker than Marlow could ever have imagined, and Marlow is himself pushed to examine his own nature, character and morality. The story is open to many different interpretations or readings but the one I wish to pursue here is that epitomized by the contemporary rendering of Heart of Darkness, removed to South East Asia at the time of the Vietnamese War, in the film Apocalypse Now. In this film the all-American hero, or avenging angel, Captain Willard, played by Martin Sheen, once more sets out to discover the whereabouts of an errant colleague, but this time the mysterious Kurtz is transformed into a renegade American colonel, once again called Kurtz, played by Marlon Brando. Colonel Kurtz is intent on turning himself into a warlord over a drug-infested corner of Cambodia. The heroic journey to eliminate the stain on America that the Colonel represents becomes increasingly harrowing as the avenging angel perceives the irrationality and destruction wrought by his comrades in pursuit of the communist enemy, and by the time he reaches the villain it is no longer clear to him who is responsible for the death and destruction; who is rational and who is not. In one scene, amidst the destruction of a Vietnamese village held by the communists (accompanied by the sound of Wagner's 'Ride of the Valkyries' blasting from the helicopter gunship's loud-speaker system), the colonel in command arranges for one of the troops to surf along a stretch of water at the point of a river that is still subject to enemy fire. 'It's pretty hairy in there sir . . . it's Charlie's [Communist] point', shouts one of the worried troops involved. 'Charlie don't surf', comes the laconic reply from the colonel. As Willard remarks to himself, 'I began to wonder what they had against Kurtz. It wasn't just murder and insanity – there was enough of that to go round for everyone.' In short, the journey is one of self-enlightenment through travelling into the heart of darkness to the place at which the traveller recognizes that Kurtz, the fallen idol, is as much a part of his own culture as Willard is. The journey can also be read as one intent on discovering the truth 'out there' but one which has become a journey of self-recognition, where to be insane is the norm and where what counts as 'the truth' and as normality lies in the external gaze of the assessor, not the internal renderings of rationality.

The analysis of management can be read through a similar frame – it has been scripted as a journey to acquire the secret of success, to drink from the 'holy grail' of managerial truth and to achieve the desired status of manager, or even better chief executive officer (CEO). Yet the journey through the maze of management texts leads in ever decreasing circles into the clear, cold knowledge that nobody really seems to be able to deliver the magic elixir. The budding manager could probably spend several years reading the management books at the airport and still be unsure as to the meaning or method of it all. In fact, one might want to consider such action as a clear sign of Kurtzian insanity in the knowledge that management fads and fashions seem to change with the seasons and that what counts as common sense one year will undoubt-edly prove to be self-evident claptrap the following year.

At this point in the management journey it begins to dawn on our weary traveller, who has gone nowhere but read a lot, that the magic elixir is not something that can be drunk and possessed, to be rede-ployed at will on return to the office. Indeed, there may be a recognition that the journey was probably never going to lead to such a solution and our executive returns home to the office, despairing of a journey that has only persuaded him or her of something that many of us would prefer not to know: that our understanding of the world – and thus the secret of management success – is imposed from without, a socially created, regulated and legitimated practice, not one subject to the measurable objectivity of facts or of truth.

This book is intended as a guidebook to the heart of darkness which I take to be management. Management is a mysterious thing in so far as the more research that is undertaken the less we seem to be able to understand. In a version of 'progressive ignorance', borrowed from Socrates, the higher the level of immersion in the waters of management the muddier the river becomes, as contradictory reports suggest a world of inordinate complexity and change that is only (temporarily) stabilized in space and time by the words on a page or the speech in a room. *If* the world of management really is as contingent and confused as the contradictory literature that piles up on my floor suggests, then there are at least two things we can do about it: first we can resort to the resplendent and worthy motto that has served most of us well for many years: 'Ignorance is bliss'. Under this strategy we smile smugly to ourselves about the inability of academic researchers to deliver the goods, that is to show managers how to manage better, and we manage in the way we always have done (and we don't make international comparisons to avoid any discomfort). Second, an alternative, and again well-tried and tested, strategy is to rely on consultants as a better bet: 'More expensive ignorance is better bliss.' Here we spend a small fortune on self-professed 'experts' (after all, if we could assess their expertise we would not need them, would we?), and if things do not quite go to plan we change the experts for better ones (that is, more expensive ones).

In this book I want to look at management through a third approach, rooted not in expertise but in recognition of ignorance, that is our very limited ability to understand and control the world, and in recognition that the quest for bliss, perfect harmony and the solution to our problems is itself very problematic in the light of our limited knowledge: 'In the world of the blind there are no one-eyed monarchs' (or 'Scepticism rules OK') might be an appropriate motto here.

The rest of this chapter is a brief theoretical journey through some contemporary theories of management and a sketch of what is to follow in the main body of the book. It is not a review of all, or even most, past or present sociological theories of management or organizations (see Burrell and Morgan, 1979; Morgan, 1986; Hassard and Pym, 1990; Reed and Hughes, 1992; Hassard and Parker, 1993; Hassard, 1993, for this). Rather, it is an attempt to situate some of the more radical methodological and epistemological developments in social theory in a managerial context.

This book does not pretend to be an introduction to *the* sociology of management, then, but *a* sociological introduction to management. The difference is that the former would require yet another grand run through the history and philosophy of many sociological traditions, whereas the latter is more concerned to outline and deploy one particular sociological approach to the substantive area considered as management. In short, the book concentrates on management rather than sociology. Sociology is my disciplinary background and provides the theoretical and methodological approach but I do not attempt to push the boundaries of sociological theory beyond their already wide compass.

Equally important, the book is not a sociological introduction to *all* aspects of management, for which a CD-ROM rather than a book might be more appropriate. Instead of providing a universally thin sociological veneer over management in general, then, this book provides an array of sociologically inspired enquiries of diverse substantive fields and at different levels of analysis. In keeping with the journey into the heart of darkness, the text sets out by providing a historical framework from which to assess the chosen subject, and proceeds to delve deeper and deeper into the managerial world. Thus, at the end of the historical scene setting, it proceeds by considering who the contemporary subjects actually are, what they do, and why they do what they do. It then steps continuously deeper, in a theoretical sense, by considering an array of substantive areas, first on appraisals and managing radical change like reengineering, two currently popular and practical dilemmas for management; and subsequently on leadership and culture, two topics with rather longer histories and more complex theoretical foundations. The penultimate two chapters, on gender and technology and on fatalism and freedom, take the journey further into the philosophical mist so that the journey itself ends not in the bright light of what we take to be reality but up against a raft of paradoxes that are reflected upon in the final chapter. In sum, the metaphorical journey ends, just as Conrad's did, back where we began, not necessarily finding any elixir but hopefully understanding why the journey went the way it did and what this might tell us about management and the role of theory.

Theory in management studies, perhaps more than almost any other academic context, arrives at the management student's door laden with moral and political baggage: theory, according to some anti-theoretical accounts, is apparently irrelevant to the 'real world' of management where decisions are taken on the basis of facts or rationality or whatever happens to be the anti-theoretician's particular animus. As I shall argue in the next chapter, the empiricist and positivist fascination with 'real facts' as opposed to 'vacuous theory' is itself particularly virulent in

Britain, it has been so for centuries, and it is not restricted to the world of management. This often becomes manifest in contrasts that are held to exist between the 'real' world and whatever is being deprecated, usually the 'unreal' world of academia. The criteria for constructing the boundary of reality have always escaped me. At the same time, debates *within* the world constructed by management theorists are often just as acrimonious as those that occur between management theorists and 'practitioners'. Perhaps the latter is an exaggeration since, by and large, practitioners of management very often do not engage in debate with theoreticians – they just ignore each other. In practice the whole circus appears vaguely ludicrous: those who argue that theory is irrelevant to the real world adopt a *theoretical* position in their anti-theoretical ardour which assumes that (theoretically) facts stand for themselves; that is, that the world of reality is self-evident and open to a non-theoretical investigative approach which will reveal the world in its transparently obvious truth. This, presumably, is why everyone agrees about everything – because everything is so blatantly obvious. On the other hand, if there are occasions where we disagree about the meaning of something, about whether something is true, about whether one thing caused another to happen, about the meaning of life – to name just a few problems – then perhaps we should consider what it is that the theories imply.

This chapter does not pretend to be neutral or disinterested but neither does it pretend to have discovered the holy grail of theoretical truth. This modesty is only partly motivated by theory itself, in that I will argue that a critical element of management lies in the way management is constructed through the accounts of various agents involved; hence what management is 'really' like is a function of the way we construct management in the first place. The other element of modesty derives from a recognition that *if* it is the case that we do not so much *discover* as *construct* management through our accounts then we can never be absolutely certain that we are right. Thus the relativist's dilemma – that everything is relative except this – cannot be transcended by dint of linguistic contortion (at least I don't know how to do it – though there may be a way). What I am concerned to do here, therefore, is to explain the consequences of certain theoretical positions and consider the heuristic limits of the constructivist approach. In doing so I hope to avoid the charge of labyrinthine linguistic complexity that so often allows the debate to founder on the reef of confusion. Naturally, my simplified version of the debate between modernism and postmodernism will, in all probability, not meet with universal approval – but that is inevitable in a world that requires interpretative effort, and anyway, if everyone agreed with *my* theoretical approach (which I imagine to be more akin to a wobbly jelly than a neat path), the project might seem rather foolish.

In the world of management the modernist–postmodernist debate hinges on two rather different substantive areas. On the one hand the debate is concerned with the most appropriate way to *describe* the current state of the world: have we moved beyond the controlled world epitomized by the machinations of the Fordist assembly line and Taylorist time-and-motion experts, to a postmodern world where flexibility and change are endemic? On the other hand, the debate surrounds the way we understand the world. Can we rely on the rational, scientific and measurable methods of the modernist scientists and positivists, or should we abandon certainty and spend more effort in understanding how particular accounts are constructed in such a way that they appear to be legitimate, to generate a transparent account of the world, while all the time masking the opacity that postmodernists claim is an inevitable result of our necessary reliance upon language?

In the (modernist) descriptive beginning was industrial capitalism, a socio-economic system that rested upon the primacy of production where the real world and the fantasy world were kept separate. According to Baudrillard's postmodern account, the contemporary world is no longer dominated by production, as consumption has displaced it in economic significance and in terms of ideological influence to the extent that productively based social classes are displaced by identities constructed through consumption. Furthermore, the division between reality and fantasy are melded into one. Perhaps both these aspects can be captured in the theme parks that proliferate across the world. These palaces are neither fantasy nor real but both and neither simultaneously, and the patrons are distinguished by their spending patterns, not by the socio-economic category fixed by professional sociologists. The patrons are what they consume, not what they produce.

In the (pre-modernist) epistemological beginning was God, and God explained everything that there was to be explained and also explained all that could not be explained; a very effective explanatory system, one might think. However, this hermetically self-sealing land of explicable and acceptable ignorance took a radical turn for the better and worse when the Enlightenment thinkers decreed that the inexplicable was no longer acceptable, particularly when Kant took his own motto, *sapere aude* (dare to know), to its logical conclusion and located the authority to explain all within human rationality, as opposed to relying upon the external authority of God. Reason not religion was then the torch to light up the unknown. I'm tempted to say, 'The rest is history', but I won't; too late.

Actually the rest, according to Cooper and Burrell (1988), is two histories. One was concerned with employing reason to ever more complicated systems of modern organization, and we can see the results across various worlds, from Lenin's application of Taylorism to modernize the Soviet Union, through the growth of huge bureaucracies across the world (as predicted by Weber), to the rise of theoretical explanations of human behaviour rooted in rational action – economics and rational decision theory being two primary contenders. The other, and much less influential, history sought to enlighten humanity rather than control it, or explain how it operated in predictable ways. This was the tradition initiated by Kant himself, carried on – or carried off – by Karl Marx, and reconstructed anew today by the likes of Habermas (Held, 1980).

The 'end of history', as Fukuyama (1992) labels the defeat of the alternatives to capitalist democracy, is paradoxically another example of the 'grand narratives' that litter all modernist accounts of the world, according to Lyotard (1984). Modernism, accordingly, rests upon progressive notions of improvement through the application of science and rationality to the extent that the best of all possible worlds is, ultimately, achievable. Precisely what this world looks like is, of course, subject to considerable dispute but the whiggish approach to historical explanation remains at the heart of modernist enterprises. That millions of people have suffered or died at the hands of many modernist 'utopians' (see chapter 5) is often taken by postmodernists as a clear indication that the entire approach is premised upon morally ambiguous foundations (see Grint and Woolgar, 1995a). Since Nazi Germany, until then regarded by many as the most 'cultured' and scientifically advanced nation in the world, decided to murder 6 million Jews and many millions more Soviet citizens, on the grounds that they were scientifically proven to be sub-human, one is tempted to agree that the links between scientific, cultural and moral progress are few and that all such meta-narratives are suspect. The modernist counter-attack is to suggest that the Allies' defeat of Nazi Germany was itself only made possible because of the horror with which this same modern and humane world reacted to the barbaric Nazi atavism.

However, much of the current epistemological debate between modernist and postmodernist approaches – in so far as there is a debate rather than an agreement not to listen – centres less on politics than on the role played by language (see Cooper and Burrell, 1988; Hassard, 1994; N.J. Fox, 1993; Clegg, 1990, for useful discussions of the debate). For Lyotard (1984) the different discourses locked into the competing meta-narratives suggest that the legitimacy of any one discourse is restricted to a localized point in space and time – in effect what counts as true depends upon where and when you are looking for it, and which version of the 'language game' is in operation.

From Derrida (1976, 1978) (and originally from Saussure's (1974) semiotic theory), postmodernist approaches adopt the term *différance* to suggest that language does not reflect the world but constitutes it. It constitutes it with regard not to the *essence* of the thing so constituted but to the difference between the thing and other things. To take an appropriate example, the word 'management' gains its meaning not by reflecting the essence of the group of people who manage but in relation to the difference between this group and the group that is managed by them – the 'managed'; one cannot make sense of the word 'manager' without simultaneously understanding the word 'managed' or 'non-manager' or 'employee'. It is, then, according to Derrida, the differences not the essences that we should concentrate on.

However, *différance* also implies that the meaning of any word is itself subject to different interpretations depending on the context, and so the move from essence to difference does not provide the solution to the problem of meaning. For instance, 'management' can mean a group of high-status individuals or a group of exploiters or a task or the butt of numerous jokes or the legitimation for one's rapid and ungracious exit from a nightclub.

Derrida also argues that logocentrism, the assumption that a trans-parent picture of the world can be secured through human thought, is problematic and that the question is not whether such a picture is true or not but how the claim to truth is constituted in and through discourse. We might, for instance, consider the way that claims to the truth in academic writings are legitimized as much through appeals to other authorities (Duck, D. (1982) and Flintstone, F. (2999 BC)) as through claims whose validity can be assessed by the reader (see if this works at home). This goes not just for qualitative studies (Atkinson, 1990) but for quantitative studies too (Woolgar, 1988a). Here, unless the reader can be bothered to read Atkinson and Woolgar (both good books actually), and then read the authorities that they cite in their own support, *ad infinitum*, you will have to take it on trust that these two works provide persuasive accounts of the alternative cases.

The critical point here is that language does not reflect the world but constitutes it. This need not mean that the world does not exist except in and through our constitution of it – as solipsism implies – but it does imply that whatever does exist we can only know by way of our constituting it through discourse. Thus, to misquote Levi-Strauss, the world cannot be known in the 'raw' – that is, in an untainted form – but only in the 'cooked', in a form mediated by language and human interpretation. Thus postmodernists pursue the 'deconstruction'

(Derrida, 1978) of claims to legitimacy to demonstrate the constructed, as opposed to the non-constructed (true, natural, objective), nature of the claim. Hence, when managers claim that they control organizations on the basis of their superior expertise or education, deconstructionists might question these claims by showing the extent to which their claims to expertise rest on their power to discipline those who question it.

The ambiguous nature of language suggests that interpretative effort is involved in making sense of the world and, following this, that the message provided by the sender need not necessarily be interpreted in an identical fashion by the receiver of the message. The flexibility that this suggests has often been held up by modernist critics as a sure sign of anarchic chaos within the heart of postmodernist approaches: if the reader writes the text, and if there are multiple readers, then all we are left with is a cacophony of contending voices. In effect, we are presented with a supermarket of interpretations and, in the absence of any consensus about what count as criteria for evaluating competing claims to the truth, any account is as good as any other. However, since these interpretations are not derived from, and do not embody, equal resources, it is unlikely that an egalitarian cacophony prevails and more likely that some voices are more equal than others – particularly those in positions of apparent power. If we want to know, then, why the orthodoxy prevails over the heresy, we should look not at the content of the argument but at the resources with which the arguments are articulated.

It is important to note here that such resources are not limited to the conventional resources that modernists might align on each side of a controversy to establish why one side won. It is not that more prestige leads to more material resources, and, since this provides for greater empirical research (the natural world can be observed more closely), it explains why research team X 'discovered' a particular star. Rather, the point is that the apparent increase in accuracy with which modernist research discovers the world is an effect of the limited discourses which provide a kernel of legitimacy for research, and within which only certain forms of knowledge can be ascribed 'truth'. In short, the canons of scientific legitimacy do not recognize heretical forms of research as valid since the methods and philosophy are invalidated by these same canons. Over time, though, as these paradigms (Kuhn, 1970) of legitimacy become increasingly tested and disputed, an alternative paradigm develops to displace the first, not to claim that the original was legitimate but only within a particular envelope of space and time, but to claim that it was always false, just as the new paradigm will always be true. For postmodernists, of course, the interesting point about the paradigm shift is not that we have progressed from error to truth, or that we have swapped one form of falsehood for another, but to consider the ways the new orthodoxy legitimates itself through recourse to the 'facts' – an alternative form of representation. In contrast, postmodern writers on management are limited in how they can provide what conventionally counts as 'expertise' to organizations. Modernist consultants may proclaim that their expertise allows them to control the organization through increasingly accurate measurement, and subsequently prediction, of the structures, cultures, people and things that make up organizations. But postmodernists will look sceptically upon any such grand narrative that pretends to reveal the inner truths of any organization, and concentrate more upon the way consultants construct particular and persuasive renderings of the organization. Where the modernist consultant displays an apparently objective account of an organization that either is stable, or will become so through the execution of the consultant's recommendations, the postmodern sceptic looks at the ways in which an unstable array of matter is (temporarily) stabilized in and through the consultant's discourse.

What, exactly, does this mean in practice? When, for example, the consultant claims that performance related pay will boost morale and increase productivity, the consultant is involved in implementing the pay scheme and subsequently 'examining its effects': 'measuring' morale, perhaps through a survey, or monitoring absenteeism rates and 'measuring' output. Lo and behold, either the productivity increases or it does not – what could be clearer than this? Well, the postmodern sceptic worries about lots of things here. First, about whether there *is* a causal relationship between pay and productivity – can we really measure something as complicated as this? Doesn't this mean that we have to assume that nothing else has changed in the meantime? That, for instance, employees' moods don't boost productivity (whatever counts as a 'mood'); that new machinery or ways of working don't boost productivity; that the exchange rate changes don't boost productivity; that the threat of unemployment if the scheme fails doesn't boost productivity? Has quality been allowed to fall since everyone is now allegedly so concerned with boosting production? Can the increase be sustained once the CEO gets hooked on another scheme? Will the employees find ways around the scheme? And so on. In effect, what appears a simple causal relationship between pay and productivity only seems so because the consultant's discourse has persuaded the CEO that everything is controlled and explained; there are no woolly bits around the edges because the organization is like a machine that needs experts to fine-tune it; it is not, as Gergen (1992) suggests, just as likely to be like a cloud, billowing this way and that beyond anyone's apparent control. Indeed, it is, for the postmodernist, precisely because organizations are fabrications constructed to impose some rhetorical order on the disorder of life that they are 'uncontrollable'.

Postmodernist approaches also suggest a decentring of authority from internal to external. That is, for instance, what counts as a good manager or leader or product or employee rests not within the requisite body or thing but in the way the body or thing is evaluated by others. It is not that an objective set of criteria exists to measure these but that the criteria are a product of the social milieu.

The radical implications of this theoretical sojourn will not be pursued further here, in what might otherwise become a rather (more) arid and contorted metaphysical desert. Instead, I want to see what difference such an approach makes when it is deployed within certain areas of management theory and practice. The aim, then, is to use a constructivist approach as a heuristic – a learning tool – that may – or may not – facilitate our understanding of management. *If* the reader ends up by appreciating some rather different nuances and concerns about management then the book will have succeeded in its aim. The development of theory ought not to be regarded as the property of the faithful, to be protected from, and practised against, the unbeliever. If the history of the social sciences, and philosophy generally, implies anything it is that no approach appears to prevail across all space at any one time, or within any one space for all time. Scepticism rules OK! (Well, relatively speaking).

The following chapters take the reader on a journey that should lead her or him or it (assuming this can be 'read' by a genderless machine) to understand not just something about management and one particular sociological approach to it, but also about the *way* we come to understand what management is – and how the *way* we understand it has implications for *what* it is. For example, if we want to know *what* directors do we might consider asking them to specify, through interviews, diaries and questionnaires what they do. After the research fieldwork we would no doubt come to some conclusions about what it is that directors do. Of course, it may also be the case that the different methods generate different kinds of data. The conventional social science response would be to seek a triangulation of the evidence, in which the different data are juxtaposed and an attempt is made to triangulate the true position from two or more different points, as one might do in any orienteering exercise. This approach is firmly rooted in modernist and positivist assumptions that the data merely reflect the real world and, providing the methods are sufficiently scientific, the data will be compatible. Thus, in our directors' case, we survey a large (that is statistically significant) number of directors and the results suggest they all work fifteen-hour days and our diary data support this.

But suppose we now adopt anthropological methods. First, we will not have the resources to observe these 'tribes' of directors so we will have to limit the number of cases to a handful. Now suppose our observations suggest that, although these directors are in their offices for fifteen hours a day, they are not 'working' all this time but socializing or organizing golf or sleeping off executive lunches or plotting the downfall of their CEOs. These data might still be compatible with the quantitative data from the survey and diaries; but suppose the directors deny the anthropologists' results and claim that what the anthropologist calls 'socializing' and 'organizing golf' is a critical function of the way business operates. Are these directors working hard for the company or just enjoying themselves at company expense? Who is to say? Now this is the crunch: *who* has the legitimate authority to pronounce upon the non-triangulated results? On the one (modernist) hand, since there is self-evidently only one truth a decision has to be made as to which party is mistaken about what directors actually do. But what if we cannot decide upon this because no one can stand above the debate, that is, there are no agreed criteria that we can use which will pronounce one side to have told the truth and the other to be mistaken? Could it be that the directors do actually believe that they are working for the company in all their activities and that the anthropologists deny this, and that what is actually going on is not something we are going to be able to decide in any objective or neutral way? In short, could it be that what the directors are doing depends on which approach one uses and which expert one believes?

The rest of this book is an attempt to deploy this form of constructivist argument in an array of different management fields to demonstrate its heuristic potential and its limitations. It is not, therefore, an extended review of postmodernism, nor does it attempt to steer a path that holds close to what might be a postmodern orthodoxy. I do, however, intend to pursue a generally constructivist line that adopts some elements of postmodernism (see Grint and Woolgar (1995b) for another attempt).

The following chapter is a historical review of the development of management traditions, set against the background of European wars, in which national identities coagulate in the venom that seeps between hostile nations. Chapter 3, 'Mimetic Pyrophobes' (fire-fighting copy-cats), explores what managers appear to do – and why they appear to do what they do. In particular, I consider the historical significance of the education of managers (or lack of it) in creating a tradition of fire-fighting that appears, at least in Britain, to have continued repeating itself since its origins in the industrial revolution. In chapter 4, a current management fixation, appraisals, is used to root the text in a practical issue and to demonstrate both the problems with conventional approaches and the possibilities inspired by constructivist alternatives. The practical application of constructivist ideas is further pursued in chapter 5 where the prospect of securing radical organizational change is configured through Bloch's (1986) 'Principle of Hope', an argument for the necessarily utopian premise of all radical change. Business process reengineering (BPR) is one such form of radical change, and this chapter takes a close look at BPR as an example of the fads and fashions that seem to keep management in a constant state of turmoil. The aim of this chapter is to consider the extent to which the 'success' of reengineering can be construed through an external focus on related ideas beyond management, rather than through the 'objective' utility of the ideas encompassed by reengineering itself. This externalist approach is also adopted for chapter 6 on leadership, which is examined in some detail to throw some uncomfortable ideas onto the tracks of the leadership gravy train. This chapter is especially concerned to explore the logical problem of investing individuals with leadership qualities, notably charismatic leadership qualities, when leadership appears to be essentially dependent upon the *post hoc* whim of the followers not the leaders themselves. The relational implications of this are further pursued in the following chapter on management and culture. Starting from traditional assumptions about culture, in which culture is an association of farmers, tools, seeds and the natural elements, I go on to analyse the way culture has been progressively reduced to human ideas and practices in which the human takes an unprecedentedly superordinate position above and beyond the world of the non-human. The circle is completed through contemporary theoretical developments in which divisions between human and non-human are radically challenged.

The theoretical issues become yet more challenging in chapter 8 which pushes the journey into more difficult waters by moving between what might be considered as the Charybdis of gender and the Scylla of technology. The first generates a whirlpool of moral and political questions for constructivism; the second appears to be a particularly hard rock to crack. At the termination of this section of the journey through a sociology of management I attempt to demonstrate how both the whirlpool and the rock can be crossed – with difficulty – but crossed nevertheless. The penultimate chapter halts the journey into the heart of darkness in an appropriately Cimmerian world of trench warfare in the First World War to examine methods of control under extreme forms of management. This is not to wander off the path of management but to consider just how much control and freedom the managers of war and the managed of war have under such conditions. *A fortiori*, if the 'poor bloody infantry' are free to do otherwise than 'go over the top' then we have to reconsider the extent to which management control is based in a fatalism that is just one of many possible forms of action. In summary, our journey to the heart of darkness begins to draw to a close with a recognition of freedom and therefore self-responsibility; we are, it appears, fated to freedom. The final chapter reflects upon the journey, especially the methods, and poses some uncomfortable questions for the writer of the journey as well as the traveller: just how much 'management' of the traveller is involved in 'understanding' this management journey?

2

The Black Ships:
The Historical Development
of British Management

Introduction

In 1852 a meteor streaked across the Japanese sky and, shortly
afterwards, four American navy ships sailed into Tokyo harbour: the
'black ships' had arrived. To the Japanese, virtually isolated from the
rest of the world for over 250 years, the black ships represented a
double threat: they were alien invaders of the Japanese homeland that
had remained 'unsoiled' by foreigners for centuries; but they were also
aliens within advanced alien technologies that the Japanese had little, if
any, knowledge of. When the Mongol hordes had threatened Japan in
1274 and again in 1281 the invaders had been expelled by the actions of
the Japanese soldiers and the intervention of *Kami Kaze*, the 'divine
wind' that twice destroyed the Mongol/Korean fleet (R. Marshall, 1993).
When European sailors made contact with Japan in the late sixteenth
century, after a brief dalliance with some of the ideas and technologies,
such as firearms, ship-building and navigation, the Tokugawa shogunate
expelled the foreigners. In 1852, however, the *Gaijin* (foreigners) posed
an immediate threat. The previous responses to external threats had
been to expel them, and to maintain the boundaries. The response in
1852 was different: this time the Japanese decided not to expel the
foreigners immediately, though this would have been possible if difficult
to achieve, but to learn from them in order to resist them. Thus the
Japanese changed their strategy of resistance from an expulsive to a
mimetic form. The first was rooted in fears for the imminent destruction

of a culturally superior people by a barbarian horde. The second was rooted in assumptions about the imminent destruction of a culturally superior people by a barbarian horde armed with sophisticated technologies. The black ships represented not just the barbarian but the technologically sophisticated barbarian. In what follows I want to consider the extent to which the development of British management can be read in a similar light.

Like Japan's (and probably every other country's), Britain's cultural heritage has been one commonly grounded in notions of superiority. Certainly by the middle of the nineteenth century the British lion appeared dominant: its army patrolled 25 per cent of the globe and its navy ruled a large proportion of the sea waves. But within another quarter of a century the proverbial black ships had arrived, this time in the form of American and German competition. The British response to the perceived alien threat was to take the first Japanese route: to expel the alien by operating closed markets and the *status quo ante* – to do otherwise would have been to suggest that British superiority was either waning or based on a problematic heritage. As in Japan, the response seemed to work: for a further century Britain appeared to survive and prosper, but only in absolute not relative terms, for the foreign competition became stronger, as did 'the other'. Not really until the 1970s does British management appear to have considered the second route. By this time the black ships had become so threatening that a change of strategy pushed a (still) reluctant management into the mimetic mode. From then on, a small but increasingly popular move to copy the black ships developed. At different times the German, American and Japanese have all been held up as the system to guaranteed success. Whether this is the case or not remains to be seen.

In what follows I begin by considering the general origins of management before concentrating on the development of a particular British form that I highlight against the backdrop of events at the beginning of the industrial revolution and during the wars with France. Taking the constructions of management traditions as a flake from the construction of national traditions, I spend some time linking the heroic figure of Wellington to his equivalent in the world of industry to see the extent to which the latter stereotypes mirror the former. The chapter then moves on to look at the clash between different social classes and interests, focusing in particular on the relationship between the aristocracy and the industrial capitalists. Finally, the focus becomes narrower still to examine the significance of the classic British company form, family capitalism. But let me begin at the beginning, with the origins of management.

Historical origins of management

The word 'management' is derived from the Italian *maneggiare*, meaning to control or to train, particularly applied to the management of horses; the Italian was itself rooted in the Latin *manus*, meaning hand. 'Herding cats' rather than horses is the image that springs to mind sometimes but management as an activity goes back much further than Ben-Hur's attempts to manage his team of chariot horses around the arena, literally at break-neck speed. The Sumerians had a system of account management that Foucault would have appreciated in its conflation of power/knowledge, though probably the most spectacular instances of large-scale management in the ancient world are embodied in the pyramids, or in the British case, in Stonehenge. These construction projects required a complex organizational system that could only have functioned through some form of effective management, though precisely what that may have been is disputed (Mendelssohn, 1974).

Management has also existed in relation to the management of war, a phenomenon which appears to be as old as humankind, and which has also required some form of managerial co-ordination. From the eighth-century BC Assyrian charioteers, whose success appears to have been dependent upon the successful management of a formidable array of logistics, to the considerably earlier siege of Jericho, and up to the recent war in the Gulf, the management of war has been, at least partly, the war between managers (Keegan, 1993).

A third source for the origins of management lies in the early religious institutions, particularly the Christian monastic organizations, like the Benedictine monasteries whose life from the fifth century onwards was apparently minutely controlled by the regulations created by St Benedict and enforced through the religious hierarchy. The requirement to keep the size of the institution to a group of around twelve generally discouraged the development of anything like the managerial bureaucracies of later and larger organizations; nevertheless, unlike the rival Cistercian monks, the Benedictines employed lay workers and hence the utility of self-imposed discipline would probably have been considerably reduced and a management system necessary (Applebaum, 1992: 195–209; B. Harvey, 1993).

However, it is to the fourth antecedent, industry, that many would turn in the search for the origins of contemporary management. The original guilds, in which craftworkers banded together to control labour supply, wages, product prices, quality and quantity, had some forms of management, though they were both small-scale and deeply embedded into the fabric of the community – to the extent that deciding where the rights of the guild started and the realm of the family ended would probably have been the subject of some dispute. It is no coincidence that medieval homes would probably have had only one 'chair', occupied by the family head, in a (board)room where a single 'board' served as the table for meals and other activities (such as board games).

Medieval guilds, which had spread throughout all the major European cities by the twelfth century, were 'total institutions' and not really corporate actors that were legally distinct from the people who worked within them. Indeed, Kieser (1989) suggests that such guilds were generally not innovative and seldom functionally specialized to the extent that we might consider certain individuals as performing what are taken as managerial activities. Rather, they were controlled by a 'master' who supervised a 'novice' until such time as the novice created a 'masterpiece' and became a 'journeyman', that is a craftworker paid by the day (from the French '*Journée*' and not the English 'journey'). These guilds were themselves moral economies (see Grint, 1991), rather than market-oriented institutions, where honour, custom and tradition were more important than increasing sales or profits. Indeed, accumulating wealth as an end in itself may well have seemed extraordinarily irrational. Kieser quotes one example of the role of the moral economy from a shoemaker's guild in Schmiedeberg, in Germany, where a master shoemaker was expelled from the guild for picking up a nail used by the local executioner to re-attach his victims' heads after execution (1989: 552). In several mining areas, in both Germany and England, the miners themselves ran their affairs as collectives without any apparent form of superordinate authority, even to the extent of administering their own law – so that Devon miners would frequently 'seize and beat up the king's bailiffs ... and hold them in prison pending the payment of a ransom' (Lewis, 1924: 36, quoted in Gimpel, 1992: 99). Self-management, then, has a very long history.

However, the monopolistic restrictions of the guilds may well have stimulated the development of functionally specialized institutions in which the producers were separated from the controllers – a development requiring some form of management. By the fourteenth century the division of labour was well under way in some areas: four hundred years before Adam Smith (re)'invented' the idea (which was still some time after Odysseus had undertaken such divided labour), Florentine cloth production had been divided into twenty-six separate operations. But if the division of labour was not an invention of the industrial revolution neither was managing recalcitrant labour: in 1345 York Minster's works' manager found himself at the receiving end of a damning indictment in which absenteeism, stolen materials, unfit workers, defective building and rotting machinery were just some of the noted problems (Gimpel, 1992: 106–8; see also Sonenscher, 1989). Should we still remain convinced that the nineteenth-century habits of work avoidance and intricate and intractable wage negotiations, so vividly depicted in the autobiographical work of T. Wright (1867), are the responsibility of the industrial revolution, we would do well to return to the fourteenth century where the problem of day wages – where the workers stopped work as soon as the supervisor's back was turned – was matched by the complexity of the system: at Caernarvon Castle in 1304 the payroll includes 53 stonemasons on 17 different daily rates of pay (Gimpel, 1992: 109).

In short, management has a history as long as human history; one might even say that humanity's distinction from other animal groups is rooted not just in the ability to use a language to communicate, and to use and develop technology, but in the ability to marshal other humans into complex organizations that, through co-ordinated action, can achieve far more than any single human could ever achieve. In other words, humans are essentially a managed species. A further implication of this is that the kind of problems thrown up in management also have a very long history; from managing military supplies to managing hunting and farming, to mobilizing a workforce and developing quality control mechanisms, management has always been, at least in part, 'just one damn thing after another'. But just as military and religious management has differed widely, even with organizations using apparently similar technologies and knowledge, so too, has business management. In the next section I want to consider the extent to which British management has an historical thread that remains relatively unchanging across time, and the extent to which this depends upon assumptions about what 'the other' is doing; what the black ships represent.

Wellingtonian management: managing the formation of national identity

In this section I will be mainly concerned with the development of British management, but the development of an archetypal British manager is critically dependent upon the differences between this archetype and 'the other', whether that other is French or American or German or Japanese. I will start by doubting whether such cultures are manifestations of some deeply rooted, and mysteriously evolved, element of the national psyche and by doubting that cultures are unchanging in space or time. We are probably all aware of national stereotypes and we probably all know many individuals from other countries who simply do not appear to fit the stereotype. That national stereotypes are both static and change across time can be seen in the current crop of stereotypes as against the historical ones: according to Pears (1993) the English have traditionally regarded the Germans as obedient but unimaginative, the Italians as greasy and dishonest, the French as dandies and egoists, the Spanish as cold and sinister, and the Dutch as worthy but dull since at least Tudor times. Yet the English themselves seem to have been transformed considerably: Erasmus in the sixteenth century regarded the English as open and emotional, always kissing each other. By the sixteenth century an epidemic of seriousness broke out, to be replaced by the saturnalian seventeenth century and the emotive eighteenth, when tears, suicides and melancholy appeared to be all the rage, that is, until Victoria took the throne (Pears, 1993: 216).

Of course these representations of British, or at least English, culture are very probably grossly inaccurate, but as Hofstede remarks, people 'grow up in a particular society in a particular period and their ideas can not help but reflect the constraints of the environment' (1993: 82). In this kind of representation, then, management culture is a reflection of national culture, which, in turn, reflects historical circumstances. The implication of this national-based cultural predisposition leads certain management theories and tools such as 'management by objectives' to be dysfunctional in other cultures (Hofstede, 1980; Evans et al., 1989).

What I want to consider here is the extent to which British management can be read as the historically constructed product of a national identity *created* at the point at which national identities became a significant part of many people's lives – that is, the late eighteenth and early nineteenth centuries – and when British industrial success appeared, at least to the British, to be unstoppable. I do not suggest that this approach explains what so many others have attempted but failed to explain – the gradual demise of British industry – but I want to see to what extent such an approach can shed new light on an old topic. The stereotypical British manager has historically been a scion of the greater national icon: in a land where background and experience are more important than potential ability, and where practical knowledge is preferable to academic 'waffle', it is the aristocratic amateur and the apprentice that prevails over the educated public expert. Where common law, tradition and legal precedent are more important than statutory law and a written constitution, it is the array of individual liberties and privileges that prevail over any form of rational social contract. And where success in all spheres of life appears to follow the evolutionary, not the revolutionary, the incremental accretion, not the radical reconstruction, it is the 'natural' change of Darwin not the 'unnatural' change of Robespierre that prevails.

To what extent has British management been moulded along these lines and where did the mould come from in the first place? Clearly, many of these alleged characteristics can be 'discovered' in the travails of the Anglo-Saxons, but they can probably be discovered in many other cultures too. The first point is to consider the extent to which national identities are constructs of particular periods, rather than manifestations of 'inherent' traits. The second is to see whether the construction of this identity can throw light on British managers and their role in the decline of British industry.

Let us begin by considering briefly the rise of the British identity. Colley (1994) suggests that the seventeenth and early eighteenth centuries were critical for the development of an identity that was recognizably British, rather than English or Welsh or Scottish or Irish. This was the era of almost continuous war with the French, and the ultimate result was not just a national identity but the founding of the Bank of England and the creation of the City as a financial trading centre. This identity is not something which reflects some kind of innate British characteristic but is constructed in the sense that B. Anderson (1983) talks of 'an imagined community'. That is, the notion of a collective identity depends upon individuals coming to believe that they have something in common with their neighbours – since they will never be able to assess this empirically given the numbers involved – and, equally critical, that something is held in common in opposition to a common identity held by 'the other' which threatens them. Hence, in the British case, the commonality construed is behind not just a physical boundary but also a religious one: British Protestantism against French Catholicism. National identity is, therefore, an invention, just as the stereotyped French are inventions. Whether there is some element of what we may call 'truth' behind the stereotype is missing the point; it is the belief that counts (anyway, how are we to measure the reality?).

If what counts as 'the British character' begins to develop around this time, when the background is one where the French Revolution and Napoleon's citizen army threaten the bedrock of English society, then it is worth considering two related issues. First, particular icons or 'heroic' individuals are constructed to reflect this 'character'. Second, British capitalism and management begin to fashion themselves on the lines of the same mould.

In the case of the individual icon, the argument suggests that those individuals who become heroes are constructed in a particular fashion so that their characters are read as flakes of the national character, or, more accurately, as fractals, in the way that chaos theory develops representations of phenomena which appear to be unrelated but at high levels of magnification reveal symmetries that are repeated at each new magnification (Gleick, 1987; Gregersen and Sailer, 1993). Let us take, as the foremost example of the period, the Duke of Wellington.

Wellington's character, under this approach, is constructed not as a reflection of any allegedly innate or internal characteristics, and not just against the silhouette of Napoleon, but through the resonances of the contemporary national character, as witnessed in the self-constructed stereotype. As Pears argues, 'the qualities he came to symbolize became built into the national consciousness as part of the essential fabric of Englishness ... he encapsulated a newly-forming vision of a national type' (1993: 217–18). What is at issue here is not what Wellington was 'really' like; as I argue in chapter 4, what people are 'really' like depends on who is asking the question and who is answering it. Rather, my concern here, following Pears, is to illustrate the way Wellington came to represent the national character, but only in and through the contrasts that could be drawn with Napoleon, which at another level are representations of the different countries and cultures. Napoleon, as portrayed by the British, was a more charismatic figure than Wellington; he was a brilliant strategist, a genius, and his troops would follow him to their deaths as and when he wished. Wellington, in contrast, represented the obverse of these characteristics; indeed, he was the living image of all that the British held to be their own: he was methodological and dedicated where Napoleon was dashing but erratic; 'Wellington was the technician of war, Napoleon was its Michelangelo' (quoted in Pears, 1993: 223). But it was that very dogged determination in the face of short-lived brilliance that marked the British from the French. Where Napoleon came from nowhere to lead a (temporary) empire as a (temporary) emperor, Wellington was both aristocratic and a loyal servant of those born to rule. Hence the danger of a radical meritocracy could be shown to be limited in the face of 'true' (that is inherited) position.

This reverence for a specific kind of heroic figure can also be gleaned from the nature of the British educational elite's curriculum at the time, and for a considerable period afterwards: heroes there were aplenty, and most of them Greek or Roman, but they were all heroes of inherited wealth and honour – and they were all dead, so the threat of 'upstart' heroes was minimized (Colley, 1994: 168). Thus Napoleon took imaginative risks in battle and through rigidly centralized control shook the world apart. Wellington's 'pragmatic improvisation' secured an incremental route to long-term, and therefore final, victory – and ensured that the world would be returned to normality. Furthermore, the 'upstart' Napoleon had to rely upon the emotional allegiance of the common French foot soldier – the kind of egalitarianism that would later lead to all kinds of troublesome political phenomenon, like democracy (Therborn, 1977). Wellington, on the other hand, seemed to thrive on his own, calling his soldiers 'scum' when he called them anything.

More significantly, since it was Wellington and the British who ultimately 'won' it was self-evident which kinds of talent and skill were the most appropriate. Over a century later Churchill and Montgomery were to reenact this same battle with Hitler and Rommel respectively – and again British determination won out over continental flair, or so the moral runs. Dunkirk is an excellent example of this: what appeared to the Germans to be an inglorious British retreat, conducted more like a farce than a military operation, was read by the British as a triumph of British steadfastness and improvisation in the face of overwhelming odds.

There are two levels at which this construction of the archetypal English hero, and the national identity which it simultaneously constructs, can be considered. At one level the timing of the development is important, for it was only subsequent to the Battle of Waterloo in 1815 that British domination of the world's economy became self-evident, hence it would have been an important historical axis around which the British economic and military domination swung. Waterloo was read as the culmination of centuries of battle against the old enemy, and it marked the dawn of the 'chosen people.' Second, it is important to note that the battle was not against the 'other' in general but the French in particular. Thus, the ideal British character was the inverse of the stereotype French. Where the French were centralizers, strategists and risk-takers, and succeeded – where they did – through inherent talent and the closely marshalled emotional support of the masses, the British had clearly to be the opposite. That is, they must be decentralizers, wary of state control, tacticians but not strategists, risk-averse, and dedicated.

In effect, I am suggesting that the British hero of the period, born from the fires of war with France, embodied not just the military image of Wellington but the industrial image of hundreds of capitalists too. That this image is itself a transient one can be seen from the difference between Nelson and Wellington: Nelson was much closer in flair and style to Napoleon than Wellington was – but it was Wellington and not Nelson who saw off the ancient French threat; Nelson, after all, was not an aristocrat.

It is, perhaps, ironic that a French observer of British management in the mid-nineteenth century should comment in a similar way about the 'peculiarities' of the British manager who was only able to operate when in direct contact with the work: experiential rather than theoretical approaches have deep roots and even longer effects (Haynes, 1988:

256). We have very little systematic evidence about the nature of British management during the eighteenth and nineteenth centuries and to suggest that British managers began to model themselves upon the characteristics thrust upon Wellington is not what I am concerned with here. What I am concerned with, though, is the extent to which the behaviour of British managers can be configured within the same kind of stereotype. That is, have British managers traditionally regarded the most appropriate way to organize work as one where pragmatism prevails; where strategic intent and centralized control are anathema; where the state's role is largely confined to keeping out 'the other' and keeping control of 'the enemy within'; and where dedication to incremental change through hard work and the acquisition of experience is preferred to radical restructuring using meritocratic procedures and the emotional support of the employees? If there is a similarity of representation between the way Wellington was constituted as an icon of the British character and the way managers have traditionally operated, might it be that they are struck from the same bronze? In short, might it be that the bronze original was imagined into existence in particular historical circumstances and that, by whatever means, the normative way to act is one in keeping with what counts as being British? Here, indeed, might be the irony of Waterloo: the victory which managed to cement the British character in place simultaneously cemented British management in place. That the cement and the character were merely part of the imaginary community is precisely the point: imaginations can change, but they can be extraordinarily resistant to change too. In the next section we move from the imagination that constructed Wellingtonian management to the imagination that sees, in the aristocratic background of the elite like Wellington, the anti-industrial worm that allegedly infected the first industrial apple.

The management of class: captains of the land, industry and insubordination

Captains of the land

The relative decline of British industry, from approximately 1870 onwards, has recently been the subject of a veritable landslide of material since Wiener's (1981) attempt to pin the blame squarely on the shoulders of an anti-industrial culture that revealed strong preferences for aristocratic over industrial interests (see also Coates, 1992). This section makes no pretence at resolving the dispute that has been raging ever since but it does attempt to consider it through the ideas introduced in the previous sections: the Wellingtonian management model and the threat from the black ship of foreign competition.

Since all societies can be construed as stratified by class, amongst other things, the critical aspect of class is not whether class societies generate different forms of culture – since all societies are riven by some form of social division – but why the actions of certain groups of people lead to the construction of an 'imagined community' of individuals whose commonality is construed through their economic position. Moreover, what is the result of such action in the development of specific forms of culture? If we consider Barrington Moore's (1966) structural explanation for the rise of democracy, communism and fascism, a crucial aspect of it lies in the role of the bourgeoisie. Thus, the more powerful the bourgeoisie, and the more the bourgeoisie had to struggle for its own rights against the state, especially in the process of industrial development, the more likely individual rights are to be either written into the constitution or at least strongly institutionalized in law. Where the bourgeoisie remained weak such individual rights failed to materialize. Of course, since it is the industrialization process itself which spawns the bourgeoisie we should not be too surprised to note the relative absence of the class in both Germany and Japan. Could it be then that where the process of industrialization is ushered into existence through a political process, rather than emanating in a more evolutionary manner through the economic action of individuals, bourgeois rights are impeded?

If the critical juncture is the timing and form of the industrialization process it would be possible to account for the rise of individualism through the struggle – or its absence – on the part of the bourgeoisie for political rights to match its growing economic strength. Where Moore sees a 'weak bourgeoisie' what we might see is a society without the industrial muscle to support a bourgeoisie. Hence, under certain conditions – political union in Germany and external threat in Japan – both societies are industrialized from above in the relative absence of a strong bourgeoisie. Once the industrialization process becomes economically viable and self-sustaining, once it begins to spawn the very members of the bourgeoisie upon whose continuation it depends, the state is powerful enough to constrain any such demands for political independence. The groups which control the industrialization process in Germany and Japan, therefore, were members of the landed aristocracy, the Junkers and the samurai respectively, who themselves used the state apparatus to discipline the peasantry and the new proletariat.

It is not, then, that different class structures led to different cultural approaches to the question of individual rights, but that the decisions of elite groups in each country to develop economic and industrial strength brought into existence industrializing processes that were used to facilitate the interests of the industrializing elite; since the industrializing process was instigated by different social groups with different interests the results were different. In Japan and Germany the industrializers were already amongst the establishment – and hence had no need to develop further political and social rights against the state. But in the British case the industrializing bourgeoisie had to fight the existing establishment and its state to secure the expansion of the franchise and political rights against the state. In the USA, since there never was a landed nobility, the bourgeoisie had a relatively easy path in constructing a culture around their own interests. One is tempted to add here that in the absence of virtually any form of stake in the development of Russia as a nation, the Russian peasantry were left with little concern for the nationalist concerns of either the czars or the Kerensky government, and provided the Bolsheviks with an opportunity just waiting for the cry of the dispossessed (see Pipes, 1994).

While Moore's approach to this is set at the level of social structures, especially social class, it is not necessarily incompatible with approaches that take a more action-oriented approach, such as Rustow's (1970) decision-making perspective. If we accept that classes are not merely groups of people with similar economic conditions but actually groups of people who imagine themselves to have similar ideals and interests and act appropriately, then we can transcend some of the structuralist and rather mechanistic assumptions made by Moore about the explanation of class behaviour. Rustow suggests that the phenomena of democracy can be traced back to a series of specific events and decisions which have a common ancestry. These need not detain us here since we are concerned not with democracy but with cultural differences. However, the important aspect is to note the way that the birth of social institutions (such as democracy or trade unions) is constructed through some form of decision amongst conflicting groups that neither side is powerful enough to dominate the other and that both groups have some form of shared identity that differentiates them from outsiders. Thus, democracy originates as a second preference but becomes a first preference over time as it begins to yield certain benefits to the participants. In the case of Germany and Japan, of course, democracy was derived not from this compromise but from an enforced order on the part of the Allies at the end of the Second World War (see Therborn, 1977, on this). However, the point is that part of the compromising procedure is an agreement on individual rights against the arbitrary action of the state (in the case of Britain and the USA), but that the cultural history of Japan and Germany has not been one where such protection was ever sustained for a long period of time.

The tradition, therefore, is one in which the relative strength of the British bourgeoisie kept a tight reign on the power of the landed nobility, and it was this establishment of individual rights against the state which facilitated the political and economic rise of the new industrial elite. Yet Wiener (1981) suggests that the industrial elite only scaled the heights of political or economic power for a short period of time, after which the aristocracy and aristocratic culture cast a spell upon the new industrial elite and turned the majority into petty nobles, safe in their new country mansions while the industrial engine of growth gradually expired.

Colley (1994: 154–5) certainly has no difficulty in denying the meritocratic pretensions of late seventeenth- and early eighteenth-century Britain, where the British aristocracy represented no more than 0.00001 per cent of the population in 1800 – just a decade after the guillotine had eliminated a large proportion of the French aristocracy that previously made up over 1 per cent of the French population. When John Burke (of Burke's *Peerage*) calculated that there were only 400 hundred elite families who were *not* aristocrats in the 1830s, and that these were nevertheless closely linked to them, and when a quarter of all MPs were married to the daughters of other MPs (there were no women MPs at the time), just how open British society actually was is clearly disputed.

In the event the continuing dominance of the aristocracy suggests that there was no 'bourgeois revolution' in Britain (B. Anderson, 1964), and the 'captains of industry' led by Cobden and Bright and the like failed to overturn the old order. By 1865 business men could still muster barely 25 per cent of the Members of Parliament. In fact the post-Corn Law administrations were, if anything, more, not less, aristocratic in their make-up. Partly this was because the parliamentary rules of the game were still constructed to inhibit non-aristocratic admittance, but it was also because northern manufacturers were unwilling to engage in the game, at least at national level, though they were powerful at the local level. Some of this absence was possibly related to the form of ownership in businesses, in which family domination was the norm and few business leaders felt confident enough to leave the office for long periods in the House. The middle class as a social group did not appear to have a universal inferiority complex; indeed, Langford (1989) asserts that even before the industrial revolution middle-class values were firmly ensconced in power. But the confidence problem in the manufacturing section appears to have gone deeper than this and to have resembled a cultural inferiority that struck even the heartiest of the 'captains'. Titus Salt, for instance, retired early from his seat in the commons, suffering from 'broken sleep ... shattered nerves and gouty twinges'. Thomas Thomasson, another mill-owning MP, warned that 'People who might think that they were very important in Bolton found themselves very little boys when in London.' Even those who made it to the top table were treated with suspicion and contempt: W.H. Smith, the 'Bookstall Man' as he was known in the House, almost did not make it to the Conservative Cabinet as First Lord of the Admiralty in 1877 after Queen Victoria noted that it 'may not please the Navy ... if a man of the middle class is placed above them' (Searle, 1993: 6–8). In sum, the representation of the culture of 'social subordination', as Searle calls it, or the absence of 'cultural capital' in Bourdieu's terms (Bourdieu and Passeron, 1977), suggests either that the manufacturers 'failed' at the national political level (however successful at the local level they may have been), or that their success only occurred through a subordinate aping of their social superiors. There is even a suggestion that, as the market for the manufacturers' goods became more and more dependent upon military, especially naval, protection, so the hostility of the manufacturing class to the imperialist ambitions of the southern elite declined, thus reinforcing the aristocratic ideal (Gatrell, 1971, quoted in Searle, 1993: 12–13).

In contrast, the successful entrepreneur in the USA operated in a rather different cultural milieu, where the general availability of land and the widespread geographical and social mobility undermined the desperate search to find a landed estate to protect the family inherit-ance. This difference is perhaps nowhere more clearly expressed than in the assumption that successful British individuals would prefer to move into public life, or the City or a profession – anywhere but into industry (at least until very recently) while Carnegie in the USA noted that 'our rich men are not interested in public affairs: they leave that to men who cannot succeed in business' (quoted in Keeble, 1992: 23). In effect: 'In an order dominated by gentlemanly norms, production was held in low repute. Working directly for money, as opposed to making it from a distance, was associated with dependence and cultural inferi-ority, (Cain and Hopkins, 1993a: 23), a concern as old as Ancient Greece (Applebaum, 1992). In the British case, the contempt for the 'sordid' world of machinery, in which one had to have direct and visible contact with the means of support, was in clear contrast to the 'invisible' income and profit making 'at a distance' which land ownership and financial dealings in the City of London, in addition to some of the more 'acceptable' professions (the armed forces, the clergy, law, medi-cine and later the senior civil service) provided. The peculiarity of the British aristocracy was its ability to marry its traditional land-owning support system with the rather newer financial and services support system. For those industrialists hoping to exchange their new money for old so that the family fortune would post-date the creator, the only real route appears to have been to purchase land (F.M.L. Thompson, 1990).

Moreover, many of the elements of this aristocratic system were the antithesis of those constructed by the new manufacturing entrepreneurs in northern England. For example, the high levels of trust alleged to have been developed through the system of 'reciprocal' obligations under *noblesse oblige* were inversely mirrored by the low levels of trust and high levels of hostility that the new factories and mechanized production systems appeared to stimulate. Indeed, the factory system was construed as alien, exploitive and disruptive, while making money through land or financial acumen was considered as a particularly British, or at least English, skill, in which no one appeared to be exploited and no-one appeared to resist or organize against it. The highly visible and 'hands-on' method of securing an income, coupled with the collapse of the boundaries between cleanliness and dirt as manufacturers 'got their hands dirty' in the muck and grease of industrial production, could not have been a sharper contrast to the world of the financial entrepreneur in the City. And while the industrial capitalists of the north secured few political victories against their more powerful southern colleagues (the Anti-Corn Law League being one of the few), the intense competition between the manufacturers undermined what little political cohesion they ever had. The *Norfolk News* may have hailed the repeal of the Corn Laws, which protected the aristocratic elite from the vicissitudes of the market, as the beginning of the end of the old order and the dawn of the period when 'The seat of power . . . has been transferred from Downing Street to Manchester . . . the mills have beaten the aristocracy' (Searle, 1993: 1), but the reality seems otherwise. In short, the factory may have been the black ship for the British aristocracy; it represented the threat of radical upheaval and the end of their own privileged and ordered existence – unless the aristocracy could, as they subsequently did, take the third strategy: not to expel the alien, nor to emulate it but to control it by adoption.

The most recent review of the role of finance in the decline of British manufacturing industry, having argued that only 6 per cent of British companies fit into the 'best performer' category, certainly suggests that the difficulty of obtaining finance has played a significant part in the decline – though historically speaking the problem may not have been so acute when most firms were not seeking the large investments that only the City could afford (Cain and Hopkins, 1993a, 1993b). Hence the concern that the lack of a German-style system to provide large-scale capital injections is premised on the assumption that British industry grew as fast and as large as the German's did; it did not. Nevertheless, the ease with which money could flow abroad and the scale of returns accrued by such investments did make life rather more difficult for the local entrepreneur. The particular problems facing small and medium-sized companies seem to lie in the risk-averse nature of British banking, which tends to insist on lending against collateral rather than assessing the viability of the business. Under-investment is not the only problem, of course: lack of commitment, inflexibility and short-termism in the face of shareholders who compare performance every three months are also acute. However, the role of finance capital appears not to be a myth constructed by incompetent manufacturers (Royal Society for the Arts, 1994).

Captains of industry

Not everyone assumed or accepted that the captains of land would become the captains of *the* land. Marx, for example, thought that the opposite would occur – that the bulldozer of industrial capitalism would obliterate status differences between capitalists and the pre-existing land-owning elite as the former simply rode roughshod over the pretensions of the latter. Schumpeter was similarly persuaded that the 'process of creative destruction' would, among other things, undermine the status of property itself because 'substituting a mere parcel of shares for the walls of, and the machines in, a factory takes the life out of the idea of property' (1976: 148). Weber was not so persuaded, given his penchant for the role of status. Indeed, it was precisely this aspect that Veblen (1953: 65) focused upon in his analysis of 'conspicuous consumption': 'the requirement that the gentleman must consume freely and of the right kind of goods ... [and] he must know how to consume them in a seemly manner'.

Mathias (1969) clearly suggests that the early industrial revolution in Britain witnessed a considerable degree of upward mobility as industrial entrepreneurs and leaders struggled to the top from all forms of background to fulfil Samuel Smiles's claims about self-help. The small capital requirements had, in Alfred Marshall's words, ensured that half the early entrepreneurs were born in cottages (quoted in Honeyman, 1982: 2). Personality, intelligence and determination, rather than inherited wealth and status, were the key to the meritocratic implications of early industrial leadership according to this orthodoxy – an orthodoxy not far removed from the Thatcher model of self-help in the 1980s. It was 'not the man of the greatest natural vigour and capacity who achieves the highest results, but he who employs his powers with the greatest industry and most carefully disciplined skill ... the skill that comes by labour, application and experience' (Samuel Smiles, 1958:

36, quoted in Honeyman, 1982: 4). (Note here the subordination of education to experience, which will be discussed in the next chapter.) Such appeals fell on receptive middle-class Victorian ears but appeared to make little impact on the working class (Pollard, 1965).

One clear explanation of the rise of the industrial elite and the displacement of the aristocracy at the helm of power lies in the vigour with which the ideology of laissez faire rose to prominence in the late eighteenth and early nineteenth centuries in Britain. As Adam Smith and Samuel Smiles between them managed to persuade most of the rest of the population that the free market was the route to prosperity, and paternalism the route to indolence, so the obligations of the rich for the poor fell from favour and with it the only possibility of reconstructing such a relationship into a high-trust culture. When the market portrays all individuals as essentially – and rightly – locked into a struggle of all against all, it is hardly surprising if the result is low trust. In Germany and Japan, the force of the free market ideology never attained the popularity that it did in the UK and, indeed, in the USA. In Germany the paternalist role of the state was evident in the social policies instigated by Bismarck in the nineteenth century, and the individualism that marked out the British (Macfarlane, 1978) and American contemporaries was equally noticeable by its prominent absence. Similarly, in Japan, where the absent bourgeoisie also failed to instigate either free market policies or individual political and economic freedoms, the state's role was to lead the country through industrialization not to watch from the sidelines (B. Moore, 1966; Grint and Choi, 1993).

In Britain, the result of this 'hands-off' policy, and its co-partner industrialization, was to develop a form of relationship rooted in low-trust dynamics and evident in considerable class-based mutual hostility. Coupled with the initial success of the British economy – which owed much to the absence of external competitors in manufacturing and to a particular form of acumen in finance – this model spawned a distinct form of management which was recognized as leadership, and which has come to be regarded by many in Britain still as *the* form of leadership.

It is important to remember here that such low-trust cultures do not live in the minds of the participants, nor do they live outside them. That is, the culture requires institutionalization for it to persist but what such institutionalization means for the participants may differ considerably for each one. Thus, it is only through the perpetual reenactment of low-trust decision making that it persists: low-trust does not survive by dint of some cultural idea but in and through the practices and language of participants. In Japan, the high-trust culture prevails not because the Japanese are in some way conditioned psychologically but because the consultative system embodies institutions that reproduce the perception of high trust. That the institutions themselves do not axiomatically create such high-trust is best seen by comparing the high-trust German system of industrial relations with the low-trust French one. Both have works committees systems but they only appear to operate adequately in Germany (see Lorenz, 1992). There have been attempts to build similar institutions in Britain, most notably through the Whitley Council schemes, but they have only ever prevailed in the public sector.

But we should also note that the low-trust between industrialist and employee, master and servant, did not necessarily undermine the relationship between the industrialist and the nobility. For example, given the critical significance of external trade for many manufacturers it was clear that they were crucially dependent upon the state providing satisfactory naval and military protection to trade routes and overseas markets. This could only be achieved by developing strong links with Parliament – controlled as it was then by the aristocracy. In turn, the revenue generated by such trade enabled the aristocracy to reduce its own tax requirement and to support a military system where a large proportion of its sons would find employment, status and a public role. The costs of supporting a military system that was to create and defend an empire were by no means inconsiderable. Mann calculates that between the twelfth and the nineteenth centuries something between 70 and 90 per cent of the English state's expenditure was funnelled into the military – and this directly correlates with the advent of war; figures that are mirrored by every other European state (Mann, 1986: 483–90). Even though these figures do not include the local state expenditure the point really is that the costs of an empire were extremely high – hence the mutual reliance between the landed and the industrial elites. In short, for all the divisions between the sides (and there were more than two), the industrial bourgeoisie and the aristocracy needed each other. As Colley notes, 'The cult of trade crossed party divisions' (Colley, 1994: 60). Furthermore, the industrial middle class did not pose a political threat to the aristocracy until well into the nineteenth century – the aristocracy may not have been enamoured of the industrialists and certainly did not want their sons to enter industry, but this did not stop them appreciating the industrialist's role in the provision of wealth and security. This was evident from the way trading companies provided the credit to pay for the succession of wars with France. For example, 40 per cent of the cost of the American war came from merchants and businesses (Colley, 1994: 65). In return, the industrialists and shop-keepers needed the navy for their export routes, and the army when internal strife appeared troublesome – for instance during particularly bitter strikes (Haynes, 1988) or the Luddite rebellion (see Grint and

Woolgar, 1995b). Even though the direct influence of the industrialists and merchants may have been limited by their virtual absence from Parliament in the eighteenth century, this did not stop them flooding the House with requests for favours, for legal changes and for tax reductions (Colley, 1994: 68). As Colley concludes:

> In short, the relationship between the trading interest on the one hand, and the landed interest that dominated the legislature and policy making on the other, though by no means an equal or an invariably tranquil one, was for much of the eighteenth century and after mutually beneficial. Trade was not only an indispensable part of the British economy, but also vital for the state's revenue and naval power. In return, traders depended on the state for the maintenance of civil order, for sympathetic legislation, for protection in peace and war, and for access to captive markets overseas. (Colley, 1994: 71)

Naturally, when the British war machine proved less successful, as in the American War of Independence and the early campaigns against Napoleonic France, the marriage of convenience between the captains of land and industry became rather more fractious.

In fact, even though the interests of the financial and landed elite often ran in parallel, the official explanation of events in the empire may have attempted to dissociate the one from the other. For example, in 1882 British troops occupied Egypt, ostensibly because a revolt by the nationalist element in Egypt had threatened British interests in the Suez Canal. Cain and Hopkins (1993a: 362–9), however, suggest that the bankrupting of Egypt six years earlier had culminated in defaulting on large-scale debts owed to British investors, including Gladstone himself (who had 37 per cent of his own private investment portfolio in Egypt) and the likes of Lord Rothschild. When the Egyptian government attempted to take control of its own budget back from the British, the gunboats moved in.

Searle's account suggests that, although limited liability was introduced in 1856, the small-scale family firm remained the norm until the 1880s. Even then, the absence of a united manufacturing class at Westminster, and the competitive and cultural pressures that inhibited such unity in the face of the disdain of the southern elite, did not disempower the northern manufacturers altogether. Although the competitive pressures that fractured the potential national unity of the group became replicated in the divisions that existed – and still exist – between the professions and between different technically based managers (Pollard, 1965; Armstrong, 1984; Child, 1969; Child et al. 1983; Lash and Urry, 1987; Reed and Anthony, 1992), paradoxically, perhaps,

the competition also facilitated the local political clout of these industrial magnates. Hence, although the national political victories of the
manufacturers were few and far between, theirs was a system that only
required a minimal interference from the state: once the Corn Laws
had been removed, once limited liability was in place, and once the
1867 Reform Act had secured sufficient leverage at Westminster for the
manufacturers, there was less concern for the relative absence of
industrial representatives. Anyway, where wages and conditions could
only be scientifically managed by the laws of supply and demand there
was no place for state intervention – and even less for trade unions.

This dual hostility is nicely captured by the reaction of *The Economist*
to a strike in Preston in 1853, where the downward pressure on wages
was explained as a direct consequence of the Factory Acts and the
solution to the strike was said to be for the union members and the
factory owners to unite against the land owners, whose representatives
had enforced the legislation out of their antipathy to all manufacturing
(see Searle, 1993: 274). Of course, given the significance of local
competition (which also extended to civic competition between cities),
and particularly the role of wages in that competition, in conjunction
with the decline of the radical aspects of early nineteenth-century trade
unionism, some manufacturers began to soften in their attitude towards
unions, helped along by the growth of piecework – though whether this
facilitated or diminished managerial control is still a matter of some
dispute (cf. Lewchuck, 1986; Drummond, 1989; McKinlay and Zeitlin,
1989).

Reluctant recognizers of trade unions they most certainly were, but
there were few employers who were intent on eliminating the movement. Given that the judicial interpretation of the law provided ample
opportunities for employers to write trade unions out of the game, such
as the Taff Vale decision of 1901, which made unions liable for damages,
and the Osborne decision of 1909, which undermined trade union
political activities, capitalism certainly had a chance to shake the still
young labour movement to death – but it chose not to do so. But then
since the system seemed to be relatively successful, to the extent that
economic growth persisted more or less uninterrupted until the 1930s,
there was considerably more to be lost than gained in any such radical
developments. The employers were also probably too divided amongst
themselves to co-ordinate a campaign against the trade unions and were
too hooked into the notions of voluntarism, which held the state at
arms length at all costs, to attempt to use the state to eliminate this
fundamental assumption (L.C. Hunter and Thomson, 1976). For
'experience had taught successive generations and governments of the
ruling class that their strategy of rule could cope with successive

admissions of new social groups to decision-making processes vital to society – provided these groups could be induced to work within the framework' (A. Fox, 1985: 270). This pragmatically based and concession-oriented approach bears a striking similarity in some ways to the idea of proportionality in the theory of the just war, in which action and reaction are limited to the minimum necessary to achieve the aim (see L.V. Smith, 1994).

A similar acceptance of the Factory Acts developed as the legislation appeared to put competition on an equal footing, without the need to undercut wages or conditions of work, and in an era when foreign competition in such areas was negligible. As this competition increased, British competitiveness began to decline, to the extent that by around 1870 a relative decline in manufacturing industry set in, though note that invisible earnings continued to grow until the First World War – buttressing yet further the advance of the City at the expense of the industrial north (Cain and Hopkins, 1993b) and further undermining the industrial investment that was considered necessary to resist the increasing competition (Pollard, 1989).

But accepting legal restraint did not mean undermining the essentially voluntary nature of the British industrial system. The informality of the British system is probably best represented by considering the legal constraints which operate upon management in their treatment of employees. Even at their most interventionist, in legal protection against unfair dismissal, for example, British managers are only required to act 'reasonably', and this is usually interpreted by the courts as acting rationally in pursuit of their own business interests. In effect, there is precious little legal intervention in Britain (see Collins, 1992). The origins of this disdain for legal intervention are many but of particular interest here is the way in which conceptions of society as 'already free' – and therefore without need for recourse to the law to enforce freedom – are a constant recurrence through history. For example, the spectre of the 'Norman Yoke', through which the originally 'free' state of England was temporarily undermined, is strongly echoed in the Leveller literature of the seventeenth century and, much later, in the Victorian literature and culture of the English middle classes (Morse, 1993). If all 'true-born English men' (*sic*) were already free why should there be a need for further laws to free them?

Captains of insubordination: the trade unions

Gradual, if unenthusiastic, acceptance of trade unionism was also facilitated by the general trend amongst British trade unionists to ignore most of the class-based calls for unity and political action that socialists had made throughout the nineteenth century. It does seem to be the case that socialism as a political ideology was important in facilitating the kind of culture within which capitalists could be resisted through a labour organization, though religion also had its role to play here; and under the conditions facing some groups, such as miners, the development of any kind of independent organization was a massive undertaking when the owners of the mine owned the very houses miners lived in, the schools their children attended, the church they prayed in, and the local state they appealed to (R. Moore, 1974). Even radicals like William Morris had warned that socialism was not merely:

> higher wages, more regular employment, shorter working hours, better education for your children, old age pensions, parks and the rest ... [if] that is all you want then I say here that this is the real advice to give you: Don't meddle with socialism. Make peace with your employers before it is too late ... consider their interests as well as your own ... make sacrifices today that you will do well tomorrow, compete your best with foreign nations ... and I think you will do well .. at any rate you will make the best of the prosperity there is left us as workmen. (W. Morris, 1983)

Yet, at least for the most part and most clearly for the first half of the nineteenth century, most managers appear to have assumed that trade unions were only agents of insubordination and indiscipline, rather than parties to an 'effort bargain' that might be mutually beneficial (Haynes, 1988: 255–60). Furthermore, as Fox put it: 'not only doctrines of economic liberalism but also later doctrines urging a mass horizontal unity of the whole wage earning class were working against much of the grain of the British trade union instinct, inclined as it was towards seeking security through exclusion of labour market competitors rather than emancipation through class unity' (1985: 64).

Thus it was 'labourism', a policy of incremental advances through the existing system, rather than socialism, originally aimed at overthrowing the system, which survived. As long as labourism provided real if intermittent wage increases (which it did for most of the period from 1850 onwards); as long as the working class was itself fractured by occupation, status and gender; and as long as the state appeared to play by the rules of the game – to 'submit to their own rules' as E.P. Thompson (1977) called it – there was little to be gained and much to be lost from adopting a more radical approach to political and industrial life (Kynaston, 1976; Grint, 1991). There were several more violent forms of protest – by the Luddites against new technology (Grint and Woolgar, 1995b); by the 'Rebecca' rioters against toll roads (J.V. Jones,

1989); and by Captain Swing rioters against farm machinery (Hobsbawm and Rudé, 1969) – but none developed into the widespread movement that Chartism became and even Chartism was snuffed out by the 'appropriate' concessions of the authorities (D. Jones, 1975).

The predominant labourist strategy was hardly novel, nor was it essentially working class; on the contrary, the English aristocracy had wielded the rights enshrined in common law to defend themselves and their privileges against the encroachments of the state and the crown for many centuries, and the early craft guilds merely reproduced what was self-evidently a successful – and ostensibly 'natural' (that is culturally English) custom. In short, a truculent and independent, rather than a radical and collective, ideology tended to prevail. In fact, Fox argues that much of this ideology has its roots in the English predilection for liberties which 'littered English life at all social levels' and which derives from the Anglo-Saxon focus upon common law rather than the continental European preference for civil law. From origins wrapped in myth and mist, it is not difficult to see how such common liberties came to be seen as (temporarily) subjugated to the 'Norman Yoke' and to set the kind of approach to social life that would result in a preference for empiricism rather than theory and, in education, for the practicalities of training and apprenticeships rather than the conceptual arenas of theory and education. This heritage was also used, for example, by the Marine Society, a patriotic organization set up in the mid-eighteenth century by merchants and essentially small-scale capitalists (in the face of a national state reluctance to take proactive action), to encourage unemployed and vagrant men, and orphaned and pauper boys, to enter the Royal Navy and fight against France. As the rhetoric demonstrated, liberty was all:

> You are the sons of freemen. Though poor, you are the sons of Britons, who are born to liberty; but remember that true liberty consists in doing well; in defending each other, in obeying your superiors and in fighting for your King and Country to the last drop of your blood. (Quoted in Colley, 1994: 97)

British capitalism, British managers and British trade unionists developed, therefore, against a background where the local actions of small-scale companies and voluntary groups compensated for the centralizing actions of the state that occurred in Germany, Japan and France.

In the USA the diverse patterns of immigrants, in conjunction with the general hostility of the federal state to labour organizations, also made the construction of class-based trade unions more difficult, and employers like Ford were not slow to take advantage of ethnic divisions wherever possible. But it should be remembered that all ethnic groups were involved in the defence of their own territory and culture and hence the employees were as much responsible for the limited popularity of class-based unions as employers were. Indeed, the only major progress made by unions appears to have been the development of 'business unionism', a highly centralized form specifically designed to limit concerns to the bread-and-butter issues of improving pay and conditions. Relatedly, the response of the American political left to this situation was more along sectarian and purist lines than in attempts to secure pragmatic advances for trade unionists. The long-term result of the often industrially militant, but not politically radical, union movement has been a gradual decline in membership and influence, as the pragmatically oriented and instrumentally directed unions and their members have courted, and been courted by, both main political parties – to the extent that there is no longer (even if there ever was) a clear allegiance between the Democrats and the trade union movement.

In the USA the anti-state philosophy did not, however, lead to the proliferation of small-scale, family-owned businesses. On the contrary, the US economy rapidly transformed itself into the premier example of 'big business'. Was the survival of the family firm, and the resistance to growth strategies that would have infused companies with both capital and professional management, a major cause of the relative decline of British industry?

Family capitalism

The gradual evolution of the firm from an ideal type where the family owned and controlled it, to another ideal type where ownership and control were clearly separated, was first noted in the seminal article of Berle and Means (1932), who argued that the separation brought with it the possibility of contradictory interests: the owners of stock seeking maximum returns and the managers seeking the long-run interests of the firm and themselves. Whether that long-run interest became manifest as sales maximization, as Baumol (1959) suggested, or maximizing growth, or whether the conflicting demands of shareholders, employees, customers and managers usually resulted in a managerial strategy that sought out satisficing options that embodied viable compromises across the different stakeholders (Cyert and March, 1963), was another matter. Nevertheless, the invisible hand of the market was clearly being displaced by the visible hand of particular stakeholder interests.

Such a visible hand highlights the prior invisible role that managers played in the development of organizations. Since neo-classical models assumed that the external market determined the actions of the agent, management could really add very little, except perhaps in eliminating the marginal or X-inefficiencies that Liebenstein (1966) subsequently highlighted as occurring within organizations when people did not act at the highest level of potential efficiency; an argument that Marx related to the difference between labour and labour power (see Grint, 1991: 94–7).

This problematizing of the neo-classical position (which assumed that the market determined the actions of any economic agent or organization; see Gospel, 1989) was also undertaken by Coarse (1953), who had originally argued in the 1930s that the large corporations then emerging could displace the market through their internal co-ordination of resources, thus (potentially) reducing transaction costs. It was upon this foundation that Williamson (1975) built his model, which suggests that under conditions of bounded rationality (that is, limited information), organizations do rather more than just maximize profits. A further aspect of this development was noted by Chandler's (1977) work, in which the internalization of markets where transaction costs are high, in effect, tended to lead to vertical integration. Large firms undertaking this internalization would also tend to develop bureaucratic mechanisms for controlling the multiple levels of organization, leading to what was called a uniform (U-form) centralized control system. Inevitably, it seemed, multiple hierarchies undermined the effectiveness of central control and even by the 1930s some organizations (such as General Motors, and before them Siemens in Germany) had adopted an alternative multi-divisional (M-form) organization, which was considerably more decentralized than their U-form competitors. It was the case, as Chandler argued, that 'the modern business enterprise became a viable institution only after the visible hand of management proved to be more efficient than the invisible hand of market forces in co-ordinating the flow of materials through the economy' (1977: 339; see C.H. Lee, 1990 – which this section is based upon – for a longer review). Indeed, one of the three 'prongs' of investment that propelled the USA to its leading position by 1913 was an investment in management (the other two being production facilities, and a marketing and distribution network). It is the absence of investment in British management that Chandler asserts to be the leading explanation for long-run failure and, indeed, Chandler is keen to point out that in many areas there is no long run – if organizations do not respond appropriately then the window of opportunities slams shut extraordinarily quickly. Some did make it – British Oxygen, Metal Box, Unilever, ICI and EMI, for example – and Chandler tends to explain these survivors through a deeper managerial hierarchy – an interesting claim in the present context when thinning managerial hierarchies appears to be all the rage. Many other leading firms did not make it. For example, in 1870 the British had all the advantages in the production of textile dyes: they were invented by William Perkin, Britain had the largest single market, and it had all the raw materials necessary, except one – chemists, and these were hired from Germany. Yet it was the German firms Bayer, BASF and Hoesch that eventually succeeded (Chandler, 1992).

In the USA the corporate structure developed much faster and more intensely than that in either Germany or the UK, with a rapid shift towards large-scale corporations from early in this century. Of course, being the home of mass production also facilitated the rise of mass labour but the history of virulent, and sometimes violent, union suppression, in conjunction with the ever open West and an almost constant demand for labour, configured to generate strong support for individual solutions to industrial problems rather than the collective solutions that were more typical in Britain. 'The American Dream', or the possibility of everyone moving from log cabin to the White House, simply makes no sense in a country like Britain where those who seek to take giant strides away from their own background are, or at least were, frequently derided as 'getting above their station', 'getting above themselves' or 'forgetting where they came from'. The response in the USA, when things were perceived to be troublesome, was more often to seek an individual solution (go West) than to seek a collective one (join the union). The response in Britain was likely to be the opposite. As Hampden-Turner and Trompenaars (1994) suggest, following Belluh et al. (1985), the archetypal American heroic figure is certainly an individual (and usually a man) but it is an individual who saves a society which he (or she) cannot join. This is probably best represented by watching almost any Clint Eastwood Western, in which the hero invariably rides out of town at the end, having just risked his life to save it.

Since the costs of labour were also high as a result of the persistent demand (hence the material inducements to many Europeans to emigrate to the USA), they rapidly became a source of conflict between employees and employers, and while Taylor sought to ally the 'right' worker to the 'right' technology, Ford tended to prefer to eliminate workers through technical advances. Given the huge size and relative prosperity of the US internal market it is a commonplace to assume that the opposite conditions in the UK inhibited this quest for technological development. In effect, while the surplus labour in Britain discouraged the search for technical innovation, the high demand for and cost of labour stimulated the American capitalist to either replace labour or at least attempt a vigorous control over labour costs. However, we should be sceptical of claims that the absence of a large-scale market, like the American one, necessarily inhibited technological innovations, since there are good counter-examples, especially in steel production (Dintenfass, 1992: 18).

But we should not exaggerate the significance of such large corporations, at least in the British context. Excluding agriculture, public administration and the armed forces, in 1907 the largest single company in terms of employees was the British General Post Office (GPO) with 212,310 employees, followed by six railway companies; Lever Brothers and Cadbury's came 84th and 85th respectively with total staffs of 4,700 and 4,683. In 1935 the GPO was still dominant with 231,877 and the largest non-railway company was Unilever, in seventh position with 60,000 staff. By 1955 the nationalized railways topped the board with 801,199, followed by the Coal Board and the GPO; ICI was the largest private company with 115,306, but, again, only the top 100 organizations could boast a staff of more than 10,000 (Jeremy, 1990). In contrast, German firms were, on average, much larger than their British counterparts and this is even more the case with US firms (Chandler, 1990).

It certainly was the case, then, that British industry was mainly dispersed in a very large number of very small organizations. At the end of the nineteenth century the average size of British companies was still a mere dozen or so employees, headed by the owner, not a professional manager. Yet the survival rate of family firms in nineteenth-century Britain was so poor that it is difficult to pin the blame for Britain's economic decline, as Wiener (1981) does, on the displacement of economic by social objectives on the part of large numbers of second- and third-generation business families: there simply were not enough of these to make a significant difference (G. Jones and Rose, 1993: 6). Anyway, by the mid–1920s Britain's largest 100 corporations accounted for the same share of manufacturing output (about 22 per cent) as did the largest 100 corporations in the USA. The irony is not just that family-owned firms were probably more efficient than much of the literature makes out, but that the more the British corporate structure resembled its American, German and Japanese competition, the less efficient it became (Dintenfass, 1992: 9):

As late as the turn of the century Britain still accounted for almost one-third of the total 'world' trade in manufactured goods. This was half as large again as Germany's share and three times the share of the United States. Seventy years later Britain's share of the world trade in industrial commodities had fallen to less than one-tenth ... By the early 1980s British imports of manufactured goods exceeded British exports – reversing a positive balance that had persisted since the industrial revolution. (Dintenfass, 1992: 9–10)

Equally dubious is the assumption that the era of 'family' or 'pro-prietary' capitalism was one restricted to the nineteenth century. As G. Jones and Rose (1993: 1) point out, 'family firms account for between 75 per cent and 99 per cent of all companies in the EC.' When Michelin, Mars, C&A, 50 per cent of Sweden's multinational manufacturers and Jardine Matheson are all owned by relatively small family groups – and Korean, Arab and Chinese industries are, if anything, even more critically dependent upon family ownership – the end of the family capitalist is still clearly a long way off, whatever the concerns that Chandler (1990) and Lazonick (1993) may have about the alleged inefficiencies of such an organizational form. For Lazonick, in particu-lar, the eclipse of first Britain by Germany and the USA, and then the latter by Japan, can be explained primarily by the shifting contours of capitalist formations. Britain's proprietary capitalism was 'appropriate' for the nineteenth century, when technology was relatively unsophis-ticated and fixed costs generally low, but the increasing competition that stimulated the search for, and development of, expensive plant soon left the British family forms stumbling; indeed, many went out of their way to avoid growth since this would inevitably have led to their becoming dependent on both external sources of finance and specia-lized management. On the other hand, as G. Jones and Rose's review suggests (1993), family firms do offer the possibility of a long-term perspective that has so often been missing from British companies.

Yet the question might be not whether managers have a long-term view but what kind of long-term view they have. For instance, the long-term view of a typical nineteenth-century textile magnate might well have been that the most important issue was keeping the firm in family hands – irrespective of what this would do to the long-term profitability of the firm. On the other hand, the Korean family firms, or *chaebols*, have managed both long-term growth and the retention of family control – though this has been achieved through state assistance to transcend the borrowing problems that typically beset family firms (G. Jones and Rose, 1993: 4). Since Japanese *zaibatsu* between the wars were similarly structured to their British family-owned counterparts but pursued remarkably different strategies (and there were as many family-owned firms in Germany as in Britain until about 1930: Church, 1993), and since the strategies of British family-owned and non-family-owned companies were remarkably similar (Coleman, 1987), one is led to conclude that the critical issue here is not the pattern of ownership but the cultural predilection for particular kinds of corporate strategy. This, of course, does not mean that British culture did not play a critical role in the decline of the British economy, or at least British manufacturing, but it does imply that family firms as institutional forms were not wholly responsible.

Conclusion

This chapter has provided a brief overview of the historical development of management, with particular regard paid to the case of British management. I began by considering the changes to British management, or lack of them, in terms of the Japanese response in 1852 to the arrival of the American 'black ships'. The portent of doom heralded by these alien manifestations spurred the Japanese to reverse their previous (seventeenth-century) quarantining of 'the other' and attempt to emulate certain elements of it in an effort to retain the sanctity of the national boundary. In Britain, the equivalent black ships – which ironically arrived only three years afterwards at the Paris Exhibition – provoked either no response or that of quarantining, in which competition was displaced or ignored. I suggest that the evidence of this chapter suggests that 'carrying on regardless' is a more appropriate description of British management history than anything else is. The slow relative decline of the British economy that began in the 1870s and accelerated in the 1970s shows some marginal signs of change but not the radical about-turn that may be necessary.

Explanations for this gradual decline have filled numerous journals and textbooks, and this chapter has merely skimmed the surface of this material in an attempt to provide a skeletal framework from which some particular areas have been highlighted. In particular, I have concentrated on the construction of a national identity during the early part of the nineteenth century, and considered the extent to which Wellington came to be constructed both in opposition to Napoleon and as a representation of the archetypal British character – in contradistinction to the French. What particularly interests me is the extent to which Wellington's character, or rather the character that we have come to associate with the man, can be read as a motif for British management. Thus the hard-working, dutiful, organized and aristocratic Wellington (as opposed to the over-talented, precocious, charismatic and meritocratic Napoleon) represents the values held dear by British management. In effect, this kind of short-term-oriented, improvising, unemotional, non-intellectual British management came to be seen as both truly British and, given the military and economic power of Britain during the nineteenth century, the rational way of organizing business.

In turn, the British social system has perpetuated this particular way of undertaking business, both in the general subordination of manufacturing industry to the interests of land and finance, and in the particular actions of the three major groups: the landed and financial elite, the industrial capitalists and the working class. While the aristocracy merged with the aspiring financial capitalists to dominate the social, economic and political life of the country, the manufacturing capitalists remained, for the most part, content to dominate only their own locale. Yet the split between these two groups was never complete, and however much their interests diverged they also needed each other. The landed and financial elite needed an empire to run, a military system to populate with its sons, and a global status to match its ambitions; for all this they needed the tax-wealth generated by industry. In turn, industry needed its overseas markets and trade routes protecting, and a state prepared, if necessary, to control local insubordination and to generate sympathetic legislation. Such insubordination as did occur was generally limited to the formation of trade unions by the working classes to protect themselves, in turn, from the onerous master-and-servant traditions that had tried to keep workers as the vassals they had once been. Yet the unions were rooted in the same libertarian beliefs that the industrialists had used to wrest some political leverage from the aristocracy – who in turn had used them to resist the absolutist pretensions of the monarchy. Sullen and resistant to capitalism and management the workers may have been, but revolutionary they were not.

Part of the reason for this may have been the relatively small-scale and family-owned form of capitalism that prevailed for most of Britain's industrial history. In the land of Wellington there were few examples of grand strategies, few cases where individual flair shook the world to its foundations, and even fewer opportunities for individuals of low birth to rise to the top of the tree. Instead, family capitalism predominated in the land, an array of small-scale organizations that may not have been as innovative or as dominant as their German or American counterparts but were relatively successful nevertheless; indeed the more British capital resembled 'the other' the less successful it became. In the next chapter I take a closer look at contemporary developments in management.

3

Mimetic Pyrophobes: What are Managers, What do Managers Do, and Why do they Do What They Do?

Introduction

This chapter introduces the reader to the contemporary sociology of management by first pondering on the identity of managers to consider whether they can be distinguished by task or context, and goes on to discuss what their tasks actually are. Having established what appears to be a consensus, the discussion then moves to analyse three rather different answers to the same question: why do managers do what they do? The first answer is the traditional one, rooted in rational behaviour within a market economy: managers do what they do because the environment requires such action: those who fail to take the required action do not last long as managers. The second answer questions the extent to which the environment just happens to be as it is and suggests that the contingencies of history are an essential element in explaining the motivation of management behaviour. The third answer suggests that we might be more circumspect in announcing any such discovery because the methods that we use to 'uncover' the truth about management seem to be implicated in what the truth actually is. In effect, the last section continues the theoretical argument sketched out in the previous chapter and considers the extent to which management is a construction rather than a discovery.

What are managers?

Most dictionaries carefully avoid the problem of defining managers by considering them as 'people who manage'. Management tends to be defined as one or more of the following: the action or manner of managing; the working of land (dialect 'manuring'); the use of contrivance for effecting some purpose; administrative skill; indulgence; a governing body; and, finally, addicted to scheming. None of these definitions is particularly helpful if we are seeking a definitive account, but they are all significant in casting different lights on what might appear to be the same phenomenon.

Another way in to the problem is to assert from the start that managers are both those people who are paid to manage – professional managers – and those people who have to co-ordinate resources in some form – just about everybody. By asserting that a position of superordination 'above foreman ... and above first level supervision in an office' is also required (Stewart, 1994: 2), Stewart immediately draws the boundary around the professional implicated in some degree of power over others. Thus we are left with what appears to be another tautology: managers are those people who are paid to be managers. Yet the tautological nature of the statement is not simply an erroneous and therefore redundant aspect. On the contrary, what counts as a manager is a critical issue, since by definition it simultaneously demarcates the target group by establishing what appear to be relatively viable boundary lines, and, more importantly, denotes the significance of the economic and the political relationships in the construction of this group. Those people who are in charge of or responsible for others, but who are not acting as economic agents for the 'owners' of the organizations (public or private), are not managers in this discourse: being a parent is not the equivalent of being a manager in this world. Those people who are acting as economic agents for the 'owners' of the organizations (public or private) but who are not in charge of others are not managers here either: a self-employed builder is not a manager. Management, in this world, then, is a superordinate position within an employment hierarchy. Those groups that dominate employment organizations are managers.

However, as I have argued elsewhere (Grint, 1991), if work is defined by the social context and not the content of the activity then we should be wary of assuming that we can define who managers are by concentrating on what they do. Let us take this further by comparing what managers are supposed to do with what parents are supposed to do.

According to Hales (1986) management's task is to lead, liaise, monitor, allocate resources, maintain production, maintain peace, innovate, plan and control. Yet parents lead their families ('this way you lot'), liaise with various people about them ('it couldn't have been our children, officer'), monitor their actions ('I'm still watching you'), allocate resources ('it cannot be pocket-money day already'), maintain 'production' ('what do you mean you don't like fish fingers?'), maintain peace ('stop arguing!'), innovate ('let's change the room round'), plan ('if we go to the library first we can buy some sweets on the way back') and control ('go to bed!'). Indeed one would be hard-pressed to find many people who did not undertake these activities at some time in their normal day. The implication is that managers do not necessarily undertake actions that are dramatically different from those undertaken by anyone else, and that what managers do is closely related to their social situation. If one acquires the status of a manager then one's actions will become regarded as those appertaining to a manager; if one is a parent then what a parent does is manage through parenting but not become a manager.

The importance of this should not be obscured by what appears to be a semantic squabble: what managers do does not depend upon the actions they undertake but who ascribes to their actions the actions of management. In effect, if managers are involved in conversation they are managing, they are not engaged in idle chatter; but if children are involved in conversation they are more likely to be deemed to be engaging in idle chatter rather than any form of management. Who managers are, in other words, depends on who has the power to constitute certain forms of action as the actions of managers.

Does this contextual answer to the question of who managers are also imply that the tasks which managers undertake are equally contextual? That is, is what managers do little different from what anyone might do – but the context within which the act occurs differentiates the manager from the non-manager?

What do managers do?

Whitley (1989) certainly agrees that management tasks are interdependent and contextual but argues that, unlike non-managerial tasks, they are also relatively unstandardized, changeable, involve developing routines and restructuring, and rarely lead to overt outcomes that can be associated with individual inputs. One might want to argue that the tasks of most soldiers in war or most orchestra players are akin to this, and if this is so then one is led back to the significance of the context within which the task occurs and not the task itself.

Given this amount of contextual baggage it is, perhaps, little wonder that managers have considerable freedom to do what they can or to do what they like (Stewart, 1982). Either way, the traditional assumption about what most managers, or rather most British managers, end up doing is undertaking pyrophobic duties most of the time; that is, they dash from one emergency to the next resolving short-term problems and crises whilst keeping 'production' or 'the system' going: they fire-fight.

Fire-fighting for managers is probably a misnomer since fire-fighters generally have to undertake a lot of physically strenuous activity with water and chemicals to douse fires. For managers the more appropriate analogy might be one where fires are suffocated with words: linguistic asphyxiation. It does, after all, seem to be the case that most management action is involved in the articulation of orders and requests to subordinates or peers (Stewart, 1976): management is about talk, if it is about anything.

Management in traditional theory, though, is task- not talk-oriented: it is the co-ordination, monitoring and allocation of material and human resources. But, as is made clear in the previous chapter, we really know very little about management activity even before the Second World War, let alone in the eighteenth and nineteenth centuries. Fayol (1949), writing in 1916, for example, suggested that managers had clear-cut duties that involved planning, organizing, co-ordinating, commanding (or motivating) and controlling. However, according to Stewart (1994), studies of what managers actually did, rather than what management theorists thought they did, only began in earnest in the 1950s, with Carlson's (1951) study of seven Swedish and two French executives' behaviour over a four-week period. The reactive socializer rather than the machined decision taker was the picture that emerged as managers fought fires with words and networks of colleagues and subordinates.

Perhaps more significantly, the differences between managers, between managerial jobs, between managerial cultures and even between the same manager in different elements of space and time appear to be as striking as any similarities, at least in Stewart's diary-based studies (Stewart, 1967), though again, the fragmented and discursive essence of managerial work is clearly evident. This apart, contextual aspects seem to be critical (Kotter, 1982; Stewart, 1994: 1), and most of the tasks seem to be accomplished through a sophisticated system of social networking rather than through the direct action of any one particular manager (Sayles, 1964).

Mintzberg's (1973) assessment confirmed the significance of the social network but tended to stress instead the informational processing and direct action of his five American CEOs. For Handy (1985) the corresponding profession is not fire-fighting but general medical practice, as the general practitioner becomes the first port of call for all kinds of problem and seldom spends more than a fraction of any day dealing with one particular case or issue. Management, then, is apparently a reactive and fragmentary task not a proactive or holistic occupation. Whether it is like this or not we shall reconsider in the next section.

Why do managers do what they do?

Why managers do what they do seems at first sight to be more controversial than what managers are or what they do. In what follows, three rather different approaches are considered. First, there is the standard argument that management action is driven by rationality, primarily that associated with the rationality of the market, whether from a perspective that is sympathetic or from one that is hostile to capitalism. Second, there is the argument that suggests that it is not so much rationality as history that drives managers to manage in the way that they do: we are all, to a greater or lesser extent, prisoners of our history: managers do what they do because the accretion of historical traditions lays down pathways that more or less constrain them to act in particular ways. In this case the argument will concentrate on the role of management education, but other aspects of history could have been chosen had not some of them been considered in the previous chapter. The final section switches this approach around to ponder on the role the researcher plays in constructing rather than reflecting or describing explanations of management action.

The rationality of management

From the beginnings of industrial capitalism in the late eighteenth century in Britain, and certainly since Adam Smith's *Wealth of Nations*, published in 1776, management tasks and causal explanations have been locked into models of rational behaviour ultimately embedded in the operations of the market: managers do what they do because the imperatives of the market require that it be done. Those managers who do not manage in this way follow the fate of the dodo – their inability to adapt to a changing environment ensures their extinction.

Weber's (1978) account of managerial rationality is rather more fabricated around concerns for changes in the development of different modes of legitimacy, in which the legitimacy of tradition is gradually displaced by that of rational administration. That is, superordinates are obeyed by subordinates less because they have always obeyed superordinates like monarchs and chiefs, whose power is premised upon ideas of hereditary distinction, and more because the superordinates, like managers, are 'experts' in their profession. They are obeyed because the subordinates recognize that it is rational to obey them. The combination of expertise with rational administration, set in an environment driven by the hidden hand of the market, sets the stage for the rise of the manager (see Grint, 1991: 104–11).

Chandler (1977) extended this explanation of managerial activity and locked it, overtly or otherwise, to the ever-burgeoning growth of managerial hierarchies, themselves a consequence, allegedly, of the increasing complexity of organizations. The division of labour, reported by Adam Smith, requires managers to co-ordinate this otherwise diffuse and centripetal network; hence managers do what is functionally required of them. A consequence of this, originally according to Berle and Means (1932) and Burnham (1962), would be that management, as a social group, would displace all other powerful groups to become the new elite in the 'managerial revolution' (see Burch, 1972; Scott, 1979; Fidler, 1981). Beyond the functional requirement, managers would maintain their position and execute their co-ordinating activities by monitoring their subordinates. Indeed, there are good grounds for assuming that many of the early developments towards factory labour were premised not on the superior technical capacity of the machinery (since much the same machinery was already in place in many cottages) but on the disciplinary effects of managers on formerly free labour. In effect, by controlling labour, management was able to achieve much higher levels of productivity than could be achieved under the previous cottage-based system of 'putting out' (see Marglin, 1982; Landes, 1986; Grint and Woolgar, 1995b).

In the absence of any objective criteria by which managers can be assessed (see chapter 4 for an account of this as far as formal appraisal systems are concerned, and Grint and Woolgar, 1995b for an account of the significance of this in assessing technological capacity), and in a world where collective action is crucial but where individual performance is critical, one might be tempted to look closely at *why* managers spend their time in an apparent frenzy of discontinuous fire-fighting, rather than in some apparently ideal state where long-term strategic thinking is undertaken, safe in the knowledge that (a) fires are much less likely to break out *because* of this planning, and (b) where fires do occur the local operators are sufficiently skilled and responsible to extinguish them without disturbing the cerebral work of their alleged superiors. Thus the context within which most managers manage appears to be one that is very conducive to the short-term and reactive self-publicist rather than the long-term and proactive altruist.

To imply that acting in the interests of the organization, rather than in one's own interest, is altruistic is guaranteed to raise the hackles of anti-capitalist labour-process or 'critical' interpretations of management (see Reed, 1990, for a longer review). Under this approach capitalism as a system is both philosophically alienating and economically exploitive, hence to act in the interests of a capitalist organization is not to manage altruistically but to participate in the further oppression of the majority of the population. Drawn originally from the seminal work of Marx and reborn through Braverman's (1974) polemic against the apparent deskilling imperative of late industrial capitalism, this approach is, nevertheless, locked into assumptions about the rational explanation for managerial behaviour. Managers do what they do because the dynamics of the capitalist market coerce them into such actions. Those that do not exploit their employees are not good – that is humane – managers but short-sighted ones, because only those who are securing the maximum amount of surplus from their employees will survive the rigours of the market. This is important because if managers could make a difference, that is could act humanely by not alienating and exploiting their employees, then capitalism as a system could provide the basis for a qualitatively superior form of existence. However, since alienation and exploitation are structural features of capitalism, not the results of individual character, they are necessary to its very survival and no amount of tinkering with the system will ensure social justice: it is the system which is inherently malicious, not the individuals who find themselves within it. Thus managers under capitalism must act on behalf of capitalism or they will become mere employees themselves. It was for this reason that Marx considered the actions of trade unions and co-operatives to be merely ameliorative not transformative.

Just how deterministic this model of management is depends upon whose model one reads: Braverman's (1974) version provides far less freedom to act than did some of Marx's original ideas, and recent developments in the labour-process approach have attempted to construct accounts of why managers do what they do in a rather more subtle way (Willmott, 1984; P. Thompson and McHugh, 1990), though some of them still tend to follow the functionalist overtones of the general 'rational' approach that explains managerial behaviour by recourse to the imperatives of the market.

In sum, although the moral assumptions behind the pro- and anti-capitalist accounts of what managers do, and why they do it, are diametrically opposite, with the traditional managerialist approach supporting the action and the labour-process approach criticizing it, the analytic framework remains similar: managers have virtually no choice if they wish to remain in employment as managers. Since workers' interests are the opposite of managers it is in the interests of managers' to exploit the workers and in the workers' interests to resist this exploitation at all points – both sides are imprisoned by the prison of industrial capitalism. This juxtaposition of opposition is most apparent when Taylorism is considered (as it was by Lenin, for example) as a technically neutral system of work management – the problem for such accounts is not what Taylorism required managers to do but why they did it (see Traub, 1978; Nyland, 1987).

Yet no general rational account of managerial action can explain managerial behaviour if the behaviour differs in space and time. If British managers are fire-fighters, is there something about the British economy which demands such a response and therefore explains it as rational? For example, compared to Japanese corporations, most British corporations have a much higher proportion of their shares in 'hostile' hands – that is hands seeking short-term rewards and disinterested in long-term progress. This might require managers to spend their time fire-fighting because the time period for measuring the performance of their company is so small. On the other hand, if this is the case, and if it is detrimental to the performance of industry generally, one might expect the 'rational' response by industry and the government to be one which alters the pattern of share-ownership or at least the power of shareholders. Could it be that the short-termism of British industry – which has a long history – is itself the result of 'accidents' of history rather than rational responses to external dynamics? This is the subject of the next section.

The rational management of history

One of the difficulties with reconciling the analytic accounts of the actions of managers with prescriptive accounts of what they should be doing is evaluating the extent to which fire-fighting is a task that management ought to spend most of their time on. There are suggestions that neither German nor Japanese managers, for example, are pyrophobic to the same extent as the British and probably American managers are. Does the difference between the national management styles (if there are any) reflect the different situations that the managers find themselves in – or is it simply because different national groups have different traditions that are unrelated to the contingencies of space and time? Or perhaps it is the very traditions that cause the production and reproduction of the contingencies: that, for instance, the massive effort oriented towards fire-fighting inhibits the concentration on alternative methods of management that would eliminate the fires in the first place.

There is certainly a strong body of opinion that asserts that the pyrophobic actions of British management can be laid at the door of the particular approach to the education of those involved in business. This tradition assumes that British management's distaste for, and consequent lack of, managerial education – which is as widely known as it is difficult to change – produced a tradition of hands-on, reactive, short-term and pragmatic management. The roots of this lie in the twin stereotyped spectres at the British feast: an aristocratic spectre that attempts to avoid any association with the world of industry and a parallel industrialists' spectre that reciprocates by avoiding any association with the world of (elite) education. The former can be unravelled by a reading of the educational format regarded as appropriate for the likes of middle- and upper-class 'gentlemen' (women were not considered fit to attend most public schools), whose education was deemed to be sufficient to cope with any problem through a close perusal of Ancient Greece and Rome; the more closely the substance of education approached the contemporary world, and the nearer it moved from the realm of ideas to the realm of things, the less useful it was deemed to be. Indeed, it smacked of the utilitarian logic that the aristocracy regarded with as much distaste as they did the equivalent idea that one should actually 'work' for one's living. If nineteenth-century working-class patriarchal shame hinged on whether working-class wives had to engage in paid work outside the home (excluding the textile regions of northern England), then aristocratic patriarchal shame hinged on aristocratic men having to 'work' at all: the greater the distance between the aristocrat and any overt means of economic activity the higher the status (see Grint, 1991).

This reverberated right through the universities of the time. For example, Oxford University did not undertake engineering degrees until well into this century, despite having its first chair in 1908, and even though University College London had a chair in 1828 and Cambridge's Mechanical Sciences Tripos began in 1892 (Guagnini, 1993). That management schools have developed in Oxford and Cambridge only in the last few years is testimony to the continuing strength of the hostility to matters of business. When the British Empire needed running, and when economic prosperity appeared to be an inevitable product of the elitist educational system, the pressure for change was minimal. Was the fire-fighting tendency of British managers related to this general distaste for business education?

The early industrial lead that Britain acquired through the industrial revolution may have provoked a reluctance to invest in new technologies and organizational forms when things still seemed to be going relatively well. But from William Fairburn's warning at the Paris Exhibition in 1855, through the Devonshire Commission of 1872, the Samuelson Commission of 1884, the Mosley Commission in 1902, and right up to the time of writing (August 1994), there is considerable evidence that people knew Britain was continually slipping behind and that the one feature that always emerged at the time, rather than *post hoc*, in the explanations for this was Britain's educational system – or rather the problems with it (see Roderick and Stephens, 1981; Sanderson, 1972). Moreover, in areas like motor manufacturing, where Britain did not have an early technological lead, it did not, therefore, have an accumulated investment – but neither did it ever catch up with the American market leaders. For example, Morris Motors, Britain's largest car manufacturer, did not develop moving assembly lines, conveyor belts or the mechanization of the assembly process until 1933, twenty years after Ford in the USA (Dintenfass, 1992: 21–6). And while the surfeit of relatively skilled workers *may* have acted to deter investment in expensive machinery in the early nineteenth century without damaging the short-term efficiency of the British economy, by the second half of the century Britain's comparative advantage now seemed to lie with unskilled, labour-intensive industries (Crafts, 1989).

A leading suspect in the search for the guilty party, in Britain at least, was a social order educated through the public schools and Oxbridge into the duties of loyalty and order, in which the newly melded amalgam of old land and new finance existed to run the empire and keep out the twin evils of labour and manufacturing (Cain and Hopkins, 1993a; Cannadine, 1992). As Cain and Hopkins assert: 'The empire was a superb arena for gentlemanly endeavour, the ultimate testing ground for the idea of responsible progress, for the battle against evil, for the performance of duty, and the achievement of honour' (1993a: 34). It was also, of course, a useful place for exporters to run to when competition became too intense on the open market – as it appeared to do in the early 1930s, when, after Britain's share of world exports in manufactured products had declined from 41 per cent to 20 per cent in the preceding four decades, Britain abandoned the gold standard and introduced the Import Duties Act (Rooth, 1993).

Equally significant for our purposes, the form of work undertaken by this elite group not only secured an invisible income at a distance but also relied upon a high level of trust, since access to information was critical to financial success in which transactions 'were both informal and efficient' (Cain and Hopkins, 1993a: 36). It can hardly be coincidental that this replicated the system of personal honour that public schools were designed to engender. Wiener (1981) argues that public schools played a significant role in turning the sons of business men against their cultural background to end up much like their aristocratic colleagues – anti-business. But Rubinstein's (1993) counter-critique suggests first that most of the sons of business men in the nineteenth century did not attend public school anyway – so they cannot have been 'infected' by the anti-business culture. Moreover, he is doubtful whether Britain ever really was 'the workshop of the world', given its limited pre-eminence at the top of the industrial tree, and wonders whether it should really be reconceptualized as 'the banker of the world', a position it has held virtually unchanged since 1690 when it vied with Amsterdam, and a claim that Cain and Hopkins (1993a, 1993b) would have little quibble with. Yet Rubinstein's critique misses some of the point: that the sons of the captains of industry were not 'tainted' by the public-school system still leaves unchallenged the idea that such sons (and it was taken for granted that daughters would not be involved) never made it to the positions of power – because they lacked the 'cultural capital' (Bourdieu and Passeron, 1977) to do so. The more important point is the absence of effect through their absence in terms not of their cultural sympathies, but of their subsequent political exclusion and weakness.

This hostility to technical education on the part of the social and educational elite, so richly reproduced in the works of Wiener (1981) and Barnett (1986), does not, in itself, explain the problem of British manufacturing, since the prejudice is common to most European nations, at least until the 1930s (Raven, 1989; Daunton, 1989; Fox and Guagnini, 1993) – the exception appears to be Sweden (Ahlström, 1993). There is certainly some evidence which suggests that the problem in Britain in particular relates to the small size of the average firm and the limited financial resources available for educational investment (R. Fox and Guagnini, 1993). Indeed, the level of investment in education necessary to develop some of the early technologies in the industrial revolution seem to have been relatively modest when 'even [the] most sophisticated machine, James Watt's rotary steam engine [1784], required no more physics than had been available for the best part of a century'; a point that a German tourist noted in his disbelief that so much had been achieved 'by men lacking any formal education for their profession' (Hobsbawm, 1962: 48).

Moreover, the danger of taking the hard line here is that one ends up with some form of conspiracy theory, or at least a version of developments which deposits all the power in the lap of the social and political elite, leaving, once again, the poor old manufacturer bereft of any leverage in the matter. In short, some of the accounts imply that the engineers and manufacturers were desperate to acquire academic credentials while the establishment, aristocratic and/or academic, were equally desperate to keep the 'upstarts' out. If the ideas about power developed in chapters 5, 6 and 9 have any utility, this theory of a systematic imbalance of power, which leaves the subordinate group literally powerless, is simply inadequate to the task of explaining what actually happened.

Indeed, closer inspection of the dual worlds of manufacturing and academia reveals them both to have been constructively involved in developing hermetic seals around their own orders of knowledge. In short, both parties were active in their mutual ignorance. Thus, where the academic establishment deemed manufacturing, engineering and business to be areas of knowledge that were unworthy of advanced study, the manufacturers, engineers and business people themselves cast scorn on the irrelevance of formal education, a system that was 'merely academic'. There was, then, an inverse mirroring by the culture of those directly involved in manufacturing: the skills involved in manufacturing could not be 'taught' through some formal academic education but could only be passed on by a system of apprenticeships, usually between five and seven years' long (Guagnini, 1993), a system which never really took off in the USA in the absence of a guild tradition and in the presence of much greater labour mobility (Elbaum, 1989). For a long time, engineering graduates found their qualifications virtually worthless. The Institution of Mechanical Engineers, for instance, founded in 1846 and embodying the elite of the engineering 'profession', only granted full membership on the basis of 'experience and practical achievements'. A marginal category of 'Honorary Member' was reserved for those whose qualifications were 'purely academic' (Guagnini, 1993: 26–7).

Just as the absence of an academic background to engineering in the nineteenth century was the dual responsibility of an elite arrogance about practical skill *and* of engineers' contempt for theoretical knowledge, so, too, the absence of manufacturing interests in Parliament was generated by an elite pretentiousness about the social value of manufacturing *and* by the manufacturers' scorn for the absence of 'hard graft' on the part of 'soft southerners'. But underlying the latter was an effective dilution of the hostility' in which the aristocratic governments of Victorian Britain consistently provided enough concessions to the manufacturers for the aristocracy to continue in power virtually uninterrupted (Perkin, 1972; Joyce, 1980).

This resistant response on the part of manufacturers to what they regarded as the pretensions of the establishment has similarities in several areas: for example, in India where road sweepers celebrate rather than conceal their work through the promotion of a macho image (Searle-Chatterjee, 1979); in English slaughter houses where the official disdain for those who 'kill for a living' is not hidden from view by the slaughterers themselves but actively promoted through their 'hunting and fishing' leisure activities (Ackroyd and Crowdy, 1990); and in British secondary schools, where the academic 'failure' of many working-class boys is celebrated in a macho culture that replicates the world of the factory (Willis, 1977).

Small wonder, then, that when William Fairburn, a leading manufacturer of the day and a colleague of Robert Stephenson, visited the Paris Exhibition of 1855 and warned the country of the superior technical design of the Germans, French and Americans, putting the responsibility firmly on the shoulders of Britain's poorer educational system, nothing much happened. In fact, a common element to the American and German systems was the internal competitive pressures, between the various Länder in the German case (König, 1993) and the various states in the American case (Donovan, 1993). Even when the British educational system took hold of the problem, in the late nineteenth century, it did so through the provision of technical colleges, rather than engineering departments in universities, which had just started to make some impact. So weak was state support that even in 1870, the high point of British economic dominance, Britain spent less of its GNP on education in science and technology than Germany did (Dintenfass, 1992: 38). It was not until the eve of the First World War that the Institution of Mechanical Engineers recognized academic qualifications as suitable for membership, though it should be remembered that in some areas, such as mining engineering, Britain remained pre-eminent until this period (Harvey and Press, 1989).

Even after the Second World War the revered place of apprenticeships within engineering itself, and the devaluation of practical knowledge by the academic establishment, remained firmly in position, to the probable detriment of both. Technical schools in Britain, after the tripartite division following the 1944 Education Act, left academic grammar schools clearly as the elite establishments, whilst the majority survived the secondary-modern system and an ever decreasing minority attended the technical schools. With the system of division remaining essentially voluntary, technical education was never going to impress the very people whose own lives had been construed through a culture that was consistently hostile to the 'mechanical arts'. The consequences have been twofold. On the one hand, there has been a polarization of attitudes towards education, with an institutionalized split between 'education' and 'training' which is manifest in the post–1944 split between grammar schools and secondary moderns, in the pre–1993 split between universities and polytechnics, and the concerns of management development professionals that management training must be 'relevant', 'skill-based' and 'competency-based' (rather than educational). This suspicion about the utility of academic approaches to business is still very much with us, as the recent ESRC (1994) and NIESR (1994) reports suggest.

On the other hand, the reliance upon apprenticeships as the mechanism for transmitting knowledge at the practitioner level has tended to ensure the replication of information rather than the development of knowledge; if knowledge transmission is restricted to learning the way one's predecessor did the job, and so on back to the beginnings of time, it is small wonder that engineering skills, even when they are transmitted, become redundant. We can go further than this, for the reliance upon a voluntary system of trade-union regulated apprenticeships, rather than a state-controlled system of apprenticeships and/or education, left Britain desperately short of skilled labour from the beginning of the century. For instance, just before the First World War a mere 7 per cent of the male population was in apprenticeships. Sixty years later only 6 per cent of all 18-year-olds left school with a technical or vocational qualification – nine times fewer than in Germany and two times fewer than Greece (Sanderson, 1988: 43–5). The result, to take one example, was that Germany had the investment in education to develop production systems that could cope with flexible demands. Since British workers were considerably undereducated in comparison to their German counterparts many British production systems were forced to concentrate upon long runs of undifferentiated products (Steedman et al., 1991).

In sum, those who were engaged in business tended to be self-taught or apprenticed individuals whose skill was measured by the degree to which they could replicate what their forebears had been able to do. It was this mimetic approach to knowledge which has been held responsible for the inability of British business to develop and sustain leading business technologies. This may account for why there appears to be such a strong conservatism at the heart of British business, but it does not explain why fire-fighting began in the first place, or why managers, rather than engineers, tend to fire-fight and to develop incremental approaches to change.

In the USA, in contrast, interest in business manifested itself in formal business schools in the late nineteenth century – over a century before Oxbridge turned its mind to the matter – in the Wharton School, established in 1881; though this was six years after the first Japanese business school, established as part of the drive to industrialize and keep out the West. By 1914 (when Japan already had the largest English-speaking technical university in the world), there were 30 American business schools with 10,000 students; by 1932 there were 400 schools with 90,000 students. American schools were matched by the efforts of corporations like General Motors' training schemes, where, as early as the 1920s, senior executives could expect to spend up to four hours a week in some form of training (Keeble, 1992: 29). In Britain, some Bachelor of Commerce degrees were in existence by the beginning of the century, at the London School of Economics (LSE), Manchester and Birmingham, though the initial funding for Birmingham came from the Canadian High Commission and the only direct external funding until after the Second World War was a donation of £5,000 – from Mitsui of Japan in 1921 (Keeble, 1992: 103). At the LSE in 1935, Beveridge, the then head, was pressed to close the commerce degree after its graduates found employment too difficult to achieve, and, after Beveridge left, the degree was (sub)merged into the BSc in economics. A Federation of British Industry report in 1947 set the issues out clearly: 'A B. Comm. course is not appropriate for full time university study, and ... the possession of a B. Comm. degree can hardly be regarded as a qualification of significant value for entry into industry' (Keeble, 1992: 109).

By 1920 the majority of executives in Japan, Germany and the USA were graduates; even by 1950 the UK only had 20 per cent (Keeble, 1992: 33,51). Still, this was hardly surprising in a nation where the employers had informed a government committee in 1928 that they were opposed in principle to extending the school-leaving age (Keeble, 1992: 67). That graduates were not considered a significant investment can be gauged by the salaries they received on first entering employment: new graduates working for Selfridges could expect 25p a week; on the railways, graduate engineers received nothing for six months; and all this against a background where the average wage in the country was £3.65 a week (Grint, 1988). Time and again businesses rejected the attempts by universities, minimal as they were, to interest them in business education; and when graduates were recruited for business positions they tended to come from Oxbridge, where there were no business degrees until very recently. Once inside a corporation, graduates seldom found themselves on any kind of fast track to promotion, Unilever and Harrods being virtually the only two major companies where exception proved the general rule (Keeble, 1992: 142). By the 1950s progress was still minimal: 80 per cent of British managers had no systematic management training, and it had been only in 1947 that the British government had set up the British Institute of Management in a belated attempt to rectify the situation – leading via the Robbins report to the first two postgraduate business colleges at Manchester and London. By 1986 a Department of Trade and Industry survey suggested that more than half of companies still had no formal management training, including 20 per cent of the largest (more than 999 employees); and the 1985 Labour Force Survey suggested that only 12 per cent of managers were graduates and 20 per cent had no qualifications at all. As Constable and McCormick suggest (1987), innate ability and job experience are *still* regarded as the most important determinant of effective management. If anything, the gap in educational achievement between Britain and the rest of its industrial competitors is greatest at the level of technician and worker rather than of management (Glover, 1992, Prais, 1981). Nevertheless, as late as the mid–1970s less than 60 per cent of the directors of large UK manufacturing companies were graduates, compared with 90 per cent in the USA, Western Europe and Japan, while the early 1990s' figures are 70 per cent and 100 per cent respectively (Glover, 1992: 323). Even within British graduate directors, there are heavy imbalances towards arts and natural science and away from engineering and technology. By the late 1980s, 85 per cent of senior managers in the USA and Japan were graduates – Britain could barely muster 25 per cent (Ackrill, 1988).

Not much seems to have changed since William Fairburn's warning about slipping standards in 1855: the 1994 British National Engineering Assembly heard its director general, Graham MacKenzie, regurgitate a complaint that has been echoing for two centuries now: 'The profession has to educate engineers in business, financial and language skills, and technical competence, to meet industry's needs. The current system is out of date' (quoted in the *Guardian*, 2 August 1994). Quite when it was 'in' date is uncertain.

What are we to make of the historical argument? It would seem fairly clear that the traditional disdain for education and preference for training on the part of the manufacturing and industrial groups – employers, managers and employees – is matched by the elite's histori-cal contempt for manufacturing and industry, a point discussed in the previous chapter. The result, at least in industry, appears to have been a tradition where mimetic replication prevails over novelty, where practical skill prevails over theoretical knowledge, where getting one's hands dirty on the shop floor secures greater respect than developing a novel and theoretically radical alternative method of managing, and where 'being busy' (or being seen to be busy) is a safer way to promotion than 'being thoughtful'. In short, the historical traditions do seem to have laid a pathway straight to the fire station and away from the ivory tower, especially when the ivory tower appears so hostile and irrelevant and the fire station so culturally compatible. There is clearly a problem for overtly rational accounts, since what counts as rational depends on who is assessing it: it may be rational for individual manufacturers to avoid educating their managers but only in the context where the political elite constructs a culture that subordinates manufacturing interests to its own. What may be rational in terms of management styles then, appears to be as much a cultural as a rational issue; indeed, rationality seems to be a culturally delimited phenomenon. British managers fire-fight because they have always fought fires and this therefore seems to be the rational way to manage.

Does this mean that we now know what managers do and why they do it? Not really; after all we do not have many accounts of what managers actually did until the 1950s, and even since then the accounts are few and far between. Moreover, we may have some ideas about why management seems to have developed in the way that it did, yet these are relatively few and many of them are mere assumption. But there is another problem with 'discovering' what managers do and why they do it: do the ways that we look at this question make a significant difference to the answers? The next section considers the critical role of epistemology and methodology.

The management of rationality

As suggested in the first chapter, one of the interesting aspects of language is that it appears to be not a transparent medium through which we reflect upon the world but rather an opaque means for constructing the world as we know it. The implication of this constructive rather than reflective form is that the world of management is one of infinite constructions, where what managers do is to construct their worlds through language and what management researchers do is (re)construct managers' worlds through both managers' words and their own (re)wordings.

We have already seen that most management tasks appear to be the result of collective, rather than individual, action, and the overt ambiguities that derive from the significance of language in management combine to generate a world where contradictory imperatives appear to develop. On the one hand, it becomes difficult to ascertain the precise contribution of any one manager to any outcome, beneficial or otherwise; yet managers are deemed to be individually responsible, and it is through an assessment of this that their position in the hierarchy is established and reviewed. On the other hand, successful management appears to require collective action, which minimizes the role any one individual can play. In effect, the more collective the group becomes the more successful it may be, but this is not necessarily in the interests of any individual manager – unless the managers can construct an account of the achievement which stresses their positive and minimizes their negative contributions. Thus, since most managers appear to spend a considerable amount of their time ensuring their own personal success (Dalton, 1959; Hannaway, 1989) but have little individual control over the collective success of the organization, and since what they do is primarily achieved through language, why managers do what they do involves reconstructing their motives from their own and others' accounts and attempting to trace what they have done through these same accounts. The result is that there is no body of objective facts to which the researcher may refer to establish the veracity or even validity of these accounts; there are only the accounts themselves.

Does this mean that the researcher can only line up the contending accounts of what has been done and why by juxtaposing them and saying to the reader: 'Take your pick'? Not necessarily; it is still possible to consider which account proves to be more persuasive without necessarily accepting that the success of the account depends upon its veracity. For example, one manager might assert that she or he was responsible for the rise in profits and this was effected through an altruistic concern for the good of the company itself. A second manager might dispute this and argue that the success was collectively achieved and that the inspiration behind the first manager's account was wholly selfish. It is probably impossible to establish which of these two managers is nearer whatever counts as the truth, and the researcher is probably not in a position to judge anyway. However, the researcher can consider the extent to which those managers who appear to be successful in their careers – judged by the speed and extent of their ascendance through the managerial hierarchy – develop different forms of account and different strategies of operating. To put it at its most extreme, if the relatively unsuccessful manager insists on the 'facts' speaking for themselves, while the relatively successful manager exerts a considerable amount of effort in actively persuading his or her colleagues about his or her own role in the action, then we might consider that the latter strategy appears to be more successful than the former, irrespective of the 'actual' contribution of each manager – whatever that might be and however it might be measured. In effect, management is directed towards what Gowler and Legge (1983) called the 'management of meaning'.

Borrowing from literary theory, one might consider here the distinction between what Barthes (1990) called *lisible* and *scriptible* texts. *Lisible* texts are written within the basic conventions of the day and are intended to be read, that is understood, in a particular way; the meaning is supposed to be clear because the possibility of constructing different meanings is reduced through the closure effected by the conventional practices of reading – they are 'readerly' texts. *Scriptible* texts, on the other hand, require active work on the part of the reader to construct the meaning; they are, in effect, written by the reader and are thus 'writerly' texts. This formulation is rather similar to Eco's (1981) approach, which distinguishes between 'open' and 'closed' texts (though Eco ironically inverts the conventions he discusses by calling those texts which he regards as coercive – in requiring a particular understanding – as 'open' while those which require the reader's constructive input he calls 'closed'. To avoid even greater confusion I shall assume that closed implies a narrowing of potential interpretations and open implies a widening of potential interpretations). This does not mean that the texts themselves have the effect of limiting or widening the interpretative flexibility available to the reader. The writer may *attempt* to limit the reader's interpretative imagination, but this may be actively resisted by the reader. It may be that a considerable amount of effort is required by the reader to generate alternative interpretations to the one implied by the writer, but alternatives are still available. It is also important to consider the link between the writer and the intended reader. That is, just as constructors of technology operate on the basis of an assumed user which they configure through a variety of mechanisms (see Woolgar, 1991), so, too, writers of texts may operate on the same basis: writers of newspapers who that consider their audience to be politically right-wing may write on the assumption that the potentially ambiguous message will be read in an appropriately right-wing way by their readers – but this does not stop a left-wing reader constructing a different account.

The point at issue for us here is threefold. First, to suggest that texts themselves determine their own understanding is to negate the constructive role of the reader in making sense of the data; it implies that the texts (facts) speak for themselves. This kind of traditional, positivist approach is one that has limited appeal in the context of constructivist epistemologies. Second, if we shift the notion of a text from a literary text to the world of management we are faced with the same kind of dilemma: do we take the discourse of managers or management researchers as the equivalent of a closed text or an open text? If we assume that writers have the ability to generate closed texts – and they are closed because they are reflections of the 'truth' – then we are faced with accepting that what management does is a reflection of the accounts that researchers provide. On the other hand, if we assume that what counts as a closed text lies in the approach of the reader but not in the text itself (since what the text is depends on the reader in the first place), then what management does is a derivative of the account but not a reflection of it. In effect, the accounts are active constructors of what managers do, and the readers then have to decide whether such accounts are plausible or not (rather than true or false). This is not dissimilar to the way the justice system operates: in theory the court decides upon guilt and innocence by reference to the truth of the contending accounts provided by the witnesses. But, since the court was not privy to the action it actually has to decide which accounts are more plausible rather than relying on being able to distinguish between truth and falsehood.

A third ramification of this is that the question of *why* managers do what they do is open to (at least) two potentially different accounts. On the one hand, a plausible positivist account might consider the dynamism of the environment and the historical traditions which generate predispositions to act in certain ways. On the other hand, it is possible to consider the question of why managers do what they do in precisely the same way as the question of what managers do. If what they do depends upon the epistemological means of securing knowledge, then why they do it is similarly constrained. If we ascertain causal explanations by traditional methods we might question the managers themselves, get them to write diaries or question their histories. But if we are concerned with the way in which the methodology that we use to generate knowledge about the world in itself affects the knowledge, then we should spend as much effort interrogating what we are constructing as what we are discovering.

How would this approach differ in practice from the previous ones? For example, when observers observe the goings on of managers, who is it that compartmentalizes the activities of managers? If we allow managers themselves to do this they may produce five hundred different categories or just one – managing. If the researcher imposes the categories then we are unlikely to see five hundred emerge as an accurate reflection of the diversity at large, since five hundred is simply too large a number to use; a more manageable number might be ten or thirty, but note that the choice of this number of discrete actions lies in the actions of the researcher, not those of the manager. We might just as well assume that everything the manager does is managing – hence there is no variety in action as such (see Stewart's (1994) useful review on this problem). Or perhaps we can distinguish between self-regarding action and other-regarding action, as Hannaway (1989) does. Again, this is a category imposition by the researcher not one derived from the self-professed actions of the research subjects. As another illustration we might consider whether a psychiatrist studying management would come up with the same account as a sociologist, or an economist, or a feminist or critical theorist.

Relatedly, we perhaps should not be surprised to find Fayol's account of management work couched in the scientific and mechanistic language that prevailed at the time in the USA. Nor should we be surprised if more contemporary CEOs fill their diaries with busyness, with action rather than contemplation. When what counts as responsible behaviour in the West is precisely the notion of filling every minute with 'useful' activities that can only be assessed by the quantity of time apportioned to them, rather than the quality of output resulting from them, and when grossly inegalitarian reward structures are felt to be in need of legitimation, being busy is likely to remain high on the agenda of most managers. Relatedly, when the alternative of strategic thinking requires subordinates to be both trusted and rewarded appropriately it may be that most managers would prefer to remain busy rather than effective, especially when being busy is considered both easier and more legitimate to measure than effectiveness. Would corporations be happy to employ executives who insisted on staying at home or sleeping all day at the office even if they appeared to be economically successful?

The contextual issue becomes even more interesting when we consider the way different managements operate. Stereotypically, British management is amongst the most short-term and reactive, whereas, for example, Japanese and German management is considered to be more long-term-oriented and proactive. As has been argued both above and in the previous chapter, it does not take a genius to note that the British love-affair with laissez faire was hardly likely to have spawned a management tradition along the lines of those of the Japanese or Germans, where long-term planning became as much a part of German and Japanese common sense as its opposite did in the UK: if the market does determine the way the economy and its organizations operate then a reactive style which keeps the state at a distance is more rational than a proactive style where the links between state and business are multitudinous. Also, if the markets generate a turbulent environment where anything might happen, and usually does, then one might consider the most appropriate person to manage this turbulence would be a manager whose general knowledge and experience of the world far outweighed whatever specialized technical skill she or he might have. But if technical specialization is regarded as a prime method of *controlling* such turbulence, rather than reacting quickly to it, then specialized management might be the answer. It is precisely this form of difference that distinguishes British from German management, according to Stewart et al. (1994).

The implication of this constructivist approach is not just that management researchers construct what managers do and why they do it (this is not the same as saying that these researchers 'fabricate' what goes on, since fabrication implies a high degree of disingenuousness), but that managers are themselves imbricated in the overlapping constructions. In effect, managers choose to represent their actions as constrained by virulent external forces that threaten to crush them at every turn – but they could have chosen otherwise. Hence the dynamic environment is one which appears to leave them no option but to exhaust themselves pumping water at the multiple fires which they continuously reconstruct around them. Alternative ways to manage are possible, but the discourse within which what counts as good management sits is one that construes proper management to be a variety known here as 'mimetic pyrophobes'. Not only are these managers inveterate haters of fire but all the role models within their world are similarly invested with this approach to management; hence managers act in a mimetic fashion to model themselves on the fire-fighters that preceded them.

Conclusion

This chapter has attempted to answer a series of questions concerning the identity, action and motivation of managers. It began by suggesting that management can best be identified by the contextual environment rather than the particular set of tasks involved in the job. It then set out the research, such as it is, concerning the nature of managerial jobs and concluded that, for Britain at least, management seems to be concerned with manic attempts to stamp out the numerous fires that break out all around the typical manager: keeping the show on the road, and managing to keep one's head when all around are losing theirs to stress, seems to be the order of the day and the passport to success. Exactly why this state of affairs has come about was the concern of the final section, in which three rather different explanations were deployed. The first is that management action is simply a response to the functional requirements of the environment: dynamic capitalist markets demand fire-fighting skills, whether the researcher sympathizes with the effects of this or despises it. The second approach problematizes this 'rationality' by suggesting that the environment is itself created by the actions of history, not the requirements of the market. This being the case, the preference for training rather than education on the part of industry itself, combined with the subordinate status of industry compared to land, acted to generate an array of traditional approaches to industrial management that buttressed the conservative and incremental in preference to the radical: short-term fire-fighting rather than long-term strategic planning was the result of history rather than rationality, according to this approach. Finally, the chapter concluded by throwing some sceptical cold water on the previous approaches and suggesting that the research process is an active constructor of the world of management rather than a passive describer of it. The next chapter takes this argument further by deploying it in and through the practicalities of managing the appraisal system.

4

From Silent Monitors: The Long and Relatively Unhappy Life of Management Appraisals

Introduction

Despite the increased interest in appraisal systems in business, a concomitant spread of appraisals from management down to manual workers (Townley, 1990, 1991; Swan, 1991), and their pervasive explosion in further and higher education in Britain, there is still precious little interest in or research on *upward* appraisal. This, in itself, may be puzzling given the extent to which many businesses now openly profess themselves to be concerned with 'empowering the workforce' (Kirkpatrick, 1992) or 'maximizing employee voice' (McCabe and Lewin, 1992), either through formal empowerment schemes, or, more commonly, as part of the move towards human resource management strategies (Storey, 1992), especially total quality management (Wilkinson et al., 1992). This chapter ponders on the absence of upward appraisals and the problems of all forms of appraisal in the light of constructivist criticisms of attempts to map and measure human attributes. It goes on to consider whether this means appraisals should be abandoned, or treated with extreme caution, or radically reconstructed in the light of such critiques towards a system where the multiplicity of voices is encouraged rather than suppressed.

From silent monitors

According to Stroul (1987), performance appraisal has been a 'staple' element of personnel management for over 35 years, though Gellerman and Hodgson (1988) add a further 15 years onto this in their appraisal of appraisals. In McGregor's (1987) celebrated article 'An Uneasy Look at Performance Appraisal', first published in 1957, he argued that appraisals had become standard practice in many US companies during the previous twenty years. Appraisal systems, of some sort at least, actually have a rather longer history: Swan (1991: 16), for example, quotes a third-century Chinese appraisal assessment. Somewhat more recently, Captain John Smith, a leader of the colonists in Jamestown, Virginia, in 1607, chose to plant corn and build fortifications rather than search for gold and find a route to the Pacific as he had been employed to do by the Virginia Company of London, which financed the expedition. The Virginia Company's appraisal of Smith was that he had failed, and he was removed in 1609. Being successful and doing what is required of you are not the same thing (Smither, 1988: 155).

Almost four hundred years later it might seem novel to use new technology to monitor and flag performances in contemporary 'high-tech' manufacturers, such as that described by Sewell and Wilkinson (1992), where any manufactured component failure 'would result in the normative sanction of an identifying or "black" mark being placed above the operator's station' (1992: 280). But the public identification of individual performance on a continuous basis is hardly recent. Robert Owen used similar 'silent monitors': a piece of wood mounted over a machine with one of four colours on to denote daily performance. Arkwright went one better and provided different dresses for different performances (Pollard, 1965: 225).

The similarities between past and present are perhaps best represented by the current developments in performance-related pay for teachers – the group usually held responsible for the allegedly falling educational standards (they seem to have been falling ever since compulsory education was introduced in England in 1870). The scheme under operation involves the provision of extra pay for those teachers deemed to be performing well by school governing bodies and the possibility of withholding increments and pay rises from those deemed to be failing by the same appraising body. This is hardly new either: in 1862 the Revised Code of Regulations, drawn up by the Newcastle Committee after a review of the education system at the time, suggested that: 'the junior classes in the schools, comprehending the great majority of the children, do not learn, or learn imperfectly, the most necessary part of what they come to learn – reading, writing and arithmetic' (quoted in Hopkins, 1979: 119). The response to this parlous state of affairs (which bears a perilously close resemblance to almost all general complaints about education ever since) was performance-related pay:

> The managers of schools may claim 1d per scholar for every attendance after the first 100, at the morning or afternoon meeting. One third of this sum thus claimable is forfeited if the scholar fails to satisfy the inspector in reading, one third if in writing, and one third if in arithmetic respectively. (quoted in Hopkins, 1979: 120)

Those anxious about the value of such an appraisal scheme may be relieved to know that the only apparent benefit was a 16 per cent reduction in the annual grant provided by the government. As Robert Lowe, the vice-president of the committee, proclaimed to the House of Commons: 'If it is not cheap it shall be efficient; if it is not efficient, it shall be cheap' (ibid.). Performance-related pay was abandoned by the end of the nineteenth century.

Such 'under-performing' teachers, and of course Captain Smith, became early victims of the behavioural appraisal approach – what you do as opposed to what you are like. Its primary alternative, the trait approach, which was developed initially by the US and UK military after the end of the Second World War (Randell, 1989), tends to be restricted to non-managerial appraisal schemes (Long, 1986). In the USA, at least, trait-based appraisals received a considerable attack at the hands of McGregor (1957), Whisler and Harper (1962) and Maier (1952, 1958). Despite some subsequent recovery (Gill, 1977), trait-based appraisal systems have generally slipped into the background over the last two decades as researchers have found few significant correlations between 'positive' traits (responsibility, friendliness etc.) and 'constructive' behaviour or action (Kane and Lawler, 1979; Gill et al., 1973). Moreover, the behavioural approach is preferred on the grounds that behaviour can, it is argued, be objectively observed while traits are merely subjective assessments. Other appraisal schemes include: written reports (500 words on why X should not have your job); peer ranking (why Y, your best friend, is better than X, who regularly beats you at squash); 'critical incidents' (what did X do when you dumped responsibility for making 500 employees redundant on X's lap); management by objectives (why did X not achieve the impossible sales target you set last year); and finally the ultimate challenge in appraisal schemes, the NMJ (not my job) scheme (X is so good at doing that subordinate job that X really should stay there and not take mine). Such approaches include a wide variety of forms of appraisal that range from written to oral and whose focus alters from process to content and all points between. However, this chapter is concerned not so much with differentiating appraisal methods as with examining what I take to be their generic epistemological basis: the quest for objective assessment.

The majority of American employees, British and American managers, and an increasing proportion of British employees are currently appraised (even if, in theory at least, it is their job performances rather than themselves which are appraised), and the most significant reasons for the increase seem to be the growth of performance-related rewards, the greater force of competition, and the general trend towards flexible production and human resource management. There are, naturally, different purposes involved in the construction and deployment of appraisal systems. Some relate existing performance to future pay or promotional potential, others are more concerned with the development of individual skills or the need to redeploy, retrain and then retain staff (see Carlton and Sloman, 1992). But whatever the purpose, they all tend to embody a shift from authoritarian managerial control to a system where employees are empowered to take on a far higher level of responsibility than before. Built into the appraisal system, of course, is an assumption that performance will improve with appraisals or that performance will decrease without appraisal. Either way there are several claims that the presence of some form of evaluation, especially in a group situation, tends to lead to enhanced performance (Harkins and Szymanski, 1987, 1989). On the other hand, there are also plenty of suggestions that a negative appraisal tends to lead to worse performance, not better, as individuals generate resentment, or decrease the significance of their alleged failures (Handy, 1985: 265–8). This is in addition to the related questions concerning the confused and confusing relationships between performance appraisal and performance-related pay. Not only does there seem to be little relationship between executives' pay and performance – at least since 1989 (Szymanski, 1992) – but at the lower level such schemes appear to produce more in the way of coercing managers into paying greater attention to their subordinates than in coercing subordinates into paying greater attention to their performance (Kessler and Purcell, 1992; Geary, 1992). Furthermore, the cultural differences that render appraisal schemes open to widely variant cultural interpretations have hardly been broached in the literature as yet.

Whitehill (1991), for example, has argued that the Japanese approach to appraisal is very different from that conventionally in operation in the USA. In the USA the use of performance appraisals to reward or punish employees, especially executives, is regarded as inevitably buttressing short-termism. But Japanese business is noted for its group-oriented structures and philosophies, as well as its long-term perspective, hence any form of individually oriented evaluation procedure is likely to undermine the corporate philosophy. Nevertheless, Whitehill's own research (Takezawa and Whitehill, 1981) suggests that even the vast majority of Japanese workers accepts the need for some form of individual evaluation – though they are far more reluctant to be informed of their alleged weaknesses than their American counterparts. Of course, the Japanese system is much more dependent than elsewhere on the seniority system, so that evaluation has a long historical perspective and is not just concerned with current or very recent assessments (though it is debatable whether their seniority system is unique: see Grint, 1993b). Furthermore, in the recent past there has been a considerable development in merit assessment in Japan (Inagami, 1983), but precisely what counts as merit is often difficult to say. Cole (1992), for example, suggests that appraisals include an assessment of holiday time taken – that is, a measure of holidays due as against holidays taken. Where the latter approaches the former the appraised is often labelled '*wagamama*' or selfish, undermining the collective responsibilities of the group. Those wishing to improve their annual performance assessment (*satei*) tend not to 'prove' their disloyalty by taking all their due holidays.

Japanese management appraisals also tend to involve self-evaluations, though seldom peer appraisals. Moreover, since appraisals are not automatically linked to career or reward – at least not in the short run – they do not, according to Whitehill (1991), invoke high levels of anxiety amongst those being appraised. Indeed, the counter-productive consequences of appraisal were explicitly why Deming, the doyen of Japanese statistical quality control methods, labelled it 'management by fear' and spoke vigorously against it, for: 'It leaves people bitter, crushed, bruised, battered, desolate, despondent, feeling inferior, some even depressed, unfit for work for weeks after receipt of rating, unable to comprehend why they are inferior. It is unfair, as it ascribes to the people in a group differences that may be caused totally by the system they work in' (quoted in Ridley, 1992: 15). It is perhaps not surprising that the values most sought after by the Japanese (co-operation, tact, loyalty to the company and teamwork), are, according to some early research by Kirchner and Reisberg (1962), those least favoured in the selection of appraisers in the USA.

In fact, there seems to be considerable, though not universal, dislike of and dissatisfaction with all performance appraisal systems to some degree; though some are clearly more popular than others, and the level of popularity seems to vary with position and the result. Crudely speaking, since there has been little research in this particular area, human resource managers are favourably inclined, line managers much less so. In the graphic words of one such line manager from County NatWest Group Ltd.: 'Performance appraisal is a load of rubbish. You decide on the rating you want in the box and then make up a few words of narrative in the other sections to justify it' (quoted by Carlton and Sloman, 1992: 86). On the other hand, appraisals designed to provide private feedback which are not entrammelled by pay or promotion issues are often far more popular. Some organizations have attempted to embody this 'safer' approach to appraisal into their own schemes: one education authority, for example, officially considers teacher appraisals to be: 'A structured process to enable the recognition of achievement by teachers and headteachers and to support their professional development; appraisal is based on self-appraisal. The appraiser's role is primarily to enhance that process' (Oxfordshire County Council, n.d.). Yet scepticism appears to remain the order of the day, and this relates to both the process of undertaking and responding to the appraisal, and the well-known 'distortions' that are likely in the assessment itself.

In the latter category, the most popularly acknowledged 'distortions' are manifest in several forms. The 'Halo Effect' (Guilford, 1954) is the result of an assessment which is based on one specific criterion that distorts the assessment of all the other criteria. Alternately, what might be called the Crony Effect is the result of an assessment distorted by the closeness of the personal relationship between the appraiser and the appraised. A variant of the Crony Effect is the Doppleganger Effect, where the rating reflects the similarity of character or behaviour between the appraiser and the appraised (Wexley and Yukl, 1977). Finally, there is the Veblen Effect, where all those appraised end up with moderate scores, named after Veblen's habit of giving all his students Cs irrespective of their quality (Dorfman, 1961). Some of the more significant social characteristics which are also alleged to affect appraisals include: the gender of both appraiser and appraised, with a tendency for women to receive lower ratings; the ethnic origin, with similarity of ethnicity between appraiser and appraised tending to lead to higher scores; and age, with increasing age correlating with decreasing ratings (Smither, 1988: 165–6).

But whatever the distortions that are likely to impair appraisals, one thing seems to be immune to all forms of bias: just as most people like to be the bearer of good news so most people dislike being the messenger of doom. This is clearly apparent in the general reluctance of managers to undertake appraisals of their subordinates which are less than enthusiastic and deemed likely to have a negative effect on that person's work effort. Indeed, it is the lack of inter-

personal skills on the part of managers (as well as a general distrust of
the validity of the system) that is often cited as their reason for avoiding
the task wherever possible. McGregor (1957), for instance, suggests the
underlying reason for managerial resistance is a dislike of 'playing god',
especially when managers are constantly exhorted to be supportive of,
rather than authoritarian with, their subordinates. In the words of
Edwards (1989: 17), 'Many managers prefer dental appointments to
playing "God" in preparing appraisals', a view supported in the most
recent ACAS paper on motivating and rewarding staff (Ridley, 1992).
Sam Goldwyn probably summed up the problem best in his heartfelt
plea to his employees at MGM (after six failed films): 'I want you to
tell me what's wrong with me and MGM – even if it means losing your
job' (quoted by Tanouye, 1990: 35). Little wonder that most people,
appraisers and appraised, approach appraisals with high levels of
anxiety. Much of this is rooted in the common assumption that
appraisals are often 'political' in nature; that is, they are mechanisms
for justifying decisions already taken and without regard to individual
merit. Those appraised also tend to believe that appraisers, like their
schemes, are often less than honest and potentially untrustworthy
(Longenecker and Gioia, 1988).

Besides such 'political' concerns there are, according to Swan (1991:
27–8), many common errors made in the development and use of
appraisal schemes, including: inadequately defined standards of performance; reliance on gut feeling; unclear performance documentation;
and inadequate time for discussion. But, since formal performance
appraisal systems have been subjected to constant criticism and reconstruction over the last fifty years, one might ask, along with Metz: 'why,
in the constant process of appraisal systems revisions, can't we seem to
get it right?' (1988: 47). In some areas, notably halo errors, 'despite
over 80 years of research ... the causes and consequences are still
poorly understood' (Murphy and Anhalt, 1992: 494). What evidence we
have certainly seems to support a justified scepticism of their utility: in
their review of executive appraisals, Longenecker and Gioia suggest
that, 'although over 90 per cent of all organizations in the US employ
some type of appraisal system, it has been estimated that less than 20
per cent of performance appraisals are done effectively' (1988: 41).
Moreover, they suggest that the higher the level in the organization the
less frequent and the less satisfactory are the appraisals – despite the
increased significance of individual performance at this senior level and
the persistent demand for appraisal of their own performance by senior
executives. This is all in sharp contrast to the claims made on behalf of
performance appraisals which, we are led to believe, can: 'increase
motivation, foster productivity, improve communications, encourage

employee growth and development and help solve work-related per-formance problems. In addition, the process can provide a systematic basis for compensation, promotion, transfer, termination and training and development' (Longenecker and Gioia, 1988: 41). Rarely in the history of business can such a system have promised so much and delivered so little.

Most of the explanations for the inadequacy of the systems tend to relate either to the complexity of the variables being assessed or to the subjective elements that non-objective systems allow to confuse the assessment. Efforts can be made to lessen the scope for subjectivity by relying upon assessment criteria that are allegedly more objective – the financial performance of a group, section or department, for example – but this can hardly be helpful in developing the skills of the appraised, and the problem remains that the rewards given to, and progress of, a subordinate are usually in the hands of a single superordinate. This may not matter too much if other appraisers are involved or if the signifi-cance of any single appraisal is marginal to the prospects of any subordinate; or indeed if the contribution of such a subordinate to the success of the enterprise is minimal (though if the latter is the case then one wonders why an appraisal scheme is used at all).

There is also a fundamental problem with appraisals of individuals by individuals: individuals only act within social situations. This not only problematizes an appraisal system grounded in assumptions about the abilities and attributes of individuals (Salaman, 1980b), but also ignores the extent to which these same individuals will have to work with their appraisers after the appraisal. Nor should we overlook the point that a major aim of appraisal schemes and performance-related pay is to limit the collective aspects of work and individualize the relationship; F.W. Taylor would indeed be impressed. But, as those who implemented Taylorism the first time round found to their cost, there are as many problems as there are advantages to individualization. As Russel and Goode (1988) have suggested, the highest level of satisfaction with appraisal systems tends to relate to those subordinates who already have a satisfactory relationship with their appraising superordinate (see also Burke et al., 1978; G.C. Anderson and Barrett, 1987; Geary, 1992). In effect, a poor relationship with your superordinate is bad for both your, and your organization's, health. But there is another aspect of the appraisal that has a fundamentally social, rather than an individual, essence: the 'reality' which we construct.

The social construction of appraisals

A major problem with all forms of assessment is the relationship between 'reality' and assessment. To what extent do assessments bear a close, or indeed any, relationship to 'reality'? There can be few people who have not experienced an assessment of some variety that appears to them to bear precious little relationship to the person they think they are. Without wishing to dive into the quicksand of personality construction it is possible to suggest that, at least as far as the assessment procedure is concerned, we are what our superordinates say we are. Since we may have no opportunity to alter the assessment it matters little that we disagree with it. Or rather, it matters little providing the assessment has no effect upon our actions.

Still, the problem remains: how do we achieve a 'truthful' assessment? For those convinced that such an achievement is possible the reliance upon an individual assessor, who traditionally is in a superordinate position, is fraught with difficulty, because the assessor only sees the assessed from one specific position. But what looks like an effective manager from above – in terms, say, of the absence of overt errors – may appear from below as an ineffective despot whose tyrannical ways and evident blunders are covered by the deft skills of the subordinates. As Kiechel (1989: 202) puts it: 'Most managers pride themselves on their people skills. Alas, subordinates may have a different view.' The problem for the realist, then, is that this individual appears to have two very different images and these are not necessarily complemented by the self-image of the individual or the images constructed by other interested parties: peers, partners, children and friends etc. The impossibility of being able to reduce the complex nature of any individual to a series of scales on a ticklist of characteristics or behaviours strongly suggests that the quest should be abandoned rather than refined yet more.

The notion that we do embody a unified centre, a fixed core of characteristics that is relatively stable, has its origins in the Enlightenment (S. Hall, 1992), in conjunction with the development of Protestantism. The latter emphasized individual responsibility and a relationship with God unmediated by priests, while the Enlightenment, preceded by Descartes, developed a model of an all-rational individual, separated from 'matter' and sovereign in his or her individual uniqueness. It is not difficult to see where this novel interpretation of humanity led, as political and legal rights became centred in and through individuals and the entire structure of modern economics became, in its essence, reducible to the rational action of individual economic agents.

The sociological critique of this model of identity, embedded as it was in the 'new' individualist disciplines of psychology and economics, was vigorously criticized by the symbolic interactionist school of sociology, especially in the writings of G.H. Mead, in which identity was perceived to be the relatively unstable result of interactions between the symbolic orders representing the individual and his or her social world. But this model was still one solidly inscribed with the image of the individual as a coherent whole in itself, separated from, even if necessarily interrelating with, the outside world. The symbolic interactionists were not the first to undermine the sovereignty of the individual. As S. Hall (1992) argues, Marxist writings, notably those of a structuralist variant, also cast doubt on the freedom of the individual in the face of capitalist economic and social 'structures'. Relatedly, Freud's work posed problems for all those accounts rooted in explaining behaviour through the rational action of individuals: for Freud the logic of the unconscious was far from the equivalent of an unconscious rationality which exists in us all from birth.

More recently the work of Saussure, Derrida and Foucault has all contributed to the eclipse of stable identity. Here, meanings are constructed through language rather than mirrored by language; identities grounded in an unstable profusion of interpretative acts are equally unstable – though armies of human scientists, including (and perhaps especially) management gurus, strive to regulate and corral their citizens, or subjects, into the 'correct' patterns of behaviour and identification (see Rose, 1990). This alternative model of identity, which accepts the ambiguity and multiplicity of image construction, also denies, or at the very least suppresses, the notion of personal 'essences'. What counts as an 'essence', for the constructivist, is what we can be persuaded of, either by the individual concerned or by others. In effect, therefore, a wider range of views about an individual does not necessarily mean that we are likely to see a consensus emerging around her or him. If, after a collective appraisal, we are left with very conflicting views, this does not mean that the method has failed or that it is inaccurate; rather, it suggests that the individual is constructed very differently by different people. If part of the aim of the assessment is to evaluate individuals for promotion or specific jobs then such a conclusion could be just as useful as one which, in the traditional manner, produces a model that fits the individual into a specific personality type. For example, if a company is looking for an individual whose job requirement includes a chameleon-like ability to play to very different audiences, then someone whose group assessment appears to be consensually constructed around a granite-like inflexibility will perhaps not be the person to select.

Such a multifaceted identity clearly poses problems for traditional assessments. Mount's work (1983, 1984), in particular, encapsulates the dilemmas, for the appraisals by subordinate, self and superordinate may often appear to be appraisals of different people. The traditional response is to resort to integrating models: to assert that these different appraisals reflect different aspects of the same (that is a coherent) individual. This still assumes that we can have a single coherent individual – even though the appraisals may be self-evidently contradictory and point rather to the notion that different people read each other very differently. However, the usual response is not to accept the fragmentary, fluid and contradictory nature of the assessment as evidence of the constructed, rather than reflective, essence of the appraisal. Instead, it is to despair at the 'imprecision' and 'subjectivity' of the assessments and seek for the 'truth' elsewhere. As Smither (1988: 166–7) typically states: 'Overall, the literature on peer assessment suggests that supervisors and their subordinates typically evaluate different aspects of performance. Consequently, it is difficult to determine if one approach is more accurate than the other.' In other words, the multiplicity of views reflects the unscientific nature of the procedure, not the socially constructed nature of what we take to be 'reality'. The consistent message is clear: only those pictures of the world which reduce it to clear, simply manipulable variables are of any practical help to managers. When such variables lead to hard, prescriptive rules – and when the implemented rules fail to generate successful outcomes – then the fault is imputed to their inadequate objectivity and inadequate clarity about the world, rather than the lack of clarity which we necessarily have as we construct, rather than discover, the world.

The assumption that others construct us, and construct us in potentially limitless ways, is critically important if the major part of the management process involves interrelating with others. In terms of assessment it is also crucial in that the relationships between individuals appear to become more tightly constrained as the status distance between the individuals increases. The result is that as we ascend the hierarchy the superordinates are less and less likely to be aware of what their subordinates think of them and their performance. This 'difference of opinion' is also replicated through the contending constructions of corporate culture, with an 'official' version and probably several 'subordinate' subcultural versions (see Fortado, 1992, on this). Of course, if the superordinate really does not care what his or her subordinates think then this may not be a problem – except that such a response may itself be an effective inhibitor of subordinate work.

The search for objective appraisals

In the absence of a social constructivist approach to appraisal one is left with a permanent enigma; a quest for the sacred and secret panacea that always manages to evade those looking for a method to appraise individuals objectively. For example, Metz's (1988) review of the problems suggests that the role of the supervisor, the level of resources, the nature of training, the regularity of feedback, the existence of clear standards and the clarity of job goals, in addition to the capabilities of the individual being appraised, are all significant variables affecting performance. The subjectivity of appraisal systems – except the one currently being displayed by the author, usually is just as popular as an explanation for appraisal failure. Galin (1989), for instance, argues that the particular leadership style of the appraiser can distort the appraisal process; hence the need to retrain appraisers to consider the significance of other variables so that the distortions can be removed. Rather problematically, this means adopting the values of the opposite leadership styles, which Galin assumes also lead to a distorted appraisal. The appraisal is thus held to be undistorted (that is 'true') if one set of 'distortions' is balanced by another counteracting set.

McGregor's transcendence of the problem was to delegate responsibility to the individual subordinate, who sets the goals and assesses progress towards them. Since no superordinate can know as much about a subordinate as the subordinate does, McGregor argues that top-down assessments are necessarily problematic. The solution preferred by Edwards is team or 'multiple rater' evaluation, which, he claims, provides an 'excellent example of fairness and accuracy in performance management' (1989: 18). However, Edwards's claim for fairness is based upon eliminating the highest and lowest rater and flagging any rating which remains non-consensual as 'unreliable'. Such unreliable ratings, Edwards claims, are 'unusual'. Since the model used by Edwards is one where five raters are involved (the supervisor plus four peers), we must assume that where 60 per cent of the raters agree then their judgement is regarded as 'fair' and 'accurate' but when less than 60 per cent agree then the rating is biased and unreliable. Note here the way that individuals are assumed to have permanent and axiomatically coherent behavioural traits. The possibility that an individual is interpreted differently by his or her colleagues is necessarily regarded as an 'unreliable' rating. In effect, the system imposes a uniformity upon the raters and, where they dispute the uniformity, it rejects their assessment as unreliable! As Edwards comments, such extremists who 'unfairly overvalue or undervalue a work associate . . . lose a voice in the process'

(1989: 19). Perhaps not surprisingly, and despite Edwards's enthusiastic support for the software supporting this system, a third of those assessed disagreed with their profile.

A similar effect has been noted in performance-related pay, where the tendency for assessors to mark in a small band around the average rather than to spread the distribution conflicts with assumptions about normal distributions. As a result some companies have introduced statistical measures to force assessors to adopt a normal distribution (Kessler and Purcell, 1992: 25–6). Carlton and Sloman (1992) also report a distinct urge by senior managers to see normal distributions and an equal and opposite urge by assessors to generate positively skewed distributions; as they note: 'the systematic overrating of staff is an ongoing problem' (1992: 87). For whom this is a problem appears not to be a question worth pursuing, but it is worth noting that this 'ratings drift' is apparently revealed through a comparative analysis which suggests, according to one manager, that: 'two-thirds of the staff in [Division] are recorded as above average when the Division is performing less well than its peer group in other companies' (1992: 89). Since it is also the case that 'Ratings drift is a prevalent problem throughout the company' (1992: 91), one wonders what the comparative criteria are and precisely how one can assess ratings drift except by assuming a normal distribution of talent, which is itself a social construction not an objective measurement.

In a similar vein, Sinclair (1988) has suggested that since personal 'moods' can affect the formation of impressions then such 'bias' should be watched for in appraisal systems. Again, the subjectivity of the appraiser undermines the objectivity of the appraisal. Presumably, only when the appraiser is not in any kind of 'mood', except an objective one, is she or he able to control her or his subjectivism. But what, one would like to ask, counts as a neutral, that is, 'objective', mood? How can we measure the objectivity of something like a 'mood'? Who measures the mood of the appraiser anyway, and what happens if they are affected by a mood? In effect, the search for objective assessment seems to lead to the most inappropriate, tail-chasing responses.

The conceptual difficulties which this tail-chasing quest for objectivity can lead to are exemplified in the theoretical solution to the problem suggested by Klein et al. (1987). For these authors the crucial problem of survey-based data and the subsequent performance appraisal interview (PAI) is that it tends to:

> suffer from an overreliance on self-reported data. Objective measure of the PAI processes is impossible unless the interviews are videotaped, an impractical strategy in most instances. Even when videotaping is possible,

the resulting measures may have little explanatory value if they do not correlate with employees' perceptions of the interview. Conceptually, it is not what actually transpires during the interview that influences an employee's reactions, it is what the employee perceives as having occurred. (1987: 277)

The problem here is the distinction between 'what actually transpires' – that is 'reality' – and 'what the employee perceives'. If the employee misconstrues 'reality' then who has a faithful rendering of it? Presumably the appraiser does – but why should his or her perception be any more accurate than that of the appraised? And who adjudicates between rival claims of accuracy? Is it a third party who has some special insight into 'reality'? The point here is twofold. First, since 'reality' is constructed in and through our interpretative processes (which are social not individual in nature, because of our reliance upon language), we are really left with rival interpretations of reality, not interpretations that can easily be judged right or wrong. Second, the significance of this lies in Klein et al.'s point about the role of these very interpretative processes which they wish to subordinate to some magical objectivity – embodied, I assume, in management. It is categorically *not* that everyone's interpretations are as good as anyone else's, there is not an anarchy of competing interpretations here and it is not the case that 'anything goes'. On the contrary, the conventional result is that the most powerfully resourced rendering of 'reality' is the one that prevails, becomes legitimate, and thereby delegitimates all alternatives. Essentially, it is usually not what the appraised thinks has transpired which accounts for his or her subsequent reward package, it is what the appraiser thinks that usually carries more weight – and with the weight the reward or the punishment.

So is there a constructivist solution to this problem? Well, it is unlikely, if a solution implies that there is, after all, a way to measure performance objectively and in a way that everyone will accept as legitimate. That being the case there are (at least) two further approaches that may be worth considering. The first is simply to accept the difficulties involved and note how they will lead to particular forms of appraisal. In effect the appraisal constructs rather than reflects the appraised and this should be borne in mind when any appraisal system is adopted and deployed. *Caveat emptor* should perhaps be required as a government 'health' warning on the front of all appraisal schemes. This is especially important if the appraisal system is geared towards altering the behaviour of the appraised in line with the appraisal: if the appraiser changes, or indeed unless one can guarantee the appraisal will be constructed in precisely the same way the next time round, then changing patterns of behaviour may be irrelevant to the acquisition of a superior appraisal (see Murphy and Anhalt, 1992, on this). Appraisal systems, then, do not so much discover the skills of those appraised as create them. To take an example close to the hearts of many readers, in academia it has long been the case that one of the simplest criteria for academic appraisal is the number of publications. The result of promoting this criterion has been to stimulate academics to 'publish or be damned'. Whether the quality of the publications suffers as a result of this appraisal criterion, or whether other aspects of academic skills, such as teaching ability, suffer in direct proportion to the effort expended on publishing, is anybody's guess. But the point really is that the criteria used are not reflections of pre-existing or objective characteristics, rather they are active in producing the characteristics which they then purport to measure objectively.

The second alternative is rather more radical and suggests that we should accept the plurality of appraisal constructions and make positive use of them. In particular, we might try to embody the principles in the appraisal scheme rather than consider them as a persistent and ineradicable nuisance. One such scheme involves inverting the traditional direction of appraisals altogether: upward appraisal.

Upward appraisal

Upward appraisal is far less popular than downward appraisal but hardly novel, at least in the USA. Most writers suggest that upward appraisal began in IBM in the 1960s, and by 1985 there were suggestions that around 20 per cent of US companies were experimenting with it (Kiechel, 1989), though a larger survey puts the proportion undertaking peer review (the less radical of the two) at 5 per cent (Buhalo, 1991). The proportion undertaking upward appraisals is probably much smaller, despite all the current talk about employee empowerment, though some large corporations in the USA (such as Pratt and Whitney, Digital Equipment Corporation and AT&T) do use it. The appraisal of teachers and lecturers by their students is also common there, and beginning to develop in the UK, but it is still rare in British companies and only a few pioneering firms, like W.H. Smith and BP Exploration, have taken it up.

Upward appraisal has its roots in democratic theory and practice going back as far as the Ancient Greeks, whose democratic institutions were open to all adult male citizens and were, with the exception of some military positions, not open to re-election. That Athenian generals seemed privileged by their potentially permanent employment should be tempered by the recognition that the upward appraisal system in operation included not just a tenured position for the successful but capital punishment for the unsuccessful (see Finley, 1963; Held, 1987).

It does not take a genius to recognize that, however limited are our democratic institutions and procedures in the political realm, democracy is not something that business usually involves itself in. In the main, the argument has swung forcefully towards the Weberian argument that efficient administration requires hierarchies of expertise, manifest by that most rationalized form of organization bureaucracy. The utility of bureaucracies as forms of administration is not something I wish to consider here (see Beetham, 1987) nor the relationship between bureaucracy and democracy in the political world (see Held, 1987; Pollitt, 1986). However, one point is clear: organizations that are grounded in images and institutions of hierarchical expertise positively discourage subordinate intervention in superordinate decision making. That is to say, while subordinates in bureaucracies may be actively involved in either ensuring their tasks are properly executed or developing routines to protect themselves from superordinate criticism, they are seldom encouraged to help superordinates solve organizational problems. As a result, a huge array of talent, skill and expertise is lost to the organization. The upshot of this approach is classically displayed in British management and trade unions. For generations management has taken major decisions without any significant input from unions or employees, and for generations unions and employees have reciprocated by delegating all responsibility to those who traditionally make the decisions. The 'irresponsibility' of the 'permanent opposition' has left the unions and employees basically impotent and managers bereft of any advice beyond that which cascades from above or seeps sideways from their peers.

Upward appraisals are problematic against this background, in so far as they inculcate an apparent reversal of roles, and they are also potentially compromised by another common problem of conventional appraisals: either the appraiser is regarded as deflating the appraisal of junior staff in revenge for some misdemeanour or to ensure the office favourite secures the best appraisal; or the appraiser inflates the appraisals of all those being appraised in the knowledge that such an exemplory set of appraisals reflects favourably on the manager who leads such a dedicated team. Naturally, the opposite tack can also be employed: a troublesome team member is provided with a first-class appraisal in the hope that he or she will secure promotion and move out. In the case of upward appraisals the appraisers may still be 'out to get' their superordinate, but if they are then the superordinate probably ought to know about it rather than be unaware of the 'conspiracy'.

None the less, the experience of T-groups from the 1960s onwards is that sometimes the 'honest opinions' of subordinates look more like the barbs on a whale harpoon than gentle and constructive nudges. This is something which is likely to occur at some time, but it also depends on the situation in which the appraisal occurs. An array of academic research on group behaviour has pointed to the likelihood of extreme group decisions in comparison to the conservative nature of individual decisions (Janis, 1972; McCauley, 1989) and certainly some writers have advocated upward appraisals that consciously avoid any form of 'active' group appraisal (Levinson, 1987). But where such an appraisal is constructed it is surely worth considering the actions which stimulated the poor review and resolving the problem, rather than suffering the consequences.

There are other consequences of a shift towards upward appraisals which may not be so self-evident but may prove significant none the less. For example, supervisors may interact differently with their subordinates, especially as the period of appraisal approaches. But this need not be considered a detrimental effect, since close co-operation between team and team leader is one of the primary aims of the system anyway. Indeed, where co-operation is not improved, or at least where there is no evident improvement in the team performance, then one might conclude either that the appraisal system is having no apparent effect or that the manager involved requires some additional help in securing the requisite improvement. Edwards (1989) certainly claims that team-based appraisals generated significant productivity enhancements amongst lecturers at Arizona State University, in Westinghouse Corporation's steam turbine generator division, and on the Salt River Project in the south west of the USA, but this does not mean that the multiple appraisal system is 'objective' or 'accurate'. If the results increase productivity there is still no necessary connection to a model of objective accuracy in the appraisal system; a system which (erroneously in the eyes of the members) regarded all members of a team as idlers – and also threatened them with unemployment in the absence of extra effort – might still generate enough motivation to secure that improvement, however allegedly inaccurate the assessment.

Upward appraisal, then, replaces the subjectivity of a single-author appraisal with the subjectivity of a collective-author appraisal. This, of course, still leaves us bereft of an objective appraisal but it is perhaps less likely to be wholly fabricated: if all the appraisals are positive then, other things being equal, the superordinate–subordinates relationship is at the very least constructive. If all the appraisals are negative then, other things being equal, there is obviously a problem with the staff–management relationship – or the manager or the staff. It may be that the manager above the appraised superordinate regards that manager as good despite the negative appraisals (or even because of them); nevertheless, evidence of the state of play is always useful. Moreover, there are (many) cases where superordinates are simply unaware of their subordinates' attitudes towards them and deny the very possibility that something is wrong. A sheaf of appraisals all pointing in the same negative direction is probably a more useful tool in the hands of someone seeking to change the relationship than is uncorroborated hearsay. This also goes for the subordinates, who may, for whatever reason, have refrained from telling their superordinate about the problematic nature of the relationship. If such problems are left unresolved and do have negative consequences for performance then the possibility of airing one's feelings may be the first opportunity for resolving the problems. If organizations, then, are serious about involving their employees in a much wider variety of tasks and responsibilities than has traditionally been the case, it would be unwise to assume that the provision of opportunities, in and of themselves, will lead automatically to an increase in employee involvement. Rather, managers must provide opportunities for employees to learn to participate in organizations that have hitherto not encouraged them to get involved in areas beyond the task level. As Pateman (1970) has argued, participation begets participation. In effect, participation is a skill which has to be learned and, in the absence of such learning experiences, individuals become, rather than inherently are, uninterested in participation. What better way to impress upon employees that their voice actually matters than embodying it in an appraisal of their superordinate?

Responses to upward appraisals

Although there are relatively few upward appraisal systems currently in existence (at least in the UK), the responses to them tend not to be that unlike those to conventional appraisals; that is, people tend to respond in one of the following two ways. First, the responses may be constructive and have positive results, in which case the system can be regarded as relatively successful. But the responses may also be negative. One way of avoiding negative responses may be to prefigure the philosophy in the construction of the appraisal system. That is, if organizations ostensibly value the opinions of all employees, including those at the bottom of the hierarchy, then a good way to demonstrate this is by asking for their suggestions in the construction of the scheme. However, the problematic reactions are generally from managers not staff, hence one needs to build their ideas – and therefore their compliance – into the scheme too. The more upward appraisal feels like a typically superordinate act the less likely is it that compliance and constructive consent will accompany it. Since the intention behind the system is to improve not eliminate management, it is incumbent upon the designers to incorporate the manager and his or her subordinates from the very start of the process.

Relatedly, the resolution of all kinds of dispute through peer review, rather than the conventional managerial resolution, seems not to produce consistently anti-management results; far from it. Reibstein's (1986) analysis of peer reviews used in grievance disputes in the USA suggests that around two-thirds of the decisions go with management, and this figure is generally supported in the review by McCabe (1988; cf. Zedeck et al., 1974). In an assessment of the peer-review system in operation at the Raritan River Steel Company in the USA, it was argued that: 'any notion that employees would always side with one another was immediately dispelled. Employee panellists are equally concerned at looking for a just decision, and often tend to be tougher on their co-workers than management would be' (Ventura and Harvey, 1988: 51). In the Raritan River Steel case a critical benefit of the peer review system was also the utility of the process in staving off union intervention, but this is not an essential element of peer review and even more contingently related to upward appraisals.

The military have also been influential in the development of peer reviews. In the American military the peer review system has become known colloquially as the SYB system – 'Screw your buddy' – with strong hints that where reviews are linked to promotional opportunities then the competitive spirit tends to prevail over disinterested assessment (*Training and Development*, July 1991). But despite the SYB system the upshot of most peer reviews is that teams also want some response to their feedback to their peers or manager. This is clearly tricky, in that the remarks will have to remain anonymous to protect the subordinates and the manager will not want his or her failings to be exposed in a way that opens him or her to ridicule. Nevertheless, the manager will need to demonstrate that the comments are being taken seriously and this may involve a team meeting to discuss the broad issues raised, rather than anything too specific. A third party may also help in this area, both in interpreting the original data for the manager and in acting as a mediator in the final team debriefing.

A third way to avoid negative reactions to upward appraisal is to explain to those being appraised from the very beginning that what is about to happen is merely the formalization of what already exists. Each and every day we are all appraised by someone and appraising others. Admittedly, such appraisals tend to be covert or at least camouflaged, but they are still appraisals. Moreover, if we are not made aware of our limitations, and are not aware of them ourselves, how are we supposed to transcend them? It would be a strange manager who refused to accede to upward appraisal on the basis that she or he was already perfect, and far more likely that refusal was grounded in fear of the consequences to her or his self-image or position within the company.

On the other hand, any overt relationship between upward appraisal and career or job security is likely to push the risks involved beyond an acceptable level and turn the whole system into a mutual supporters' club: subordinates provide glowing references for their manager in return for subsequent favours. If the criterion for success is future activity, rather than positive feedback from subordinates, then this cynical mutuality is considerably less likely and less important anyway.

It is perhaps worth emphasizing at this point that, as mentioned above, the reviews are not likely to be totally negative. On the contrary, most managers are likely to get some kind of positive feedback from their subordinates and it may well be the first time that such feedback has occurred. After all, few subordinates bother to tell their manager that they are doing a good job, and most are likely to remain silent until something goes wrong. In effect, since managers tend to hear nothing but complaints – on the assumption that no news is good news – it may well prove a useful fillip for many to hear from their staff that they are actually pretty good at their job.

It is also worth bearing in mind that some areas of managers' jobs will be beyond the experience of most of their subordinates and consequently should not be evaluated by them. This too can be used as a constructive advance rather than seen as a problem, since it may highlight areas that subordinates were hitherto unaware of, and thus unable to relate to, in their accounts of managers' actions (Norman and Zawacki, 1991). W.H. Smith's experience suggests that employees are well aware that management is concerned with more than being pleasant to subordinates and that sometimes harsh decisions have to be taken. That said, it did raise a lot of questions about the interpersonal skills deployed by managers (*Financial Times*, 10 February, 1992). Moreover, it confirms the point that upward appraisals should be seen as an additional element in the appraisal armoury, not as the sole occupier of the position left vacant by a displaced downward appraisal.

This still leaves a major stumbling block in the shape of unpersuaded or suspicious managers. But if the underlying philosophy of the upward appraisal system is one which espouses the single cultural model – the image of a team or a crew in a lifeboat – then a system as potentially disruptive as this is only likely to succeed where those nominally in charge take the plunge too. After all, if feedback about performance (or at least the level of honesty) declines as one climbs the hierarchy, then CEOs are likely to know very little about their image within a company. If, as the CEO may imply, the medicine is entirely safe and positively health-enhancing, then let us see the CEO directly involved too. On the other hand, if upward appraisals are not involved in any change towards a more participative style then subordinates might be justified in questioning the intentions of the superordinates: are they concerned with empowering subordinates or just exploiting them in more subtle ways?

The possibility of excessive resistance to upward appraisal should not be exaggerated: there is, after all, much evidence that all managers seek regular feedback on their performance (Longenecker and Gioia, 1991). Indeed, were managers to insist on shooting the messenger all the time, or at least ensuring they never delivered their message, one might begin to wonder what precisely was so damning – and whether something should be done about it.

Conclusion

This chapter has considered the relatively long and generally unhappy life of performance appraisal schemes. Despite the application of several generations of specialists in the field, the ineffectiveness and alleged inaccuracy of appraisal schemes has tended to lead those seeking to improve them deeper and deeper into the labyrinth that promises an objective solution to the subjective problem. I have not argued that we should therefore abandon the existing appraisal methods; indeed, if they coerce managers into a greater consideration of the efforts of their subordinates then at least some useful purpose may be served by them. On the other hand, the approach developed here suggests that it might well be more productive to retrace our steps out of the objectivity labyrinth and accept our subjective fate. This is particularly so in the light of theoretical developments made in social constructivism, which pose a vision of reality that is imposed upon the world rather than one that reflects the world. The upshot is not that we should abandon appraisal schemes but that we should consider them more sceptically and more reflexively. Indeed, one way to move beyond the present impasse is to embody the subjective approach into the performance assessment schemes by developing upward appraisals. This is particularly apposite in the wake of contemporary movements to empower the workforce, to secure more participative styles of management, and to promote teamwork. Upward appraisals are neither simple to adopt nor automatically popular with those being appraised, nor are they a panacea for all manner of managerial problems. But like the search for an objective appraisal system, the search for a panacea is itself a distracting problem, not part of the solution. If upward appraisals do not solve all management problems, then the tenacious grip of 'objectivity' on downward appraisals merely adds another problem to their already burdensome load.

5

Reengineering Utopia: Managing Radical Change

Introduction

This chapter develops a constructivist perspective on the management of radical organizational change. It begins by considering the case of business process reengineering (BPR or reengineering) and develops a model of radical organizational change within which BPR can be reconsidered. Reengineering rapidly became the business buzz-word of the early 1990s and this examination of the phenomenon sets out to consider the claims made by proponents of reengineering and the novelty of the elements. It disputes some claims to novelty and internal coherence and sets up an alternative model of radical organizational change that grounds the explanations for reengineering's popularity through an externalist rather than an internalist account. That is, its popularity might best be explained not by considering the uniqueness or 'inherent' rationality of the ideas involved (an 'internalist' account), but rather through the ways in which the purveyors of reengineering manage, in and through their accounts, to construct a series of sympathetic 'resonances' or compatibilities (an 'externalist' account). These are construed to exist between their ideas and popular opinion, or *Zeitgeist*, and also between the novelty of the ideas and the cultural antecedents. The alternative model of change developed also suggests that radical change is most likely to fail where it is construed as a method and goal of change that is premised wholly upon rational and linear analysis, where the decision making is incremental, where the methods of execution depend wholly upon assumptions about rational individuals, and where its legitimizing characteristics are regarded as self-evident and lie in its internal and objective value. Radical change, it is argued, might be better configured as a Utopia, and it embodies the same kinds of possibility and problem that Utopias throughout history have manifested. In effect, the chapter argues that for organizational change to work as a radical and long-term alteration, the focus should be more on changing the way managers think and work than on changing the way the organization operates. Furthermore, the methods by which radical change might be achieved have to be more firmly rooted in the current cultural climate.

Accounts of reengineering

The claims

Although management theory is historically replete with claims about revolutionary innovations – and many people could list a dozen without too much effort – few innovations have acquired quite so much hype in such a short period of time as business process reengineering (BPR or reengineering from now on). 'Reengineering is new, and it has to be done', according to Peter Drucker on the cover of Hammer and Champy's book, *Reengineering the Corporation* (1993b), and it is 'the management world's most fashionable fad', according to the *Financial Times* (22 June 1993). Rothschild argues that: 'In the greatest burst of creative destruction since the Industrial Revolution, the highly evolved Machine Age economic ecosystem is being smashed flat and replaced by organizational forms and economic species never before seen' (1992: 17). Or, according to Janson, 'Reengineering is a radically new process of organizational change that many companies are using to renew their commitment to customer service' (Janson, 1992/3: 45). Reengineering, according to its self-proclaimed progenitors Michael Hammer and James Champy, is nothing less than 'a reversal of the Industrial Revolution' (1993a). 'It isn't about *fixing* anything [, it] means starting all over, starting from scratch' (1993b: 2). Or, as Hammer put it even more forcefully a little earlier: 'Don't automate, obliterate' (1990). Indeed, so novel and so crucial is reengineering alleged to be that 'the alternative is for Corporate America to close its doors and go out of business' (Hammer and Champy, 1993b: 1). Hammer and Champy's book had been in the American top 10 of best-selling non-fiction for fifteen weeks by September 1993, according to the *New York Times* poll, and there is every reason to assume that its popularity is still increasing amongst executives seeking radical solutions to a fundamental business problem (*Bankers Monthly Report*, April 1993).

So what is the problem that faces corporate America and what is the reengineered solution? The problem appears to be that the USA has developed systems of production that were remarkably successful in their time but are no longer suited to a changed world. The successful systems that the USA first promoted were rooted in economies of scale: 'Most companies today – no matter what business they are in, how technologically sophisticated their products or services, or what their national origin – can trace their work styles and organizational roots back to the prototypical pin factory that Adam Smith described in *The Wealth of Nations*, published in 1776' (Hammer and Champy, 1993b: 11). From Smith onwards, the development of most industrial nations, has, according to reengineered history, been one where modern business bureaucracies have spread the organizing principles of the pin factory to the office, the assembly line, and the corporate headquarters: specialization, deskilling, functional division and hierarchies rule OK!

This development has been fuelled by (virtually) unremitting demand to the extent that producers have dominated the market – until now. But the present growth of competition across the world, from old and newly industrializing nations, has seen the displacement of producer domination by customer domination; and the old systems of production have proved themselves inadequate to the new task. When customers were merely the consumers, the last in the chain of production, shoddy goods and poor service were apparently accepted. Now, customers are dominant, and, while the producer-dominated system ensured that no single person was ever responsible to the customer, the current breed of customer demands responsibility and quality. The problem, as the reengineers see it, is that the functional divisions that once proved so successful actually prevent organizations responding adequately to the changed conditions. The result has been a gradual decline in American competitiveness and a sharp increase in the market share taken by consumer-oriented systems like those developed by the Japanese and associated Asian 'Tigers'.

The linchpin of the new approach advocated is manifest in the full title: 'business process reengineering'. In effect, the idea is to develop systems built on teams that are configured to mirror the processes that the business actually works around rather than the functions it may use to execute these processes. It is a shift from vertical functions to horizontal processes. In Harrison and Pratt's terms: 'A business process is a sequence of activities that fulfils the needs of an internal or external customer' (1993: 7). Thus, to take a simple example, if the business is concerned with selling books by post then a customer wanting to buy books from different departments, pay for them by credit card, and have them delivered by special delivery, should not have to be switched through departments that deal with different categories of books, then be switched to a new section that deals with accounts, and then find themselves trailing through the telephone network in an attempt to have the books sent out. In the reengineered business one phone call secures the ear of an individual who, within a team, is wholly responsible for looking after the requirements of this customer: 'one-stop shopping' comes of age, and hence the term 'process'.

Before I describe my understanding of reengineering, what, precisely, does it allegedly offer the adopting organization? According to Ligus (1993), reengineering promises to:

> Drive down the time it takes to develop and deliver new products, dramatically reduce inventory and manufacturing time, slash the cost of quality and win back market share ... The following changes are possible: 30–35 percent reduction in the cost of sales; 75–80 percent reduction in delivery time; 60–80 percent reduction in inventories; 65–70 percent reduction in the cost of quality; and unpredictable but substantial increase in market share. (1993: 58)

All this can be achieved, apparently, by closing the distance between supply points, production, assembly and customer, by decentralizing, using process teams, building awareness, developing a vision based on strategic objectives, smashing functional barriers, creating involvement, streamlining information systems, and a few other assorted odds and ends. Unfortunately, it also appears that the majority of reengineering projects fail: 70 per cent, according to Rothschild (1992) and CSC Index, a leading reengineering consultancy (Stanton, et al., 1993), a figure remarkably close to the alleged failure rate of total quality management projects.

There do appear to be clear benefits when reengineering works: a much quoted example from Business Intelligence reports a radical overhaul of a specialized insurance company in which lead times fell from three months to one month for new customers and from two weeks to fifteen minutes for existing customers (quoted by Caulkin, 1993). More recently still, some academics have begun to insist that the focus of reengineering should shift from internal to external processes (Short and Venkatraman, 1992), while some of the leading consultancies involved have begun to articulate arguments which suggest that reengineering is not a total solution after all (if it was then presumably such consultants would soon work themselves into oblivion), but 'a component to a solution' (Treacy, quoted in Cafasso, 1993). Indeed, Stalk and Webber (1993) suggest that a major problem with strategies focused on time-based competition is that once all companies are involved no one secures a competitive advantage through it, but all are operating at frenetic and unsustainable speed. Let us, however, descend into the entrails of reengineering before worrying overmuch about its potential replacement.

The substance and historical antecedents

Although there are now many accounts of reengineering there appears to be a basic consensus about the critical issues involved. According to Hammer and Champy's (1993b) account, which is by far the most popular in terms of book sales if nothing else, these can be reduced to ten current practices that need reengineering:

1 a switch from functional departments to process teams;
2 a move from simple tasks to multidimensional work;
3 a reversal of the power relationship: from superordinate to subordinate empowerment;
4 a shift from training to education;
5 the development of reward systems that drop payment for attendance in favour of payment for value added;
6 a bifurcation of the link between reward for current performance and advancement through assessment of ability;
7 the overturning of employee focus: from concern for the boss to concern for the customer;
8 changes in management behaviour: from supervisors to coaches;
9 the flattening of hierarchies;
10 changes to executive behaviour: from 'scorekeepers' to leaders.

In fact, a considerable amount of attention has focused upon changes to information systems, but I want to concentrate here upon the generic features of reengineering rather than a particular application of them. In what follows I outline some details of the issues in each practice and then suggest antecedents that cast doubt on some of the claims to originality. However, my concern is not (just) to contest the originality of the ideas but to examine why an ensemble of ideas, which are not in themselves particularly innovative, appear to have taken some sections of business, especially in the USA, by storm.

A switch from functional departments to process teams

According to Hammer and Champy, the progenitor of the 'disease' that appears to have afflicted American industry is Adam Smith. Smith's discussion of the division of labour in his *Wealth of Nations* suggests that radical efficiencies of scale can be achieved by breaking the process of work down into its smallest possible unit. The resultant functional divisions of the labour process are then mirrored by the functional divisions within a company, so that the entire work process becomes fragmented and bureaucratized in a way best described by Weber (1978: 211–54). The result is not only increased specialization and alienation amongst the workforce, but an increasing, and increasingly labyrinthine, gap between customer and producer.

For reengineering advocates the problem has two dimensions: the irresponsible individual and the functional divisions that allegedly generate this state of affairs. The reengineering solution, therefore, is to switch from functions to processes: to move from producer-oriented specialization to consumer-oriented integration. Because the product or service that is sold is ultimately the result of an integrated process, not disintegrated functions, reengineering stresses the holistic aspects of work at the expense of the atomistic aspects; and because a major problem for processes is that individuals are seldom able to complete them, reengineering fixes very firmly upon teams not individuals.

However, this is hardly novel, for the historical antecedents of the shift from functionally divided individuals to process teams are manifold. We can stray back towards the nineteenth century – well after Adam Smith had dealt the apparent death blow to all work processes without extensive divisions of labour – to note that only the British shipyards adopted the specialized and highly divided squad system, while German, American and eventually Japanese yards maintained a much more process-oriented approach (Pagnamenta and Overy, 1984). Even within the same country and industry there were wide variations: woollen cloth was produced in the early nineteenth century using a high division of labour in the 'putting out' system in the west of England but a very low division of labour in Yorkshire (Randall, 1991). But probably the two most obvious counter-examples of the originality of this idea are the non-functional team-based approaches adopted by Volvo at Kalmar in 1974 (Berggren, 1989, 1992) and, before this, by the Durham miners at the heart of the composite long-wall mining system so famously captured by Trist and Bamforth (1951) during the early development stages of the Tavistock Institute's socio-technical systems theory.

Adam Smith's division of labour, and its attendant consequences, may, then, have held sway over the minds of many up until rather recently, but there have always been successful counter-examples and there is little that is especially novel in the reengineering 'manifesto'. What is new is the vigour with which it is advanced and the revolutionary potential with which it has been endowed by its promoters. We shall return to this later.

A move from simple tasks to multidimensional work

An inevitable result of this shift from specialized and functionally discrete individuals to integrated process teams is the development of multidimensional work and its corollary, multiskilled individuals. This, according to Hammer and Champy, cuts out a lot of non-value-adding labour, particularly that concerned with monitoring others' work, and it also eliminates the work that is created by the previous functional division so that 'people will spend more time doing *real* work' (1993a: 10, original emphasis): 'As a result, after reengineering, work becomes more satisfying, since workers achieve a greater sense of completion, closure and accomplishment from their jobs. They actually perform a whole job – a process or a sub-process – that by definition produces a result that somebody cares about' (1993a: 10). There are several related facets of this: first, deskilling is out and multiskilling is now in; second, multiskilled work is inherently more satisfying; third, the removal of functional divisions eliminates the monitoring processes that functional divisions require.

The case of multiskilling being a novel development can only be advanced by those taken in by Braverman's (1974) romantic critique of industrial capitalism. While there have undoubtedly been policies of deskilling along the lines suggested by Taylor, it is not self-evident that these are the *only* policies adopted by companies. Indeed, given the degree of technical and organizational change that has occurred over the last two centuries it is inconceivable that new skills have not been developed.

The second point suggests that reengineered people are more satisfied than unreconstructed, deskilled people – and the novelty of this should, in and of itself, be enough to persuade sceptics. But one only has to recall the Quality of Working Life Movement and the Job Enrichment Schemes of the 1970s to acknowledge that enskilling people is not a new response to crisis, and that such enskilled work does not axiomatically result in more satisfied employees. In fact, a whole battery of organizational research from Goldthorpe et al.'s (1969) analysis of 'alienated' employees onwards has suggested that 'inherent' interest is not necessarily a crucial factor for employees. Perhaps equally signifi-cant for reengineers, J. Kelly's (1982) review of such enrichment schemes in the earlier phase suggests that there is little, if any, connection between workers with satisfying jobs and high levels of productivity.

The third point suggests that the removal of functional divisions eliminates the need for reintegrating surveillance duties. Perhaps, but who ever said that surveillance was just about integrating divisions? We do not have to accept Foucault's argument about society becoming ever-more the subject of surveillance to acknowledge that surveillance, particularly through information technology, is alive and kicking across the corporate world: from the speed and accuracy of supermarket till operators to assembly line workers and machine operatives; monitoring is not a functionless, and therefore outdated and discarded, process (Foucault, 1979; Zuboff, 1989; F. Webster and Robins, 1993).

A reversal of the power relationship: from superordinate to subordinate empowerment

> A task oriented, traditional company hires people and expects them to follow rules. Companies that have reengineered don't want employees who can follow rules; they want people who will make their own rules ... Within the boundaries of their obligation to the organization – agreed upon deadlines, productivity goals, quality standards, and so forth – they decide how and when work will get done. (Hammer and Champy, 1993a: 10)

Empowerment, of course, can hardly be seconded to the exclusivist banner of reengineering, since the idea has had an independent, and relatively successful, life of its own for several years now. But again, the origins of much of this approach can be read into previous organiz-ational research of one form or another. Reengineering's version of empowerment seems to embody several related aspects. First, rule-bound behaviour can be very dysfunctional. This may well be the case, since an array of theoretical and empirical studies has suggested the same thing, from Weber (1978) himself, through the early works of Merton (1957) and Crozier (1964), to Batstone (1979) and Mitchell and Parris (1983). The second aspect is that, accepting that 'working to rule' usually means little gets done precisely because people have always to interpret which rule needs applying in each circumstance, teams should (subject to performance agreements) decide for themselves the best way to organize and execute the work process. Naturally, this might imply that the team may decide to return to functional specialization, but, assuming it does not, is this a novel idea? Well, only if we can ignore the history of many of the most hierarchical organizations, such as the armed forces, which have had tactical autonomy for group leaders on the ground for many years; and only if we can set aside the history of many collective forms of organizations, from producer co-operatives to anarchist communes and all stages in between (Miller, 1984; Mellor et al., 1988; Brannen, 1983). Third, the idea of devolving responsibility, within agreed limits, to process teams is precisely the organizing principle around which the semi-autonomous work teams of Volvo and SAAB have been organized. Fourth, and perhaps most fundamentally of all, the idea of inverting the power relationship between superordinate and subordinate is itself dependent upon a particular conception of existing power relationships. The reengineering assumption about traditional organizations is that power flows down-wards from superordinate to subordinate, so that the causal explanation of action suggests that subordinates act because superordinates are powerful. But we might profitably regard power as the consequence and not the cause of subordinate action (see Latour, 1986, for a fuller account of this).

The upshot of this is that, contrary to the reengineering assumption, subordinates *already* hold the key to power, while the superordinate must persuade them that they do not, if she or he is to remain in 'power'. Hence, whereas reengineering suggests we should reverse the current status of power relationships, this approach suggests that what is necessary is rather to *reinterpret* it and to accept that the subordinates are already powerful. This is the shift from training to education which forms the fourth leg of the reengineering project.

Shift from training to education

'Traditional companies typically stress employee *training* – teaching workers how to perform a particular job or how to handle one specific situation or another. In companies that have reengineered, the emphasis shifts from training to *education* – or to hire the educated ... people who already know how to learn (Hammer and Champy, 1993a: 11, 12, original emphasis). It is undoubtedly the case that Taylor advocated exactly the traditional strategy (though Taylor seems to have largely slipped by Hammer and Champy) and there is considerable evidence that much of the education of those about to enter employment is itself of the 'training' rather than the 'educational' form. But not all. Writing in the 1860s, Cardinal Newman decried the shift from a broad, classical education to a narrow, technical training (Watson, 1993: 8). One hundred and thirty years on there is, avowedly, a class-related system of education in Britain and there is indeed a tradition of training rather than education for the masses, manifest across a whole range of institutionalized divisions, from the post-war division between grammar and secondary modern through the friction between GCE and CSE examinations, right up to the current division between A-levels and National Vocational Qualifications (Dintenfass, 1992; Haralambos and Holborn, 1991). Of course, the stigma of 'practical' knowledge persists elsewhere, manifest in the hierarchy of knowledge implicit in the lethargic and unenthusiastic acceptance of engineering, technology and management studies as academic disciplines in their own right (see chapter 3).

This hierarchy was challenged much more successfully by other – mostly non-Anglo-Saxon – nations: by Germany and France especially, but even more so by Japan which has always had a tradition of seeking educated generalists rather than experienced specialists in its recruitment strategies. As a nation that had no natural resources except for its people, it is hardly any wonder that the Japanese chose to invest in education rather than training from an early date.

In effect, reengineering's concern for education at the expense of training may be welcome, and it would be remarkable if British business and trade unions came out strongly in full support of a traditional liberal education, but it is hardly a novel idea.

The development of reward systems that drop payment for attendance in favour of payment for value added

> Worker compensation in traditional companies is relatively straight-forward: people are paid for their time ... Paying people based on their position in the organization – the higher up you are the more money you make – is inconsistent with the principles of reengineering ... [in which] performance is measured by value created, and compensation should be set accordingly ... [and] substantial rewards for outstanding performance take the form of bonuses, not pay raises. (Hammer and Champy, 1993a: 13)

Ignoring the point that many companies do not pay people for their time but by their performance or 'by piece', and avoiding the sticky problems for those people whose value-adding activities are actually very difficult to measure (teachers, police officers, soldiers, civil servants, nurses etc.), the focus on bonus payments is certainly not novel: the Japanese regularly pay bonuses worth around a third of annual salary to their employees (Whitehill, 1991: 179, 180). Moreover, by focusing narrowly on the measurable 'value added' there is a very strong possibility of ignoring those aspects which appear more resistant to the accountant's, often short-term, gaze. Prioritizing value-added work may mean downsizing a plant to such an extent that when new orders arrive they cannot be met: the short-term focus of value added may lead to long-term failure. This latter example is doubly significant because it is resonant of a problem that has affected, and infected, both British and American industry for many years. In fact, many of the previous attempts to solve the problems of productivity have run through a similar series of strategies' starting with piecework in Taylor's scientific management. Focusing upon value-added components is not wrongheaded, but taken to an extreme, and to a predominant position in strategic terms, it merely substitutes the problem of short-term profitability for the problem of inefficient work practices.

A bifurcation of the link between reward for current performance and advancement through assessment of ability

> A bonus is the appropriate reward for a job well done. Advancement to a new job is not. In the aftermath of reengineering, the distinction between advancement and performance is firmly drawn. Advancement to another job within the organization is a function of ability, not of performance. It is a change not a reward. (Hammer and Champy, 1993a: 13)

Ever since Peter and Hull (1970: 22) derived the 'Peter Principle' of hierarchical incompetence ('In a hierarchy every employee tends to rise to his [sic] level of incompetence'), there have been growing concerns about the system of measuring and rewarding performance. The problems of this have already been discussed in the previous section, so the focus here is upon the bifurcation of the two and the method of measuring potential.

The first issue can only be considered novel within a particular segment of an organization. For example, in most large organizations, irrespective of the management structure, only a small proportion of those employed will ever reach managerial levels, and the chances of anyone becoming the CEO are sharply circumscribed by that individual's class, gender, ethnicity and education, to say nothing of networking abilities and what may be conceived of as intelligence or talent. So for the vast majority of people there is no need to introduce a new divide between advancement and performance because there will not be, and never has been, any real prospect of advancement.

Second, and what reengineering is really concerned with, then, is the level within which advancement has been considered normal. While non-reengineered company executives expect performance to be rewarded by promotion, reengineered company executives should not. Since many delayered companies no longer have the career channels that were previously open to aspiring executives, it should be self-evident that promotion is not a natural consequence of past perform-ance. Indeed, this is one of the reasons that performance-related pay has become so popular recently as organizations seek to (re)motivate their now upwardly immobile executives (Kessler and Purcell, 1992; Kessler, 1994).

In short, the division envisaged is by no means a fallacious one, but it is not an innovative one either.

The overturning of employee focus: from concern for the boss to concern for the customer

> Reengineering entails as great a shift in the culture of an organization as in its structural configuration. Reengineering demands that employees deeply believe, for instance, that they work for their customers, not their bosses. They will understand this concept only to the extent that the company's practices of reward and punishment reinforce it. (Hammer and Champy, 1993a: 14)

Although Smith's division of labour allegedly facilitated the develop-ment of a dramatically effective system of production, it did so only as long as customer demand could not be satiated; that is, as long as competition remained weak. But the rise of competition highlighted the problem not just of boss-centred organizations but of how to create a new structure on the basis of customer needs. One of the problems with customer-dominated organizations is that they tend to assume that simply mapping and measuring customers' existing demands will gener-ate sufficient data for them to react in a way that is in tune with the changing demands of customers. The point is that customers do not always know what they want in the abstract, nor is there always a uniform customer demand. If companies had waited for customers to demand the invention of the video recorder, or the internal combustion engine for that matter, we might not have developed such technologies. In short, to adopt a term from Woolgar (1991), customers are constantly configured in a myriad different ways by producers to the extent that there is probably never a time when it can be valid to say that 'the customer gets what she or he wants.'

The problem really is that the reengineering approach is too reductive. It reduces the determinants of action to two: boss or customer. Since there have always been organizations totally dependent upon customer, rather than boss, and since there have always been organizations where the two are indistinguishable, the novelty rides on the fervour behind the approach rather than the approach itself.

Changes in management behaviour: from supervisors to coaches.

'Work teams, consisting of one person or many, don't need bosses; they need coaches. Teams ask coaches for advice. Coaches help teams solve problems ... This is a different role than the one most managers have traditionally played' (Hammer and Champy, 1993a: 16). One could argue that this is part and parcel of the empowerment drive and therefore not unique to reengineering, but I think this misses the historical point. We need not go back to nineteenth-century factories to consider whether the widespread use of subcontracting actually prefigured this switch from supervisors to coaches.

But the more influential precedent was set out quite clearly by Roethlisberger and Dickson (1947) in their account of the famous Hawthorne experiments. Take, for example, these comments, not from the academics/consultants giving prescriptive advice but from the supervisors at the time:

> Most of them felt ... that their chief function was to facilitate the task of technical production ... The consensus of opinion was that the day of the 'bully' and the 'slave driver' had gone, and the day of the 'gentleman' and 'leader' had arrived. It was rather difficult, however, for most of the supervisors to articulate this new conception of leadership. For some of them it meant 'to get around and say a cheery word', for others it meant 'to treat the employees as you wish to be treated' ... 'to give them service' ... and 'to keep them satisfied' ... The gist of all their remarks was that subordinates could not be forced into cooperation ... Satisfied and contented employees were a necessary prerequisite for effective collaboration. (1947: 347–51)

As the training material noted: 'The thing for the supervisor to accomplish is to get the employee to analyze the case himself instead of the supervisor attempting to point out just where the employee is wrong' (quoted in Gillespie, 1991: 149). Or, in the words of Mayo, 'Normal supervision had been replaced by "continuous interviewing" and this would result in "a new and undreamed of era of active collaboration, that will make possible an almost incredible human advance"' (ibid., p. 151). Whether it was successful or not is difficult to assess (see Gillespie, 1991), but the theory underlying the new supervisory arrangements clearly prefigured the reengineered coach of sixty years later.

The flattening of hierarchies

> When an entire process becomes the work of a team, process management becomes part of the team's job. Decisions and interdepartmental issues that used to require the meetings of managers and managers' managers now get made and resolved by teams during the course of their normal work ... With fewer managers, there also exist fewer management layers. (Hammer and Champy, 1993a: 16)

There is little that is problematic about this aspect; teams can make supervisory management less relevant, though this is not an axiomatic aspect of process teams – the convention with mines has usually been for coal teams to manage themselves underground and for the control mechanism to rest in piecework with wages based originally, for example, on the number of coal barrows filled per shift (Dennis et al., 1956). Rather more recently the whole experience of Volvo and SAAB, in their experiments with semi-autonomous work groups since 1974, has been to filter out management from the decision-making processes of the team. In effect, teams have played an important role in organizational life for at least the last two hundred years, and many of them have operated without immediate managerial supervision, adopting forms of 'high' rather than 'low' trust (A. Fox, 1974) or 'Responsible Autonomy' rather than 'Direct Control' (Friedman, 1977).

Whatever the historical precedents for delayering organizations and replacing hierarchies with teams, it is not an unproblematic development. This is particularly so where delayering strips out managerial cohorts rather than thins them. If the process is one of stripping then not only are vast amounts of expertise and loyalty lost to the firm but there are proportionately fewer proving grounds for junior managers. In effect, it becomes increasingly difficult to evaluate junior managers or plan their moves through the ranks to the top because there are so few intermediate positions in which to evaluate their potential; an issue set to complicate the other reengineering requirement to assess future potential separately from past performance. This is compounded by the transformation required in managers themselves, considered next.

Changes to executive behaviour: from 'scorekeepers' to leaders.

> In a reengineered environment, the successful accomplishment of work depends far more on the attitudes and efforts of empowered workers than on the actions of the task-oriented functional managers. Therefore, leaders who can influence and reinforce employees' values and beliefs by their words and their deeds make the most effective executives. Executives have overall responsibility for reengineered process performance without having direct control over the people performing them ... Executives fulfil their responsibilities by ensuring that processes are designed in such a way that workers can do the job required and are motivated by the company's management systems – the performance measurements and the compensation systems, for instance – to do it. (Hammer and Champy, 1993a: 17/8)

The issue here is not that executives who can influence employees through their words and deeds make good executives: this is a truism of the most irrelevant kind. Rather, the issue is that the new managers now have to influence people without directly controlling them. It is not self-evident where the dividing line between these two strategies lies: what is 'direct control' in the unreconstructed company? Can there be a form of control which does not involve some form of influence and persuasion? One can control someone directly, without seeking to influence them, by pushing them off a cliff, but this is hardly a viable human resource tactic in an organization based on free contract. One assumption is that what reengineering really means here is that more effort will have to be made in the persuasion stakes and in the construction of self-activating motivational schemes. But isn't this exactly what Taylor had in mind when he tried to develop piecework rates that would motivate workers without the need for close supervision? Isn't this just what Herzberg and Maslow tried to develop? The end result may be different but the attempt to generate self-controlling and self-monitoring systems of management is as old as management itself.

In sum, there is precious little that is novel in BPR. But then two questions follow: first, why is it so popular? Second, why do so many attempts appear to fail? In what follows I argue that one way of thinking about the high level of popularity and failure can be understood through four axes that represent different ways of understanding the world, taking decisions about it, executing those decisions and, finally, legitimizing them. The model of this interaction is represented in figure 1.

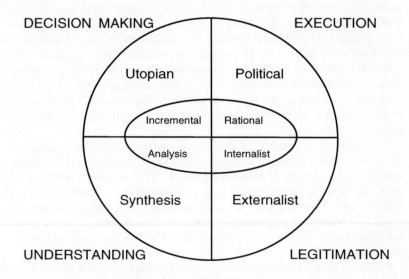

Figure 1 *Reengineering change*

Analytic versus synthetic understanding

From at least the period of the Enlightenment we have traditionally sought to explain the nature of the world by a ritual system of purification; that is, by imposing boundaries between phenomena as a way of managing their complexity. Thus we distinguish between 'us' and 'them', between humans and animals, between living things and non-living things, between animals we eat and animals we do not etc. The entire analytic method is based upon such a premise, since the world is so inordinately complex that the only way we can make sense of it is to impose boundaries around phenomena. We then take these to be 'real', that is 'natural', existing within the phenomenon itself rather than being attributed to or imposed upon it by whoever has the power to construct such boundaries (Latour, 1993).

The logical end result of such an approach can best be demonstrated by considering how Treasury models of inflation 'work'. Since inflation is a complicated issue to measure, let alone predict, the analytic method deems it best to assemble an array of variables that operate relatively independently only at the level of abstract theory. Once the critical variables have been isolated and their effects measured, the next trick is to combine them together in a sophisticated melting pot, known colloquially as a computer, which assesses the relative strengths of the variables and comes to a concluding number that predicts future inflationary trends. Naturally, the prediction is critical for government policy and, equally naturally, it is invariably inaccurate. The typical response is to add in yet more variables, to fine-tune the software, and to develop an ever more accurate predictor that strangely seems to fail yet again.

The problem, of course, is that more variables mean precisely that – more not less variance; indeed, the whole scheme can be thrown completely off course if there is a change in 'confidence', an intangible creature that appears completely uncontrollable. Perhaps, though, rather than accepting that we may as well count the seeds left on a dandelion 'clock' as pay computer analysts and economists vast sums of tax-payers' money, we might reconsider whether the approach itself is problematic.

Partly, it may be worth considering the extent to which analytic ways of fragmenting the world also embody forms of linear logic, in which one variable effects another in an invariant way. If the world is better described as one in which non-linear logic prevails, we should consider first, the extent to which variables are indeed independent of each other or are, in fact, construed to be independent only through our own inability to conceive of the world in more complex and interdependent ways; and, second, that this interdependence introduces an element of unpredictability and instability that actually makes prediction at best a method that requires more resources than is justified and at worst theoretically a nonsense. A good example of this kind of problem is reconstructed by Luecke (1994) in his account of the Battle of Midway, which the Japanese lost as much by chance, misfortune and an over-zealous adherence to linear logic, as by anything the Americans did.

The other aspect of the analytic approach that is problematic relates to the ritual purification through boundary imposition that separates humans from all else. Hence, for example, power becomes located within humans, either individually or collectively: Napoleon won the Battle of Austerlitz, while Wellington won the Battle of Waterloo – or, perhaps a little more generously, the respective commanders *and their troops* won their respective battles. Yet battles are only won through a combination of things: leaders, soldiers, guns, uniforms, transport, food, bullets, pay, ideals and many other things in between. The sight of Wellington strolling along the site of Waterloo completely naked, supported by thousands of naked, hungry, dispirited, weaponless, transportless men, would hardly have won the day. Even if we establish the elements of war through a process of sophisticated analysis this does not necessarily ensure that we can explain the unfolding of events: Hitler should not, at least on a paper analysis, have been able to overcome the Allied forces in France in May 1940 quite as easily as he did, but his holistic strategy compensated for his analytic weakness (Bartov, 1991). An analysis of the Mongol army at the gates of Vienna in May 1242 would have suggested that Armageddon was indeed at hand for Western Europe – but the death of Ogedai Khan led to an immediate return for the Mongol invaders (R. Marshall, 1993). In short, sophisticated analysis cannot compensate for the complexity of organizational life.

The consequence of this argument for reengineering relates to its holistic nature: reengineering stands or falls on the strength of the relationships it forges within the processes. Hence, just as the strength of a chain is determined by its weakest link so reengineering's strength lies in the novelty of its multiple linkages. One might argue that the linking of issues is precisely the innovation claimed by systems theorists, again, over forty years ago (Bertalanffy, 1950), though there is a more radical interpretation available which undermines the division between the social and natural worlds and speaks of the world of 'hybrids', phenomena that combine human and non-human. If we consider reengineering's success to be rooted in this recognition and promotion of hybridization then perhaps this may explain some of its success.

The second innovative element of the model, then, suggests a strong link between technical and organizational linkages, between non-human and human. The traditional socio-technical approach, of course, was premised upon precisely this dual axis, in which the optimal state was one where the discrete technical and social systems were not necessarily individually optimized, but melded together to give the optimal form of alloy. However, the promise of socio-technical systems was rarely realized, and one of the reasons seems to have been the reluctance to reconstruct the technology in line with the social systems, rather than more typically reconstructing the social system to fit with the technical one.

Rather more radical are the ideas of actor–network theory (Latour, 1993; Callon, 1986; Law, 1986, 1991; Cockburn and Ormrod, 1993; Grint and Gill, 1995), in which the boundaries between elements are replaced by hybrids that dissolve boundaries. The traditional asymmetry of explanation, in which human action is accounted for by processes that are fundamentally different from those that explain the actions of non-humans, is replaced by the principle of symmetry. In other words, and to take a single example, we should no longer consider 'interests' as an unproblematic causal variable for human action but not for the action of non-humans (see Callon, 1986, for the most startling interpretation). The point here can be taken either as a claim that non-humans have interests too or that it is very dubious to attribute interests to humans for precisely the same reasons that we do not conventionally attribute interests to scallops. The resulting account of action tends to consider human actors as remarkably weak in comparison to the hybrids that unite humans and non-humans; in effect, technology can make society more durable, and the social world is held together by more than just social ideas. Finally, and critically, that the capacity of the hybrid network – what the machine–human amalgam will do – cannot be read off from the claims of the constructors or the actants themselves but must be assessed both in the performance of the network and through the interpretative accounts of those involved in the assessment. There are problems with these approaches, but they need not concern us here (see Grint and Woolgar, 1995b). What is important is to note the potential utility of such an account in comparison to analytic models. *If*, as actor–network theory suggests, the world is composed of relatively boundary-less hybrids, and *if* the capacity of these hybrids depends upon the action and interpretation of the actants, then the stable and predictive claims of analytic and unilinear logic models are subject to severe doubt.

What reengineering can potentially do is start from the premise that boundaries imposed between functions and between different forms of resource are precisely that, imposed rather than exposed. As soon as the analytic divisions (between human resources and marketing, between machines and people) are constructed, our capacity to develop better ways of working are undermined, because these divisions impose what is essentially an artificial division between humans and non-humans. According to the model, then, we simply do not live in a world where people and things are separated: there are no humans without technological supports and there are no technologies that operate completely independently of humans. A critical advantage of the BPR approach, then, is to break down the barriers and start from the assumption that everything has to change, and change together. In effect, the approach is synthetic, that is, it synthesizes a multitude of disparate elements into an unstable but effective hybrid. (A more radical extension of this approach can be found in Latour, 1993.)

Incrementalism versus utopian decision making

Although each individual aspect of reengineering can be seen as merely a restatement of previous deliberations, there is a case for asserting that its novelty lies in the total package not the individual elements. Reengineering, in this account, is successful because of its *sui generis* nature: its holistic differentiation from, and superiority over, the analytic elements which have come before. This is plausible to the extent that the whole is greater than the sum of the parts. Indeed, one could argue that it is the radical extent of the change required that explains both the success and the failure of reengineering. That is, the high degree of uncertainty and risk involved weakens the nerves of those attempting to reengineer, so that they seek more conservative and instrumental approaches to change that appear both less risky and more plausible. This, of course, is precisely the argument made over thirty years ago by Lindblom's (1959) account of 'disjointed incrementalism' or 'muddling through' and the associated 'satisficing' behaviour described by Simon (1947). These incisive critiques of rational decision making imply that decision makers approach organizational problems not with a clean sheet of paper and an ideal, but with a set of existing customs, practices, structures and policies (see Jabes, 1982). Reengineering's innovation, therefore, may lie in its denial of this incrementalist orthodoxy that has prevailed for thirty years. Of course, day-to-day management *is* concerned with incremental change, that is, change at margins, small modifications to existing policies, procedures and methods. The bulk of the operation remains the same. The result over time, however, is a body of traditions, customs and practices that may appear to mirror the organizational sclerosis that Mancur Olson (1982) attributed to declining nation states.

In essence, the ideas imply that only an attack upon all fronts simultaneously, in which every possible institution, ritual, practice and norm is subject to critique and reconstruction, is likely to succeed. Where conventional plans for organizational change concentrate upon one or two areas (payment systems, or training, or customer focus, or just-in-time, and so on), reengineering mobilizes the entire workforce in a complete and universal reconsideration and reconstruction. Moreover, not only does reengineering require radical decisions, it also requires radically and culturally congruent decisions. That is, where decisions are made that have important consequences for the way an organization operates it makes little sense to generate wildly disparate decisions; for instance, to promote teams rather than individuals but simultaneously to generate a pay-and-reward system that recognizes only the efforts of individuals. In short, only those organizations that reengineer corporate strategy, management methods, reward systems and organizational structure in a congruent fashion are likely to succeed (Business Intelligence, 1994).

The premise of the argument, therefore, is that incrementalism is itself a barrier to change. This does not mean that all attempts to change should be utopian in their scale and direction but rather that the idea of utopian thought should be considered rather differently from its traditional one as fit only for dreamers, fit for 'nowhere' (Grint and Hogan, 1994a; Grint and Hogan, 1994b).

Reengineering is a particular form of utopian thought: it attempts not to improve the way business currently operates (though some of the reengineering focus upon business processes implies this: Business Intelligence, 1994), but to rethink it. More importantly, it asserts that the critical feature of reengineering is that associated with reengineering management rather than production processes (Padulo, 1994). It seeks not to enhance the efficiency of functions but to examine whether functions are the best way to run a business. Moreover, it does this against a background in which the larger danger is not in radical change but in not changing at all or not changing sufficiently radically. The danger, then, is the danger of obsolescence, which, by holding to established and traditional norms, allows more innovative firms to move ahead – to adopt new technologies, markets, training and reward systems.

There are several elements of traditional utopian thought that are worth considering in some detail. First, the traditional format, either in novels such as Huxley's *Island*, or the original *Utopia* of Thomas More, tends to constitute utopias as islands of perfection in an imperfect world (Badham, undated). The isolation is important in that it ensures an impenetrable barrier against worldly corruption and facilitates social experimentation. Marx regarded utopian socialism in exactly the same way, as islands of dreams that might serve as demonstrations that the world could be otherwise but as ultimately doomed unless the ideas and the practice spread rapidly across the boundaries. For reengineering we might consider the extent to which similarly radical experiments in alternative organizational forms tend to occur within organizations that are considered to be on the brink of collapse, and the minds of the doomed inhabitants have their attention focused on survival. Alternately, where organizations do not appear to be in immediate crisis, reengineering experiments are often executed within a delimited and heavily monitored 'island'; should the experimental Utopia fail, little has been sacrificed; should it succeed, the success can be used to persuade others of the need for radical change. Paradoxically, in the latter case, the utopian island must simultaneously demonstrate that it can work – but only if the rest of the organization does not 'infect' it. Yet if it, in turn, does not 'infect' the rest of the organization then it will be deemed to have failed. In other words, the boundaries around the Utopia must be permeable – but not in both directions.

The second element of utopian thought is to demonstrate, paradoxically, its eminently practical essence. One particular form is akin to the anthropological mode of research: defamiliarization – making the world strange as a device for scrutinizing it – as opposed to detailing an alternative. This shifts the debate from prescription (and there is enough of that around at the moment) to estranged (re)description. There is no specified end project in this form of utopian thought but merely an examination of the present in the light of potential, and plural, alternatives.

How does this work in practice? First, detail another organization, not to suggest that it is better than the current one, but to focus attention back on the first by comparison. This may seem equivalent to the current vogue of benchmarking best practice, but it can be used in this guise for two different purposes: first, to demonstrate the contingency of the current world or organization; second, to avoid considering Utopias as idle speculation or day-dreams: the alternative may not be here but it must be hypothetically possible. Hence estrangement, or defamiliarization, serves to provide an alternative that is not as detailed as current 'reality' but that is useful as a device for critically examining it and engendering the realization that the present can be changed in favour of a better alternative – not necessarily the one on offer.

It may be, then, that reengineering requires the kind of utopian thought discussed but much of the practice of reengineering still rests upon the traditional practices of incremental thought. Both utopian and incremental skills are necessary; the latter ensure the newly reengineered organization operates effectively and can be altered to suit the particular conditions it faces at the time, but to get to this stage requires utopian thought.

There are, of course, dangers in utopian thought and decision making too – indeed, Utopia in the political world has traditionally had a bad press, though the criticism has tended to take two rather different forms: one rooted in a fear of the inevitable consequences of failure; the second rooted in a fear of the unintentional consequences of success. The case for utopian thought and the significance of its application in reengineering, rests on two principles through which I attempt to transcend the case against utopian thought.

In the first place, Utopia is quite literally unrealizable, and hence thinking about it is not just a waste of resources but raises expectations that can never be met and must subsequently be managed. This is particularly appropriate for reengineering, where the claimed improvements are qualitatively different from, and in advance of, the kinds of claim made for less radical policies of change. Where the reengineered, but not revitalized, organization results, the deflated and frustrated utopian thinker and practitioner must, to use an old sociological term, be 'cooled out' to prevent the depression either becoming progressively worse or becoming endemic to the organization. In effect, utopian thought here is regarded as essentially destructive; it is a regressive, negative and corrupting concept that is always looking to some far-off romantic past or future that never really did or could exist. This philosophy suggests that, since we have to live in the present and plan for the future, we should avoid Utopias, including reengineering, like the veritable plagues they necessarily bring down on all who attempt to think about or implement them.

To challenge this lack of 'realism' we can turn to utopian theorists Frederick Jameson and Ernst Bloch. In Jameson's *The Political Unconscious*, Utopia is conceived of as fantasy grounded in reality (see Grint and Hogan, 1994a, 1994b, for a fuller account of this). That is, although utopian thought always exists 'outside of time' and might therefore rightly be considered as divorced from reality, history and society, the articulation of Utopia itself occurs within a specific time and place. In effect, the expression of utopian desire is always contextualized and can therefore be developed for that specific time and place. In other words, utopian texts and ideas should be seen as cultural constructs, not as ahistorical and acultural phenomena.

Relatedly, Bloch's *Principle of Hope* (1986) considers the significance of the German term *noch nicht*. This translates as both 'not yet', implying a future orientation, and 'still not', rooted in the present. The 'still not' focuses attention upon the steps taken towards an alternative – or not taken as the case may be – in the present. The 'not yet' focuses upon the ultimate future goal: the utopian vision. In managerial discourse this might be translated as the difference between vision and mission. The vision is the ultimate goal while the mission is the path. The juxtaposition of present and future, absence and potential presence, draws attention to current shortcomings and therefore acts as a necessary step to change (Levitas, 1990: 85). In Bloch's terms, it creates an 'anticipatory consciousness' – a precondition for, not an inhibition of, change. Hence, Utopias are not normally unrealistic but merely different from the existing reality: a potential reality waiting to be made real. Utopian thought, then, only makes sense – and especially practical sense – if it is considered as a way of thinking about an alternative but achievable reality. This kind of approach can be demonstrated in the development of Disneyland. Had Walt Disney not had the 'utopian' dream of Disneyland, it would not exist; the issue is not that it was a shame that Disney did not live to see Disneyland (as the popular version has it), but that it wouldn't exist without him having seen it in his utopian imagination.

The second argument against utopian thought is not that it is inherently unrealizable but the very opposite: that the danger lies in its realization – the Utopia becomes dystopia. Where our first principle suggests that we should all free up our thought processes, our second principle does not deny the danger of dystopia but rather attempts to transcend the problem by avoiding the cause. The fear of dystopia has enough solid historical support to warrant serious concern. Indeed, such concerns can be summarized in the phrase: 'The road to hell is paved with good intentions.' For management, such Utopias may be the CEO's latest dream, which involves all members of staff wearing the same uniform or watching endless 'corporate vision' videos that ought to come with a plain wrapper to avoid scaring the children. Here Utopia becomes a straitjacket that warrants no deviation, that considers all protest as a sign of indiscipline or conspiracy or worse; it becomes the nightmare rather than the dream because it implies that the originator of the dream has a universal wisdom that simply cannot exist.

In the business field we can consider a litany of gods that failed, or at least failed to revolutionize our businesses on a permanent basis: Taylorism, Fordism, management by objectives, measured day work, payment by results, collective bargaining. We might even note how these gods recur in time when today's executives forget yesterday's Utopias. For example, individual payment systems were an essential principle for F.W. Taylor, and they were tried and found wanting because of the inevitable tendency to decay which appears to undermine all such schemes. That they are now back in favour is not the issue, but we should not expect them to last indefinitely any more than they did last time.

The implication of this, and a possible explanation for reengineering's high failure rate – though it appears to be no higher than that of anything else – is that the very radicalism of reengineering, that is, its utopian essence, is simultaneously what makes it so difficult to achieve and, when achieved, makes its productivity achievements so high (see G. Hall et al., 1993). In effect, reengineering has to be utopian to work at all, and if it is utopian then it is possible to achieve the results hitherto regarded as impossible. But, since we know that all previous management revolutions have ultimately proved less and less viable over time, we should recognize that this organizational atrophy implies that the only permanent revolution is exactly that: permanent revolution.

Execution

The third aspect of the circle in Figure 1 is often regarded as the point at which the utopian dreams of the revolutionaries and reengineers become impaled upon the spikes of reality; where idealistic decisions are progressively deracinated into pragmatic compromises: it is the place of execution. Yet, paradoxically, much of the failure to execute decisions lies not in the irrationality of the decisions but rather in the irredeemably political context in which the execution of decisions occurs.

It has been a convention of Western thought since the Enlightenment that the same rationality that persuaded us to think in analytic rather than synthetic terms also operates to persuade us that rationality, rooted in reasoned individual action and the application of scientific principles, is the means by which individuals are persuaded to execute decisions made by others or to change their opinion, their attitude or their behaviour. Indeed, almost all textbooks on management behaviour suggest that persuasive accounts are those which are deemed to be rational. Yet when we get close to organizations they appear to operate along political or moral lines rather than those that we might otherwise recognize as rational.

The original responsibility for this confusion lies at the feet of Adam Smith, whose work captured and promoted the transformation of an economy run along moral lines into one run along market lines. The traditions that made up the moral economy have a- very long history and involved fines for overpayment of wages or overpricing of goods, prohibitions on the export of materials for making cloth (including the emigration of skilled workers), and a whole host of regulations covering industry (see Grint and Woolgar, 1995b; Bland et al., 1933).

One historical illustration will suffice for our purposes here. Smail (1987, 1991), for instance, has argued that the 1806 British Parliamentary Committee appointed to consider the state of the woollen industry at the time was a seminal point in the development of a new discourse through which the old moral economy, articulated through what he calls a 'Corporatist Discourse', was displaced by the new laissez faire economy, articulated through what he terms an 'Industrial Discourse'. As Smail notes, the old discourse is nicely reproduced in the 1555 Act Touching Weavers: 'No Woollen Weaver using or exercising the feate or Mistery of Weaving ... shall have or kepe at any one time above the number of Twoo Wollen Loomes' (quoted in Smailes, 1987: 53). The new discourse, on the other hand, inverted the concern from collective to individual and supported: 'The right of every man to employ the Capital he inherits, or has acquired according to his own discretion, without molestation or obstruction' (ibid.). It would seem that Smail has probably exaggerated the significance of this single episode (see Randall, 1990), but the point is that the committee does represent the increasing influence of the new discourse, and by the time of the trial of the Luddites in York, six years later, the argument that technical development represents rational progress appears to have become common sense for the establishment. For the Luddites, and those who followed in their resistance to economic and technical changes, the old discourse (which had prevailed for some five hundred years) that talked of moral obligations, reciprocity between all, and the protection of craft rights was decreasingly effective against the new discourse of the factory entrepreneurs. This new mode of thought sought to strip out morality from the economy, divest itself of all taint of collective interests, and facilitate the unfettered pursuit of private interests. This old discourse never actually died (and its persistence can be seen in the work of Noble, 1983), but after the Luddites it became progressively less influential amongst the establishment and, perhaps equally significant, amongst the representatives of the working class.

When one considers the significance of this argument to the present day, it is reasonable to view the difference between what the texts say about organizations and what managers say about organizations as the difference between the official and the unofficial line on them. The former sees organizations as rational bodies driven by the rational desire for profit maximizing and with decisions executed by rational individuals acting rationally in pursuit of rational organizationally defined objectives. This is quite different from the unofficial line, where organizations are considered as political institutions run by Machiavellian Princes in pursuit of what appears to many to be their own private interests. Hence, decisions are effectively executed by (successful) political infighting, by (successful) networking, by making the right friends and the right enemies, by going to the right school and university, by choosing the right parents, gender and ethnicity and by a whole host of related aspects that have precious little to do with any form of rationally legitimated criteria for ensuring success.

If this is the case in organizations, and if this approach – which is political and moral rather than rational – is extended from explaining managerial behaviour and success, then it might seem viable to consider how this impacts upon attempts by managers to introduce organizational change. In this approach, the desperate search to explain the failure of yet another management initiative by inadequate consultation or communication or whatever is missing the point. If managers operate politically rather than rationally in their lives, and succeed or fail on political rather than rational criteria, then we might consider the extent to which change programmes, such as reengineering, succeed or fail on the same grounds. In effect, explaining the rational implications of continuing the traditional way of doing things, and the rational effects of a reengineered process, may be considerably less effective than setting out to achieve the same ends through a political process. In short, this might mean moving from a campaign to persuade people through an appeal to their minds to one to enrol people through an appeal to their hearts.

However, the reversal of a causal explanation of execution does not account for the way certain forms of decisions appear to derive their legitimacy from sources beyond the appeal to logic. In other words, the way that organizations work and the direction in which they move and change appears to depend as much upon changing fashions as upon any evolutionary or linear progression towards better ways of managing. In the final section here, I want to consider the last dichotomous axis of the reengineering debate, and assess the extent to which the predominance of the rational has prevented us from assessing the degree to which the success of approaches to organizational change can be linked to the predominance of resonances which the new vogue appears to set up between itself and other, related, ideas.

Legitimation

I have already argued, at length, that there is a problem with assuming that the internal rationality of an idea is sufficient to ensure its acceptance, let alone execution. Here I want not to rerun the problems of rationality but to consider the extent to which we might focus upon the congruence of 'new' organizational or management ideas, such as reengineering, with other, ostensibly unrelated ideas beyond the world of business; that is, the way new approaches render an account of the problem and solution that sets up sympathetic 'resonances' with related developments. BPR's or reengineering's popularity, according to this approach, also lies in the resonances it 'reveals' between old and new business systems previously right but now inappropriate. Hence it:

> isn't another imported idea from Japan ... capitalizes on the same
> characteristics that made Americans such great business innovators: indi-
> vidualism, self reliance, a willingness to accept risk and a propensity for

change ... unlike management philosophies that would have 'us' like 'them', [it] doesn't try to change the behaviour of American workers and managers. Instead, it takes advantage of American talents and unleashes American ingenuity.' (Hammer and Champy, 1993b: 1–3)

To arrive at this conclusion a certain amount of cultural manipulation is required, if the resonances between the idea and the particular culture concerned are to be clear. For example: BPR is supposed to be about teamwork not (American) individualism. It is supposed to be about starting to risk change – so how can change be an element of the US culture? It is supposed to be about radically increasing the level and content of supportive social networks, not about American individual self-reliance. In effect, what counts as significant aspects of culture can be interpreted afresh by those who seek to change it – an important note for BPR consultants eager to work outside the USA.

It also resonates with the increased power of transnational corporations (TNCs) in the age of globalization: to compete with the Japanese, Western TNCs must generate similar levels of loyalty, increasingly disembedded from the concerns of nations or nationalities. This is particularly so in the light of the collapse of old stabilities such as the Cold War and US political and economic domination, and the political and economic turbulence that appears to increase daily. One way to restabilize the present is by reinterpreting the past so that radical (and the word 'radical' no longer bears the left-wing political resonance it once had) innovations prosper when marketed as the way to return to former glories.

In effect, then, since all the elements have been around for varying amounts of time, the issue is not so much whether the elements are novel but whether the packaging and the selling of the package are what makes reengineering different. This is the equivalent of subordinating internalist accounts to externalist accounts; that is, concerning ourselves less with whether the content of reengineering is radically different and demonstrably superior to anything that went before (which it appears not to be from the analysis above), than with *why* the package is effective in its particular envelope of space and time. That is, why did reengineering take off at the very end of the 1980s and in the early 1990s, and why is it so popular in the USA rather than anywhere else?

Clearly, if the reengineering approach failed to convince its target population that its analysis of the problems was accurate, then its prescriptive advice would probably not be heeded. But I want to argue here that the persuasive utility of reengineering, the reason for its popularity, rests not in the objective validity of the constitutive elements or the whole – the internal novelty and validity of reengineering, as it were – but in the way the rendering of the problem and solution provided by reengineering generates a resonance with popular opinion about related events – an external explanation, one might say. This does not mean that the ideologies are functional responses to the requirements of capitalism, or anything else for that matter. Rather my argument is that these ideas and practices have to be read as plausible by those at whom they are targeted, and for this 'plausibility' to occur the ideas most likely to prevail are those that are apprehended as capturing the *Zeitgeist* or 'spirit of the times'.

There are precedents for this in the popularity of previous managerial philosophies (see Rose, 1990). For example, Taylorism and Fordism can be understood in relation to the contemporary development of social statistics: the rise of the eugenics movement in the USA and its attempted legitimation through scientific measures of IQ (Kamin, 1977; Karier, 1976a, 1976b), the high point of pre–1914 beliefs in the efficacy of scientific rationality – soon to be radically disturbed by the events of 1914–18 (Pick, 1993); in the light of the changes in disciplinary and temporal schemas adopted originally in armies and prisons (Foucault, 1979); and, of course, in the development of assembly line systems, or rather disassembly line systems, in the Chicago slaughter houses, then 'processing' 200,000 hogs a day (Pick, 1993: 180). One might want to go further here and suggest that the kinds of mechanical tactic adopted by the British army at the Battle of the Somme in 1916, for example (Winter, 1979; Ellis, 1993), are precise replicas of scientific management displaced from the factory to the killing fields of Flanders. Relatedly, the human relations reaction to Taylorism and Fordism can be read as a shift from the 'rational individual' to the 'irrational group', as the development of communism and fascism appeared to be explicable only through an assumption about the fundamentally irrational needs of people to belong to groups and to construct their group identity through the destruction of 'the other'. In the military field, again, the 'new' common sense that began to prevail towards the end of the Second World War was that, as in the factory so in war, group cohesion and the solidarity of a relatively small 'primary group' were what motivated people (Shils and Janowitz, 1948); a claim subsequently disputed by Bartov (1991), who suggests that the Wehrmacht's cohesion on the eastern front, beyond the barbarism of the military system itself, was the result of a powerful organizational culture – another resonance from the present.

The defeat of fascism and the arrival of the Cold War provided fertile ground for the reconstruction of neo-human relations in the form of democratic individualism; the Soviet 'evil empire' was neither democratic nor individualist, and, particularly in the UK (Donovan Commission, 1968), the informal primary group, so long propounded by the human relations school, appeared to be the cause of the problem of economic malaise, not the solution. This time the alternative was written in the language of Lewin's democratic leadership, or McGregor's Theory Y version of responsible employees, and Maslow's and Herzberg's quest for self-fulfilment through work. Finally we can posit the arrival of the fourth wave, the 'cultures of excellence' approach where the limits of modernism and Fordism are perceived as the stimulus to change. Reengineering, in this perspective, is the summation of this fourth wave (see Grint, 1994, for a more detailed account).

Reengineering, therefore, provides what can be considered as a new discourse with which contemporary developments can be simultaneously explained and controlled. The language of reengineering renders opaque developments apparently clear, not by providing a more objective analysis of the situation and the solution but by giving a persuasive rendering of these. Moreover, part of the persuasive essence lies in the resonances that it 'reveals' between the old and the new, particularly between American past glories and future conquests. However, for this to be achieved successfully the world has to be conveyed in ways that make reengineering appear as an appropriate response.

Reengineering's historical narrative, at least that provided by the originators of the term, Hammer and Champy, asserts that the current business systems were not always wrong but are no longer appropriate. To assert that what America has been doing was always wrong both fails to explain why it has become such a successful economy and implies that American culture was and is inappropriate. It is clearly advantageous to argue that blame for the current state of affairs lies in the actions of 'the other' (that is, foreign competition) if one is intending to persuade one's own customers of the viability of change. The second manoeuvre, having persuaded Americans that they were right the first time, is to suggest that the current conditions, although responsible for the problems facing American business, are, paradoxically, ideally suited to turning the tables on 'the other'. Thus the two major problems in such an account are transcended. American industry is weak now *because*, rather than despite the fact that, it was so strong before; and American industry will be strong again because of, rather than despite, American culture.

We can assume from this rhetoric that reengineering is not only a way of fending off the attacks of 'the other' (that is Japan), but also a mechanism that will allow America to regain authority over 'the other' – primarily because the American culture is uniquely suited to the reengineering approach. The Japanese, already under attack in books from Tolchin and Tolchin's *Buying into America: How Foreign Money is Changing the Face of Our Nation* to Michael Crichton's *Rising Sun*, may be emulated but they must not be imitated.

This obviously poses related problems for other cultures and suggests that only American corporations are likely to experience the full benefit of reengineering – unless, of course, reengineering can be reconfigured in such a way that its resonances lie not so much with cultural changes that restrict its utility but with changes that expand its utility beyond the US shoreline.

Nor is it coincidental that the rise of functional accounts of organizations, and subsequently integrated systems approaches to organization, developed at a time of organizational, especially business organizational, stasis, or even more appropriately the long boom which survived from the end of the Second World War to the oil crisis of 1974. When growth is considered strong and the future appears secure, what hope for the management guru who wants to experiment with radical innovations? But when old stabilities like the East–West conflict crumble in the Berlin Wall collapse; when American, and even Western, economic domination withers under pressure from Japan and the Asian Tigers; and when the long boom turns into the long collapse, the conditions for organizational radicalism are set fair. This is particularly so when, in the absence of the 'evil empire', the legitimacy of the 'victor' rests on much less stable grounds. The reconstruction of national boundaries, then, may, if anything, make the 'foreignness' of economic competitors even more significant and the search for radical remedies more frenetic.

The response by the USA has been twofold. On the one hand, the global competition now threatening the country has seen first President Bush and then President Clinton warning their fellow citizens that America can no longer fend off the competition alone and must itself join trading blocs, such as the North American Free Trade Agreement (NAFTA). The possibility of US-based corporations exporting what the AFL-CIO call 'millions' of jobs to Mexico, to take advantage of cheaper labour and laxer health and safety legislation, has provoked a storm of criticism and considerable public outcry at the potential loss of, or slur on, American identity (Tisdall, 1993).

On the other hand, the fall of the 'evil empire' has freed some of the language of change, so that 'radical' change no longer implies shifts to the political left, and talk of giving power to the employees no longer embodies the failure of management or capitalism. Hence, where several prior attempts at organizational change have concentrated upon partial and very specific aspects of the organization – total quality or human resources etc. – reengineering gains strength from its radicalism.

Where these have been tried and found wanting, most appropriately because they are not just partial solutions but *foreign* partial solutions, then the time is ripe for radical overhauls.

However, a crucial aspect of temporal resonances is that there must be a juxtaposition of the old and the new. That is, although an element of novelty is critical this must not be regarded as a complete break with all that has gone on before; thus Hammer's concern to remind potential American customers that the novelty element is actually an historically rooted part of American culture. Success can be achieved not through breaks with tradition but through a radical return to tradition. This paradoxical juxtaposition is itself hardly novel. Max Weber makes a strong argument for precisely this enmeshing of the present and future with the past in his analysis of charismatic leadership, particularly that associated with Jesus Christ. Weber argues that it was only because the apparently radically innovative ideas of Christ's message were so deeply embedded in Jewish culture over a long period of time that they found any resonances with the population (see chapter 6). The parallel with reengineering and American culture is clear: radical innovations prosper best when they are marketed as methods to return to former glories. Moreover, the return of this former glory will be constructed in a reengineered environment which is ideally suited to American culture: it will comprise powerful corporations that vie with nation states for supremacy; it will require individual dedication and loyalty to an ideal of a kind which many other nationalities may find difficult to achieve; it will require the construction of new identities from across many boundaries where origin and history are less important than an attitude of mind; and it will be a land of opportunity for bootstrappers. The reengineered future is the land not of the sullen or lethargic employee but of the dedicated corporate warrior; it is a reengineered neo-feudalism, a total way of life.

Conclusion

This chapter has disputed the analytic claims to novelty espoused by reengineering's supporters but accepted that the holistic and, in particular, the hybrid nature of reengineering's approach, implies that there is something different about it. By dividing the way managers operate into four segments (the analytic revenge?), it suggests that reengineering is most likely to fail where it is construed as a method and goal of change that is premised upon rational analysis, where the decision making is incremental, where the methods of execution depend wholly upon assumptions about rational individuals, and where its legitimizing characteristics are regarded as self-evident and as lying in its internal and objective value. Reengineering, it is argued, might be better configured as a Utopia, and it embodies the same kind of possibilities and problems that Utopias throughout history have manifested. In effect, the chapter argues that for reengineering to work as a radical and long-term change the focus should be more on reengineering the way managers think and work than on reengineering the way processes operate. Furthermore, the methods by which reengineering might be achieved have to be more firmly rooted in the current cultural climate.

To summarize, whatever the concerns over the uniqueness of reengineering – and the development of an holistic account that locks human and non-human hybrids into complex networks is certainly an interesting way of considering reengineering, even if it is not something reengineering supporters articulate – my main point is not to suggest that the lack of novelty implies reengineering is mere hype, or that it will fail because it is not novel. On the contrary, novelty is no guarantee of success and, anyway, many of the ideas embodied in reengineering do, so its adherents claim, facilitate greater levels of efficiency. Rather, my concern is to suggest that we look beyond the content of reengineering if we wish to understand why it appears to have taken parts of the USA by storm and why it has done this at a particular time. For those seeking to encourage British or Japanese or any other form of industry to reengineer, the appropriate strategy may be to reinterpret the national culture so that it resonates with those aspects allegedly required by reengineering.

As part of this process I want to suggest that utopian thought should be brought back in from the cold, especially since the ending of the Cold War has taken the chill off many Utopias. Utopian thought is destructive, but only in the sense of the creative destruction that is necessary to change the present in and through imagining a better future. There is little doubt that 'historically' many people have suffered at the hands of utopians, whether within business enterprises that required almost religious adherence to the corporate code of a utopian CEO, or within the confines of a dystopian political system, where the future starts with Year Zero. However, utopian thought can serve as a valuable heuristic mechanism through which the *status quo* can be considered in a much more reflective way. Here, Utopia becomes the estranging device that marks out the problems of the present and offers an array of potential alternatives without the usual prescriptive coercion beloved of those peddling or seeking simplistic solutions. Utopia does not have to mean 'Nowhere' in the sense of never existing; it can mean 'Nowhere' in the sense of nowhere *yet*. The point is not that we should strive for the unrealizable but that we might consider 'what might be' as a first step towards 'what will be'.

If the world is in a constant flux then the issue is whether we should respond by abandoning the dreams of a better future or suffer the consequences of attempting permanent change. The danger of somnambulism, sleepwalking through life when all around is changing rapidly, appears as much more of a risk. One only has to consider the proportion of organizations that survive by remaining static and immune to change to know that this is a recipe for disaster: the danger is not that of moving slowly but that of not moving at all.

But where does this leave the average manager or indeed the average person? I suggest that three things should be borne in mind. First, change and stasis are the responsibility of each one of us: to believe otherwise is to be guilty of 'bad faith' – the illegitimate denial or displacement of responsibility. Second, managers might try a thought experiment which can be extremely useful in provoking new avenues of imagination: imagine what your perfect job and perfect organization might look like – and then compare them with your account of reality: are there gaping holes between the two that might be filled, or at least reduced, by practical measures taken or suggested by you? Third, don't get hung up on the practical details of the utopia; the critical issue is to use the utopian ideal to make the current situation appear strange and in need of justification so that improvements might be made.

In short, BPR's success can hardly be explained by the novelty of its individual ideas, but may have something to do with the holistic and synthetic hybrid amalgamations of these. It might also be explained by the resonances that can be established with related events and movements elsewhere. Indeed, I would argue that probably the most important aspect of successful organizational change is getting people to read the world in a different way, persuading them that Utopia is both possible and necessary. However, to get there, the drive for reengineering will need to stop concentrating upon reengineering the operational processes in isolation from the way management thinks and works: the Utopia is one where management is reengineered. Only then could what Trotsky (1969), in a different context, called 'the permanent revolution' occur.

6

The Alchemy of Leadership

The *Value*, or WORTH of a man, is as of all things, his Price; that is to say, so much as would be given for the use of his Power: and therefore is not absolute; but a thing dependent on the need and judgement of another ... And as in other things, so in men, not the seller, but the buyer determines the Price. For let a man (as most men do) rate themselves at the Highest Value they can; yet their true Value is no more than it is esteemed by others.

(Hobbes, *Leviathan*)

Introduction

'Seldom in the history of human sciences has so much been written with so little effect', or so Churchill might have written had he been concerned with examining leadership rather than attempting to execute leadership. This chapter concerns the alchemy of leadership. For centuries attempts were made to turn base metals into gold, and each time the experiment failed a new one replaced it in an apparently never-ending cycle of failure. One might regard leadership studies in a similarly jaundiced way. Between January 1990 and January 1994, 5,341 articles were published on leadership just within those journals covered by the BPI/INFORM international database (around 800 English-language management journals). That is getting on for four every day, or five a day if we exclude weekends: approximately every six hours, somewhere, someone publishes a paper on leadership in English. Assuming each paper to have an average length of, say, ten pages and pretending that we get just over three pages to a metre, if we laid the papers on leadership over this four-year period from end to end we would have about 16 kilometres of leadership material. Now the point of this wearisome trail is not the time it takes to get from the beginning to the end but the value of the journey. Are we any closer to uncovering the alchemy of leadership? That is, are we now in a better position to understand, and presumably enhance, leadership?

Leadership is a topic that has been studied extensively through numerous interdisciplinary approaches, including political theory, management, psychology, sociology and education. Yukl (1989) provides an in-depth survey of theory and research on managerial leadership yet he acknowledges that there is precious little consensus on precisely what it is, how or whether it can be instilled into individuals, or even how important it is. It is difficult to settle upon a consensual definition of leadership let alone a consensus about the substantive phenomenon itself or its effectiveness (Lieberson and O'Connor, 1972), or how leadership can be taught – if at all (Conger, 1993). As Stogdill (1974: 259) argues, 'there are almost as many definitions of leadership as there are persons who have attempted to define the concept' (quoted in Yukl, 1989: 252). Yukl's own diagnosis of the field goes deeper than the question of definition to assert that 'most of the theories are beset with conceptual weaknesses and lack strong empirical support. Several thousand empirical studies have been conducted on leadership effectiveness, but most of the results are contradictory and inconclusive' (1989: 253). One might think that with this apparent fetish for leadership, coupled with the number of data floating around, some kind of consensus, about the basis of leadership at least, would eventually precipitate out – providing the data reflect the phenomenon and do not construct it. If the latter is the case then we might expect the confusion to increase as the quantity of data increases. What is clear is that there appear to be no reliable predictive theories of leadership; leaders are recognized *after* certain actions have taken place, but even this recognition is insufficient to provide a solid guide to leadership skills, let alone how to distinguish management from leadership.

There are many who argue that management and leadership are diametrically opposed. Bennis and Nanus (1985) distinguish between leaders doing things right while managers do the right things, while Yukl (1989) proposes that leaders influence commitment while managers merely carry out position responsibilities and exercise authority. But, in the former case, who is to assess what counts as 'right', and in the latter, can one exercise authority without influencing commitment (one way or the other)?

Certainly, leadership has usually been separated from 'management', with the former being construed as the process of constructing a vision and then cajoling one's subordinates to follow it; management, on the other hand, is much more of a routine administrative affair, using the battery of managerial aids to facilitate the journey outlined by the leader. Organizations with too many leaders and not enough managers are likely either to tear themselves apart in the search for different goals or to wither as the supply lines are stretched beyond the capacity of the managers to manage them. Organizations with too few leaders may be well administered but on the road leading to oblivion.

It is also worth considering not why have we become so interested in leadership now but why we should expect leaders to make a difference anyway. After all, the industrialization and subsequent globalization of the world have been associated with ever larger organizational units: factories, towns, armies, schools, hospitals, prisons etc., have all expanded throughout the last two centuries, yet we still keep faith with a model of organizations that attributes much of the success to the actions of individual leaders. Undoubtedly the rational individual at the heart of Descartes's division between mind and matter (the Cartesian subject), Locke's 'sovereign individual', Hobbes's warlike individuals and also, in classical economic theory, Adam Smith's entrepreneurs and utilitarian theory's individual calculators all played their part in the attribution of causality and responsibility to individuals (S. Hall, 1992). But the entire modernist movement also pushed society towards 'massifications' and science, and simultaneously projected the impersonality of the mass forward in a way that many regarded as entirely at the expense of the individual, a view probably best represented in the sociological writings of Simmel (Frisby, 1984) and the novels of Kafka. This paradox, of the mass nature of organizational life and the individualized nature of experience is also mirrored in Foucault's concern for the escalating regulation, isolation and disciplining of the individual by the increasingly organized and centralized system of institutions. The implication of Foucault's claim about the disciplining role of institutionalized expertise is that we should expect to see an ever increasing attempt to develop 'scientifically proven' normative models of individuals; in this particular context, of leaders. Thus, the attempts to model the necessary traits, personality and skills of 'the ideal leader' are likely to continue irrespective of problems in generating the appropriate empirical evidence to support them. Indeed, given Foucault's notion of the 'regime of truth', in which knowledge is made 'true' by those who have the power to enforce such a conception of the truth, we should be surprised if there were not commonly accepted 'truths' about leadership ('Leaders are born not made', 'We have to have leaders' etc.). The quest for the secrets of leadership is likely to go on, then, and just as likely to generate a new list of 'dos' and 'don'ts' every other week.

What we are not concerned with here is providing a summary overview of all the perspectives on leadership (for which we are ill equipped in disk space, to say nothing of any other resources). For those thinking of reading such a book on leadership, Bass and Stogdill's *Handbook of Leadership* (1990) has 1,182 pages; probably enough in weight alone to persuade any insubordinate subordinate that superordinates know best. Those looking for a rather briefer review should try Yukl (1989), and those looking for an interesting attempt to unlock the 'secrets' of history, particularly for contemporary leadership, might try Luecke (1994).

R. Heller (1993) argues that three attributes distinguish leaders from 'also-rans', which I assume means managers who do not lead. First, and most important, they are successful – though precisely *who* attributes success to any particular action is crucial here, as Thomas Hobbes notes in the quotation at the beginning of this chapter. Second, they know what they want to achieve (or rationalize what they have got when they have got it?) and concentrate on this one thing to the extent of making the end justify the means. Third, they express the will of the people and leave them better off. Expressing the will of the people is always an interesting claim, and one that virtually every leader makes; whether their actions *do* express the will of the people (whatever that is and however it is measured) seems to me to be an enormous problem.

On the other hand, one of the most popular approaches to leadership claims that there are some traits that are intimately related to leadership skills: self-confidence, initiative, energy, emotional control, and inter-personal, technical and conceptual skills of various kinds etc. (Bass, 1981), plus competitive spirit (Stahl, 1983). It should not take a genius to recognize that even this brief survey of the attributes allegedly necessary for leadership implies that they are probably restricted to the likes of Supergirl – to say nothing about the tensions that exist between some of the traits. For example, one might argue that the last thing a risk-taker needs to consider is how to balance this tract with pragma-tism, how to be assertive and decisive while remaining empathetic and a good listener, and how to remain aloof from his or her peers and subordinates and expend energy on networking simultaneously. The difficulty of establishing precisely what are the requisite traits is captured in the alternative interpretations placed upon apparently identical behaviour: the point at which a decisive move becomes precipitate, or a tactful decision becomes a weak decision, lies in the interpretative understanding, not in the move or decision. Similarly, even if self-confidence can (a) be measured accurately, and (b) be correlated with leadership skills, this does not tell us whether an action which results in an advantage to the actor leads to self-confidence or whether only self-confident actors act in this particular way. Even the claim that leaders need strong interpersonal skills is questioned by research into what subordinates think their leaders lack – interpersonal skills (see Grint, 1993a)!

If we just take one, relatively popular list of essential qualities for leadership we can be faced with real problems in trying to extrapolate it from a specific situation. For instance, such a list might include: trusting your subordinates, developing a vision, keeping your cool, encouraging risk, being an expert, inviting dissent and simplifying. Only the vision and the simplification attributed would fit well with Stalin or Hitler, yet these two were regarded – for relatively long periods of time – as extraordinarily effective leaders.

Stalin might also be used to test another traditional division between leadership and management, the former being concerned with change, the latter with stability. Can we still rest assured that the change–stability division can be safely adopted to distinguish leadership from management? What about a leader such as Stalin who 'led' by preserving the status quo? Is an officer whose actions, in defending a salient under attack, manage to keep the defensive line intact a leader or a manager? Is a CEO who leads by refusing to change with every new management fad and fashion merely a manager? There is no change necessarily involved, but there is plenty of personal risk. Or what of the inverse example, in which an officer or manager implements a change of tactics – devised elsewhere – that results in a breakthrough; in effect where change is merely the result of managing? All these examples undermine the essentialist divisions between management and leadership, but they also lay the groundwork for an alternative. In the military case, for instance, whether the officer demonstrated 'leadership' or 'management' could be the subject of some dispute. Since the allocation of military medals for valour is critically dependent upon the rank of the individual concerned, rather than any apparent bravery, one might be prepared to argue that the higher the rank the braver the individual, and not the higher the rank the greater the access to the medal cupboard (Holmes, 1987: 355–9). In sum, the causal relationship between rank and what counts as leadership appears to mirror the relationship between rank and bravery: because an individual is in a position of authority he or she is recognized as being braver and manifesting better leadership qualities than someone lower down the hierarchy. Many at the bottom of the hierarchy may resent and reject such an equation, but their voices are generally too weak to carry much weight with those who 'recognize' (that is construct) bravery and leadership.

In what follows I set out to answer the question, 'What is leadership?'

by considering leadership in six ways. First, I lay out the issues of culpability and responsibility that leadership seems to require. I follow this by considering the most popular form of leadership, as a phenomenon which is best considered as embodied in charismatic individuals: the loneliness of command represents this approach, and I will consider the extent to which an isolated individual can ever become a leader. Third, I consider leadership as an activity that can only be understood and improved by considering the multiple contingencies that surround leaders. Fourth, I extend this to consider culture as a significant contingency. Fifth, I switch the focus away from leadership as an individual achievement towards a consideration of the significance of followers. Finally, I extend the change of focus to consider the methodological implications that underpin leadership studies and the way leadership is actively constructed by those who are the followers.

Culpability and control

> We want a few mad people now. Look where the sane ones have landed us!
>
> George Bernard Shaw in the character of Poulengey in
> *Saint Joan*

Conventional Western notions of leadership are usually predicated upon notions of individual responsibility and culpability. Hence aphorisms like: 'The buck stops here', as Truman is alleged to have said, a staking of responsibility that has long since disappeared as American presidents forget what they were responsible for and British ministers forget whether they ordered their civil servants to draft amendments that wreck legislation. The ultimate destination of this acceptance of personal responsibility for decisions taken by, or on behalf of, oneself is Louis XVI's rather more arrogant aggrandizement of the entire state apparatus in his 'L'état, c'est moi!' Of course, those that claim complete ownership and/or control over something tend to be held responsible for all the effects, and we can see the consequences of this in the way Western governments deny responsibility for mass unemployment on the grounds that the global market is beyond their national control. The contrary was the case in the USSR, where state control also meant state responsibility, and a system that corralled both citizen and state into a much tighter cycle of dependency, responsibility and culpability.

However, the point I wish to consider here is whether our notions of leadership appear as they do because of the taken-for-granted assumptions about personal responsibility. For example, people who commit crimes are (sometimes) arraigned before the courts and, where found guilty, are punished with due regard to their level of personal culpability for the crime: children under certain ages (and this depends upon the particular society) are deemed not to be responsible for their actions, as are those who are considered to be mentally unstable. Relatedly, the early English Factory Acts were imposed upon factory owners but only to 'protect' women and children, 'for it is not desirable that the state should interfere with the contracts of persons of ripe age and sound mind' (Peel, quoted in Taylor, 1972: 44). In effect, only men were capable of administering their own contracts of employment.

The precise level of responsibility for individuals is, however, not simply something derived through a perusal of the legal system. Conventionally there is a political division between the right, which believes individuals are the unit of analysis for explaining crimes, and the left, for whom the particular social milieu is the level of analysis that must shoulder the blame. We can trace the left's position in writings like that of C. Wright Mill's *Sociological Imagination* (1970), in which individuals erroneously believed themselves to be responsible for events that were caused by social developments beyond their control, and therefore responsibility. Unemployment and divorce are two that he considers, but illicit drug taking, violence and many other examples would do just as well. The upshot of accounts that locate the causal determinants of criminal action in social conditions tends to be policies that call for the amelioration of iniquitous conditions, with much less emphasis upon individuals, who are regarded (in good Althusserian fashion) as mere 'bearers' of the structures that oppress them. Since crimes are the symptoms of a structural disease, the focus is on eliminating that disease (capitalism, inequality or whatever) rather than blaming the 'victim' (the unemployed, the poor). The apparently arbitrary location of causality in these accounts is nicely captured in Butler's *Erewhon* (1970), which inverts Victorian assumptions, so that crime is beyond anyone's control and subject only to help by trained experts, while illness is an individual responsibility punishable by the courts (see Woolgar, 1994). Of course, there is always a pluralist compromise to be made: conditions provide the potential for individual action but individuals are the final arbiters of their own fate; or the opposite: individuals are the potential agents but the environment is the final arbiter of an individual's fate.

This division between attributions of causality can also be seen in the explanation of leadership appearance. Thus, at its most extreme, 'come the moment come the man' accounts point to the structural conditions which *require* the emergence of a leader to suit the times; Winston Churchill provides probably the best example in British

history, where the leadership of a relatively obscure and deeply unpopu-
lar politician is conceived of as being the appropriate – and inevitable –
result of perilous war-time conditions. At the other extreme, accounts
of the rise of leaders are firmly located within the charismatic powers
of particular individuals, and it is the actions of these individuals
that shape the conditions rather than are shaped by them. The pluralist
line in this arena is composed of either the 'conditions plus the
individual' or some version of contingency theory, in which the particular conditions are regarded as more appropriate for a particular
form of leadership. Either way, there is still a strong tendency to
regard the individual leader as personally responsible for the actions of
subordinates. Thus we talk of Nelson's victory at Trafalgar, Napoleon's
routing of the Russians and Austrians at Austerlitz, or ICI's turn-
around by John Harvey Jones. Contrarily, football managers are held
responsible for the failure of their teams; government ministers are
supposed to resign where their civil servant's blunder is deemed to be
sufficiently damaging to the government; and, in the military world,
'There are no poor soldiers, there are only poor generals', there are
'lions led by donkeys', but there are never (to my knowledge) 'donkeys
led by lions'.

The 'imperative of example', as Keegan (1991) calls it, is apparently
crucial to military leadership since soldiers must be led rather than
pushed into battle. Or in his terms: 'those who impose risk must be seen
to share it'(1991: 43), as the likes of Wellington and Nelson had done,
in sharp contrast to the 'chateau generals' of the First World War who
'fought' far behind the front line. Indeed, for Keegan, it was precisely
this division between leaders and led that stimulated the mutinies which
rippled through all the major armies between 1917 and 1919. In fact,
Keegan argues that the elaborate hierarchies developed by the various
armies served to hide the origin of the commands, so that an order to
go over the top would be given to those who were about to execute the
order by an officer who was himself about to undertake precisely the
same action. By implication, were the command to be delivered from
50 miles back from the front line by a general just off for a spot of
riding before lunch, those poor souls at the front might not be so willing
to sacrifice themselves. If ever there was a parallel between the
development of industry and war it was here: as Taylor and Ford split
thinking from doing on the assembly lines of production in America,
Haig and Ludendorff split thinking from doing on the (dis)assembly
lines of destruction in Flanders.

Of course, the decoupling then required some form of recoupling to
ensure the execution of commands. In American industry this was often
developed through the powers of instant dismissal allotted to super-

visors; on the European battlefields of the time, it was reconstructed through the leadership role of subalterns, supported by non-commissioned officers (NCOs) and the military police. In this way, the troops were not so much 'pushed' over the top by distant orders from chateau generals as 'pulled' over by young subalterns and 'pushed' over by the disciplinary system, which ensured a rather more certain death for those that refused than for those that went (see chapter 9).

There are also cases where naked coercion on the part of a superordinate can persuade subordinates to perform acts above and beyond what they might regard as their normal course of duty. For example, it is a commonplace to assume that the success of armies is primarily rooted in the social solidarity of small fighting units. As Cochrane wrote of his experiences in the Second World War: 'Men are inclined to do what their comrades expect them to do or, more accurately, because nobody wants to fight, they do what they imagine their comrades expect them to do' (quoted in Holmes, 1987: 359). However, there are examples from the Second World War, of the German army on the Russian Front, for instance, where military leadership was secured through a systematic policy of terror (15,000 executions of German soldiers for 'indiscipline') and had little to do with the construction of any form of consent through social solidarity (Bartov, 1991). As Voltaire commented on the execution of Admiral Byng in 1757, after he failed to relieve Minorca, the execution was considered useful 'pour encourager les autres' (see Babington, 1985, for an assessment of similar British executions in the First World War). However, this does not mean that it is possible to control an organization the size of an army through the permanent application of nothing but terror. As discussed below, the contingent nature of power relations is better cemented through consent than through coercion and, despite the popularity of approaches that stress the 'professionalism' or 'apolitical' nature of the German army (especially on the Russian Front), it seems more likely that many of those involved were willing rather than unwilling adherents to the cause of National Socialism. As Sajer, a soldier on the Russian front, recalled his officer saying: '"I would burn and destroy entire villages if by so doing I could prevent even one of us from dying ... life is war, and war is life. Liberty doesn't exist." Upon hearing this ... speech by their company commander, Sajer tells us, "we loved him and felt we had a true leader, as well as a friend on whom we could count"' (quoted in Bartov, 1991: 117). This nihilistic faith in the ultimate 'male' practice of war still had its organizational and 'moral' problems. For members of an organization that systematically murdered and terrorized the population of the occupied lands in the Soviet Union, it might seem strange that German soldiers concerned themselves with the ethical aspects of the tactics employed by their Soviet enemy. However, as one soldier wrote back from the front: 'When I go back I will tell you endless horror stories about Russia. Yesterday, for instance, we saw our first women soldiers ... And these pigs fired on decent German soldiers from ambush positions' (quoted in Bartov, 1991: 154). Nor was this misogynist approach the only form of ostensibly irrational reaction on the part of men in war. According to Dixon, the failure by the Allied forces to develop convoy protection schemes in the Atlantic during the early parts of both world wars – on account of the 'feminine' implications of 'mothering' little ships when the warships could be out hunting the enemy – unnecessarily served to increase shipping losses for the sake of a masculine image (Dixon, 1979: 210).

Even macho military leadership involves rather more than naked coercion for the most part, for although the threat of capital punishment may be available, and although military discipline is consistently more coercive than most civilian systems, civilian leaders seldom have to persuade their followers 'over the top'. In the words of General Patton: 'If you want your men to fight to the death then lead them. Troops are like spaghetti; you can't push them around, you have to pull them' (quoted in Holmes, 1987: 346). A similar sentiment was expressed by troops in the Peninsular War: 'our men had divided the officers into two classes; the "come on" and the "go on"; for as Tom Plunkett in action once observed to an officer, "The words 'go on' don't befit a leader, Sir"' (quoted in Holmes, 1987: 343). Of course, such kinds of proactive leadership from the front do have their consequences: the casualty rate for German infantry officers in the First World War was 75 per cent; the casualty rate for British officers in the line was, on average, twice that of enlisted men. Indeed, on the first day of the Somme 50 per cent of other ranks were killed or wounded and 75 per cent of the line officers suffered the same result (ibid.). However, the point here is whether all forms of leadership actually require people to lead from the front, to encourage by positive example, or to ensure the required action on behalf of her or his followers by dint of their commitment to her or him, rather than to secure the required action by threat or coercion.

The more significant aspect of military organization, the preference for group loyalty above all else, is often deemed to mark the fundamental irrationality at the heart of Nazi organization which Hitler used to meld the party and army into one. As he admitted in 1927, it was belief, not rationality, which drove people into action: 'What motivates people to go to battle and to fight and die for religious ideas? Not cognition, but blind faith' (quoted in Bartov, 1991: 120).

Machiavelli certainly appears to be rather more cynical, or perhaps honest, than this in his assumptions about leadership and the answer to his question: 'whether it is better to be loved than feared, or the reverse'. Conventionally, Machiavelli is regarded as the ultimate cynic, for whom leadership equates with doing whatever is necessary to maintain control. But his argument can also be read as an account of the practical problems of princes seeking to rule according to their own principles of justice. Hence, 'Cesare Borgia was accounted cruel; nevertheless, this cruelty of his reformed the Romagna, brought it unity, and restored order and obedience. On reflection, it will be seen that there was more compassion in Cesare than in the Florentine people, who, to escape being called cruel, allowed Pistoia to be devastated' (Machiavelli, 1975: 95). In effect, then, for Machiavelli, the moral equivocation that others had about the tactics of leaders such as Cesare Borgia were falsely grounded: one cannot maintain the ascendancy of love when one is about to be murdered; better to be cruel so that love can be re-established later than allow murder and anarchy to prevail at all times. A cynical liberal's response to Machiavelli's legitimation of cruelty might be to trot out the 'Well he would say that, wouldn't he' line, or a more sophisticated concern that means cannot be separated from ends. But, for my purposes here, it is important to retain the significance of the point for the question of leadership, and it is especially significant when trying to unravel that most 'popular' yet mysterious form of it: charismatic leadership.

Charismatic leadership

> An army of lions led by a sheep is no match for an army of sheep led by a lion.
>
> Daniel Defoe

Leadership, and particularly military and political leadership, has often been linked directly to charisma, that most elusive of qualities that allegedly marks out particular individuals who possess divine and/or inspirational qualities that the rest of us do not possess and cannot acquire. The idea that charisma is a possession of an individual is rather commonplace. We talk not of charismatic situations but charismatic people. We may find it difficult to define precisely what charisma is, and many of us may never have come across anyone with it, but we probably all know of someone who once met a charismatic leader, or we have heard stories of such leaders: the Christs, Muhammads, Ghandis and Churchills of the world. During the 1970s and 1980s some business leaders did appear in the same charismatic guise: people who turned companies round to achieve global success, such as Harvey Jones at ICI and Iaccoca at Chrysler or people who started with nothing and built up vast business empires, such as Bill Gates at Microsoft or Richard Branson with his Virgin Group. The 1990s appears not to have produced a similar clutch of charismatics – not even amongst the religious cults, where charismatics were in danger of becoming commonplace at one point.

The value and virtue of charisma can be gleaned from the famous quip at the beginning of this section, 'An army of lions led by a sheep is no match for an army of sheep led by a lion', erroneously attributed to Churchill, but actually first articulated by Daniel Defoe. We might want to consider just how far we can push the idea that charisma – or for that matter leadership *per se* – can be a possession of an individual. Let us imagine the mighty Churchill himself, the charismatic war-time leader of Britain who, allegedly, 'mobilized the English language for war' (though if he did so it was primarily through the printed word and not through broadcasting, since his radio broadcasts during the war were few and far between: Ponting, 1994). The first problem we have with Churchill is explaining the apparent absence of charisma before the Second World War – though this is disputable, since the undoubted unpopularity of the man may be taken as one form of charisma. But what happens when we transport Churchill to Defoe's desert island before Friday arrives. Can Churchill sport his charismatic qualities in the absence of an audience? To whom does he offer up his famous 'V for victory' sign? Who listens to his rousing calls for fighting spirit? How would we know? What do charismatics do that mark them off from the rest of us when there is no one to appreciate that special turn of phrase, that elegant sweep of the hand, that rousing voice? My point is that to talk of charisma as a possession becomes a contradiction in terms on the desert island, unless, of course, the possession remains latent, awaiting the arrival of Friday. But, latent or not, charisma has a hard job emerging when there is no one to be impressed. It is, as Willner (1984) argues, not 'what the leader is but what people see the leader as that counts in a charismatic relationship' (quoted in Pauchant, 1991: 509). One could go further by deleting the charismatic element altogether, but the point remains that without followers there is no leader. Further, this is a useful reminder of the problems of considering power as a possession rather than a relationship. How can the marooned Churchill store charisma or power (Foucault, 1980)? Over whom does he have power through his charisma?

There is something else profoundly disturbing about Defoe's/ Churchill's quotation, and the disturbance sits at two distinct levels. On the one hand, Churchill's preference for the army of sheep led, presumably, by a lion like himself implies that the docility and stupidity from which this relationship allegedly derives are essential qualities of followers, and a necessary element of any effective organization that operates like an army. In short, followers must be like sheep for the lion to operate as an effective leader; should the sheep disagree with the lion then chaos will prevail and the capability of the army will be severely reduced. If ever there was a metaphor for the leader as hero and the follower as slave this is it.

On the other hand, to follow the metaphor through, would we really expect a battle between 500 follower-lions plus one leader-sheep versus 500 follower-sheep plus one leader-lion to result in favour of the latter? Would not the army of follower-lions, left leaderless by the vagaries of their leader-sheep, simply operate at an individual level as more than effective destroyers of the enemy follower-sheep? What would the army of follower-sheep do under the charismatic leadership of their leader-lion – lick the enemy lions to death, or bleat a lot to gain their sympathy? Indeed, would not the army of sheep (prior to being mauled by the army of lions) tend, as Bertrand de Jouvenal claimed, 'to beget a government of wolves'? This being the case, perhaps we should consider the extent to which existing models of leadership are premised upon militaristic notions of superordinate control that are themselves built upon preconditional follower subordination. If, as contemporary developments suggest, followers are a more important element of the organization, then perhaps we need to consider ways of challenging armies of sheep to slough off their woollen coats and to adopt the mantles of leaders themselves.

A related issue of the sheep – army connection is that soldiers or followers are never responsible for their actions; only the leaders, charismatic or otherwise, are responsible. Again, the individualist essence of the approach ensures that the bad army is theoretically impossible – there can only be bad generals because only leaders act and take decisions; followers merely follow. The naiveté of this view is only matched by its popularity. By implication, an army of wretched murderers that engages in genocide is not responsible for its actions – only the commander is. We have certainly seen this approach used by soldiers of various kinds in defence of their own actions, but since the Geneva Convention it has not been upheld as a legitimate defence. In the business world the implication remains the same: subordinates cannot be held responsible for their actions since responsibility is the prerogative of management. For this reason, training need not be delivered to the subordinates but should be reserved for management, and when the training fails to deliver the promised results the response is more or different training – but still not for the subordinates. After all, charismatics are, perhaps more than any other forms of leaders, personally responsible for the actions of their followers.

It is hardly coincidental that concern for the responsibilities and powers of charismatic leadership tends to arise during periods of economic, social, political or military crisis. Some of the earliest research into charismatic leadership considered the way that Hitler and Stalin appeared to manipulate the masses through the power of their ideas and personality, linked to economic, social or political crises of the time (Adorno et al., 1950; W. Reich, 1972, 1975). Either such individuals rise to power because of their charisma during such crises, or the crises catapult them from 'ordinary' (that is, non-charismatic) leaders into charismatics. Since there seems little evidence that Hitler, Stalin or Churchill (allegedly three of the most charismatic leaders of the twentieth century) were endowed with charismatic qualities from birth, we might usefully remain sceptical of internalist accounts that seek evidence from within the individual rather than from without them. This need not imply that anyone propelled by fortune into a leadership position under dire circumstances will become charismatic. On the contrary, not many charismatics are instant failures; as I mentioned above, success is a prerequisite for any form of leadership and an essential condition of charismatic leaders. The (potentially) charismatic leader who is suffocated to death by the fumes of a number 40 bus on his or her way to the forum might get some sympathy for going down as an extreme asthmatic but would probably not go down as a great charismatic.

Weber (1978) was certainly aware of the situational features that encouraged the recognition of charismatics, but he tended to argue that charisma was as much historically located as contemporaneously deployed. Jesus, for example, only came to embody charismatic characteristics because he embodied so much of Jewish tradition. Similarly, part of the explanation for the success of Hernán Cortés's attack upon the Aztec Empire was the extent to which Moctezuma believed Cortés to be the embodiment of Quetzalcoatl, the fair-skinned and bearded god destined to return and wreak vengeance upon the Aztecs (Sahagún, 1978). What charismatics do, then, according to Weber, is not to revolutionize society – to change it out of all recognition from the past – but to reclaim the past from the present (1978: 630–4) during 'moments of distress' (1978: 1111).

If theorists of charisma disagree upon the extent to which it is a novel or an historically embedded phenomenon, many of them do agree upon the need for leaders to maintain their charismatic influence. Nothing appears to wane faster than the charisma of a failed leader. This implies, again, that the nature of charisma lies not within the charismatic but in the reproduction of the relationship between leader and follower so that the follower is continually persuaded of the charismatic nature of the leader. In effect, charismatics are continually remade, not born; their charisma does not exude naturally from their bodies but is the result of careful management. Take, for example, Horatio Nelson, portrayed as a 'natural' leader, a born charismatic; he owed his early career development to a paternal Captain Suckling, and he:

> took care to foster his own legend. He understood and practised the art of public relations. After actions at sea he excelled at writing what he called 'a famous account of your own actions'. He arranged for these despatches to be leaked immediately to the press, directing that where he had written 'I' and 'my' the third person should be substituted, to give the impression that some other hand had written them. (Adair, 1992: 36)

Yet Nelson's leadership style was probably closer to what Bass (1981), following J.M. Burns (1978), called 'transformational' leadership. Where charismatics tend to induce high levels of dependency amongst their followers, transformational leaders appear to operate along the reverse principle, empowering not disempowering their followers; securing adherence to a body of ideals not allegiance to an ideal body.

Clearly the difference between the two is more one of degree than kind, and one might be hard pressed to find business leaders for whom their followers have unquestioning loyalty and willing obedience. We can take this a stage further by asking who establishes whether followers follow because they believe their leaders to be divine in some sense or because they believe themselves to have little option. Many soldiers followed their leaders 'over the top' in the First World War without any apparent belief in the divinity of their officer corps; yet from an alien's view it might well have seemed to be closer to the behaviour of lemmings than of humans, and consequently only explicable through some mystical relationship between officers and soldiers (see chapter 9).

The final piece in the charismatic jigsaw is the relative absence of women charismatics. Of course, there have been women leaders to whom the term 'charismatic' has been applied – Joan of Arc, Boudicca, Elizabeth I and Mother Theresa spring to mind – and it may be that women charismatics are proportionately no fewer than women leaders are. However, it does seem more likely that the general confinement of charismatic leadership to the military and political field has disproportionately reduced the numbers of women charismatics. We might also note here the significance of the Christian churches, and most other major religions, in relegating the role of women to a subordinate status, and the effect this may have had on restricting images of leadership to those of men (Ruether, 1992). This position is most clearly developed in Pawson's (1992) diatribe against women, rooted in his argument that patriarchy is inscribed in the relative development of men and women: since Eve was constructed from Adam's rib it stands to reason that women should be subordinate to men. On the other hand, since humans appear to have been derived from primeval sludge, perhaps we should all prostrate ourselves in the mud and seek divine, nay charismatic, guidance on this one.

Contingent leadership

> My centre is giving way, my right is in retreat; situation excellent.
> I shall attack.
>
> General Foch

If charismatic leaders are the archetypes of leadership, and assuming they are not stranded alone on a desert island, then there is a problem in trying to account for their fall from power within social situations. If charisma is a possession, or even a label which followers attribute to behaviour, then it is hard to understand how anyone can lose it (oh dear, I put my charisma down somewhere and I seem to have lost it, as Steve Woolgar would probably say). On the other hand, if it is a relational issue then how does it seem to disappear when the parties remain stable? That it does apparently disappear can be evidenced from the decline of Churchill – from the charismatic war-time leader to the resident of the outer reaches of the back benches during peace. This kind of development was, in part, responsible for a rather different perspective on leadership, summarized as 'the contingency approach', in which the kind of leadership required is that deemed most suitable to the (contingent) situation. In fact, the approach covers a multitude of different kinds of contingency: whether the leader is oriented towards task or affiliation; the level of follower maturity; the level of crisis; and all steps in between. In this section I will restrict the discussion to those contingent approaches that appear to have secured some degree of (contingent?) popularity. I will then go on to consider the nature of responsibility and the methodological implications of contingency mapping.

Let us begin by perusing one of the most traditional forms of contingency explanation: that leadership is contingent upon one's choice of parents rather than anything else. If, as shall be argued later, leadership is an interpretative achievement rather than an individual quality, then arguments about the innate or learned essence of leadership can themselves be subsumed under the same individualist and essentialist doctrines that problematize the previous approaches. However, nowhere has the argument for inherited leadership ability been refined better than with regard to its occurrence within the British army. Until 1871, commissions (and promotions) were generally purchased rather than achieved by any form of examination, and between 1860 and 1867, 80 per cent of the 4,000 commissions were bought (Dallas and Gill, 1985: 13). The purchase system was abandoned in 1871, but the social class background of officers changed little over the next fifty years. Whatever effect this may have had on the quality of the officer corps, and irrespective of the pervasive class hostility at the site of industrial work in Britain, the class division between officers and troops did not seem to undermine the leadership role of the officer corps in the front line. As Fortescue, a leading army historian of the time, noted in 1923: 'No one is quicker than Tommy Atkins [the archetypal trooper] at spotting the "gentleman"; it may sound snobbish, I dare say it is snobbish to say so, but the fact remains that men will follow a "gentleman" much more readily than they will an officer whose social position is not so well assured' (quoted in Dallas and Gill, 1985: 14). Whether this was an accurate assessment at the time or not, the possibility of acquiring respect through position was not something that Australian officers could enjoy. As a young officer in the First World War wrote: 'It is remarkable how our Australians stick to their officers when they have proved their gameness. They hold off until they see a man properly tested and then they love him, but if he fails then he's right out wide in their estimation' (quoted in Holmes, 1987: 353).

In fact this kind of contingent explanation of leadership has remained relatively dormant. Probably the most influential of the contingency approaches has been that of Fiedler (1967, 1978). Crudely reduced, Fiedler's suggestion is that leaders can be divided into those who are task-oriented and those who are affiliation-oriented; which particular leadership style is effective is dependent upon the situation. Primarily, Fiedler's suggestion is that during both crises and 'highs', the task-oriented leader is the more successful of the two, whereas the affiliation-oriented leader performs best during periods of stability. We might construct suitable scenarios for each of these that would see crises being most suitable for the kind of leader who pursued the goal of the group irrespective of her or his level of personal popularity, whereas a leader during a stable period would develop her or his personal relationships with followers rather more vigorously than the goal itself. Margaret Thatcher, never a leader to court popularity for the sake of it, might demonstrate the utility and problems of this approach. At one level it appears to explain why demagogues operate best in crisis and why Churchill failed in peace. But Thatcher was a shrewd 'creator' of crises and, as Orwell's *1984* so clearly suggests, a permanent crisis is something which is both politically useful in cowing opposition and often difficult to disagree with in the absence of much information. In effect, since what counts as a crisis – and therefore what counts as stability – is not something about which we necessarily agree, to assume that the crisis/stability contingency can explain which form of leadership is most appropriate is to misunderstand the created nature of crisis and stability.

Hersey and Blanchard's (1982) 'situational leadership theory' is a slightly more complex version of this kind of approach, in which the particular style of 'appropriate' leadership depends not upon the external situation but upon the nature of the followers: where followers are defined as being of 'low maturity' they are required to have high levels of supervision at the task level but a low level of relationship-oriented supervision. As the maturity of the followers increases, the shift towards lower levels of task-oriented supervision and higher levels of relationship-oriented supervision occurs. The same kind of problem that affects Fiedler's approach affects the assessment of 'maturity', and several recent attempts to verify this model empirically have been less than successful (see Norris and Vecchio, 1992). Moreover, it would be worth starting from first principles as described by many of the neo-human relations authors of the 1960s and 1970s: if you treat employees as children they may very well respond in childish ways. Hence, to take as given a certain level of employee 'maturity' is itself to invite this question: what kind of leadership treats adults as having low levels of maturity, other than a leadership which is itself 'immature'?

A further possibility, explored in depth in chapter 5, is that the criteria for leadership can change to the extent that our interpretation of prior leadership itself alters over time. It is not, then, that leadership is contingent upon the situation – in the sense discussed above – but that as time elapses so our interpretation of the leadership at a particular time alters. Thus, for example, whether Winston Churchill was the 'appropriate' leader for the British during the war is less contingent upon the war-time conditions than upon the predilections concerning leadership espoused by particular groups at a particular time. In other words, Churchill may be regarded as a great leader during the war itself and subsequent to it, but during the 1990s, when racism has become much less socially acceptable, Churchill may appear as a man who was primarily driven, and therefore tainted, by a racism that undermines the claim to 'great' leadership status – even during the war (Ponting, 1994; A. Roberts, 1994). Indeed, if much of the early interwar work on leadership stressed traits, and the irrational desire of the mass to be led by a charismatic leader, we can see the 'style' approach of the early post-war period (which tended to support participative and democratic leadership styles over laissez faire and authoritarian styles) as the democratic response to the military defeat of 'irrational' political leaders (A. C. Brown, 1964; Likert, 1961). The shift from 'leaders' to 'situations' continued through the 1960s to end up with the work of Fiedler (1978) and the whole contingency approach to organizations and leadership, in which the most appropriate form of leadership could only be derived from a careful analysis of the particular situation. As Czarniawska-Joerges and Wolff (1991) note, by 'the 1970s, charismatic leaders were distinctly out of fashion ... the unpretentious "managers" took the place of leaders'. Or in Crozier's phrase, interest had shifted 'from the government of men to the administration of things' (quoted in Czarniawska-Joerges and Wolff, 1991: 532). Perhaps a good example of the utility of this model can be seen in the rise and fall of the 'heroic entrepreneur/leader' in the 1980s. In Britain the 1980s belonged to the Tiny Rowlandses and Alan Sugars of the business world; at least during the middle of the decade, rapid expansion and large profits could easily be accumulated through adroit action on the part of such 'swashbuckling' types. However, the economic gloom of the late 1980s and early 1990s seems to have dealt such a leadership style a rather swift and cruel blow, with more swashbucklers walking the plank than capturing heavily laden treasure ships (see Buckingham, 1992; Cowe, 1992).

A related form of leadership analysis, cognitive resources theory (Fiedler and Garcia, 1987), stresses the relationship between crises and leadership styles, in that experience is more significant than intelligence for periods of crisis and the reverse operates in periods of stability. These contingent approaches to leadership nevertheless seek, and usually fail, to provide dependable predictors of the 'correct' leadership behaviour for certain situations. As Yukl declares, 'With few exceptions, it is still not possible to make confident predictions about the optimal behaviour pattern for a leader in a given situation (1989: 263). One might add that if leadership behaviour could be predicted in a given situation then the whole notion of volitional leadership would become redundant. The predictive model could simply be wheeled on stage and anybody capable of following the rules would be able to lead successfully. Two further implications of this assumption are that once the model was perfected, competitive advantage in any area would be difficult to establish and, perhaps equally interesting, human leaders could be replaced by computerized leaders (who would be less likely to fail to follow rules and more likely to analyse complex, 'rule-rich' scenarios correctly).

The other side of this equation, which reduces leadership to the fulfilment of pre-specified rules, is the possibility that leadership is actually insignificant anyway – except to leaders, of course. We have already posed the possibility that interest in managerial leadership rose at precisely the time the legitimacy of property rights as a leadership criterion began to collapse. Certainly Pfeffer (1977) has argued that the most important criteria for organizational success are beyond the reach of leaders anyway. For instance, political leaders tend not to accept the responsibility for their country's economic woes, which are attributed to the world economic situation, yet maintain that they have a role to play in steering their respective countries towards economic success despite their apparent powerlessness.

Stewart (1982) has also offered a version of the contingency model of leadership. She argues that the kind of managerial leadership necessary is dependent upon the nature of the work being undertaken: its predictability, the speed of execution required and the degree of initiative allowed. The broad implication of such contingent or situational models of leadership is that the form of leadership required under condition X may not be the most suitable for condition Y. This is clearly considerably more flexible than many of the other models we have already considered; so is the solution to the determinist conundrum a contingent determinism? Note here the repetition of determinism, for herein lies the weakness of the contingent account. What appears as a flexible explanation for differential leadership skills is actually just a more sophisticated form of determinism. It is not that several forms of leader appear to succeed in the same situation but that, given a specific situation, a specific form of leadership is *the* most suitable. In effect, the situation determines the leadership, but not vice versa. This might be satisfactory – but only if we could agree upon two things: first, which leadership was most appropriate in each situation; second, what the situation was. Do situations remain impervious to interpretative readings? Do we all *know* what a situation is really like, or do we have to interpret innumerable variables to come up with an educated guess? If we still have to interpret the situation, and the appropriate leadership for it, then we are still unable to claim that the key to leadership has been secured. The problem is simply that the situation is just as much of a social construct as the essence of leadership.

Let us take another military example to explore this issue of rule-based leadership premised on objective assessment of the situation. According to Bartov (1991: 12–3), in 1940, an 'objective' account of the German and Allied forces lined up against each other would not have predicted the collapse of all but the British at the hands of the Germans in the space of a few weeks. The Wehrmacht used 2,445 tanks against the

Allies' 3,383, and even though the *Luftwaffe* deployed greater numbers of aircraft (4,020 versus 3,099), the critical issue seems to have been their concentration of armour, which provided the means to punch an enormous hole in the Allies' defensive shield. But this also opened the German advance to a crushing flanking manoeuvre that would have cut the advanced armoured divisions off from their supplies. The flanking attack never came, but the real point of the example is to question the notion of an objective assessment of the situation. If Hitler had used this method he would not have secured victories quite as easily as he did; if the Allies had ignored 'objective' calculations they might have saved the world a lot of blood. But they did not. Instead, Hitler deployed an approach outside any notion of rationality that the Allies would have recognized; his approach was not to be honest with his troops, to tell them that they were outnumbered and the whole scheme was hare-brained, but to strangle doubts at birth, to construct an image that only recognized success and to render all sceptics impotent through their patent slur on the character of the German forces. In Bailey's pithy phrase: 'if the educated mind is the mind that entertains doubts and asks for evidence, then the art of leadership is (among other things) also the art of diseducation' (1992: 154). The problem with this lies in the assumption that the opposite of diseducation is the equivalent of the truth. Without claiming that leaders are most successful when their simplifications are merely a tissue of lies (since the implication is that we can have an objective truth by which to measure the lies), it does not appear axiomatic that the greater the conscious degree of distortion from their 'real' interpretation, the greater their skill as a leader. The skill lies in the persuasion, not the relationship between persuasion and truth, because what counts as the truth is itself a matter of persuasion.

Collective followership

> There go my people. I must find out where they are going so I can lead them.
>
> Alexandre Ledru-Rollin quoted in Peter (1978)

One of the problems with any attempt to model leadership patterns lies in the bifurcation between leaders and followers. Compared to the enormous outpouring of material on leadership there is a dearth of material on followership (cf. Follett, 1949; Kelley, 1988; Lundin and Lancaster, 1990; C. Lee, 1991; Flower, 1991; G.R. Gilbert and Hyde, 1988; Alcorn, 1992; Buhler, 1993). Any attempt to establish what kinds of leader and leadership style exist, without reference to the related forms of leadership legitimation, implies that leaders operate in a vacuum; they can be analysed by focusing upon them as individuals to establish the kinds of inherent or acquired skill and competency that make them leaders. But this focus upon the leader as an individual misunderstands and misrepresents the nature of leadership: it is not something which individuals *have* but a process that is present only in its deployment. There are close parallels here to the writings of Foucault and Latour on power, though this debate is covered later in this chapter. The implications of this are twofold: first, it is not theoretically viable to consider the form of leadership in isolation from the form of follower-ship; second, we should shift the focus of our concern away from the 'character' or 'personality' of the leader and towards the mechanisms by which actions through which leaders are legitimated are undertaken by followers.

If, as is conventional in most companies and countries, leadership is defined as an individual attribute – skills which individuals possess to a greater or lesser extent – then the focus of concern in an enterprise tends to be more upon managers than upon employees. The implication of this model is that the leadership skill of a manager is something which is contained within the body of that manager: a good manager/leader (and I recognize that these two things are not necessarily regarded as identical) is good irrespective of the situation within which he or she operates. Conversely, as the aphorism goes: 'There are no poor soldiers, there are only poor generals.' The problem with this is the implication that leadership is a property which can be deployed by its owner under each and every circumstance, rather than assuming that leadership is the result of a specific social interaction – in other words, that some individuals have a capacity for leadership that is objectively verifiable and exists irrespective of its expression in specific circum-stances. In effect, then, whether any individual demonstrates some pattern of action, which others construe as 'leadership', is something which can be measured by isolating the individual. Yet Rommel would have had difficulty persuading a bunch of British schoolchildren that he was their appropriate leader for the summer camp or that they should follow him 'over the top'. If nothing else, the example suggests that leadership is premised upon a basic linguistic similarity: unless followers can be persuaded by words (and by words they can understand), the limits of leadership are probably quite narrow. Nor would Rommel have been able to exhibit leadership qualities without the requisite troops and weapons. Whether somebody in a superordinate position manages 'to lead', then, is critically dependent on persuading his or her subordinates of the validity of the leadership. It follows that, unless managers do not actually need subordinates in order to execute work functions, the success of managers can be enhanced or undermined by their ability to persuade their subordinates to act in specific ways. In short, a manager is more likely to be effective only to the extent that he or she secures the active compliance or consent of the followers.

A clear line can be drawn between this search for active consent and the development of close personal relationships in small teams, though it is perhaps unusual to see this line redrawn within organizations that pride themselves on their machismo. For example, according to Townsend and Gebhardt (1989: 12), 'a person who would call himself or herself a leader of [US] Marines must be capable of loving and being loved ... A platoon commander ... must truly love his men if he wishes to be known as a good leader.' This form of relationship between leaders and led, which the US army distinguishes from the specific leadership pattern, is one which allegedly distinguishes between military leaders and civilian managers. Thus, despite the authoritarian leadership style that armies around the world are renowned for, the US Marine Corps regards its own leaders as carers, whilst civilian leaders tend to be mere managers – people who get things done but do not care about the people doing it. This concern for the subordinate, rather than just the subordinate's actions, is also reproduced in descriptions of military leaders sharing the rigours of the campaign trail with their troops (Nibley, 1987), most famously reconstructed, perhaps, in Shakespeare's *Henry V* where Henry spends the eve of the Battle of Agincourt wandering through his troops' quarters:

> The royal captain of this ruin'd band
> Walking from watch to watch, from tent to tent,
> Let him cry, 'Praise and glory on his head!'
> For forth he goes and visits all his host,
> Bids them good-morrow with a modest smile,
> And calls them brothers, friends and countrymen.
> (*Henry V*, Act IV, Chorus, ls. 29–34)

This focus upon followers – in and through which leadership is developed – goes back much further in history than Henry V, and was the direct concern of several Ancient Greek philosophers concerned with supporting or denying the assumption that the only kind of good government is self-government. This assumption does not necessarily imply any form of direct democracy, or even participatory democracy, but it does imply that the best way of legitimizing management is by a process through which subordinates have some say in the actions of their superordinates. Much of this actualizing model is derived originally from the ideas of Pericles (Thucydides, 1972:145–7), Aristotle (1981),

Rousseau (1968), Marx (1968), and John Stuart Mill (1982), and more recently redeveloped by Macpherson (1966, 1977), Pateman (1970) and Held (1987, 1989), but the details need not detain us here. Suffice to say that William Lovett, himself a Chartist leader, regarded leadership *per se* as a problem, not a solution to the issue of participation in political life, for: 'so long as the people of any country place their hopes of political salvation in *leadership of any description*, so long will they be disappointed' (Andrews (ed.) *Routledge Dictionary of Quotations*).

While the anarchistic implications of Lovett's claim are not ones that many business leaders would support, there is a considerable body of research which has long suggested that different styles of leadership are associated with different forms of follower behaviour. For R. White and Lippitt (1960), of the three forms of leadership they considered (autocratic, democratic and laissez faire), the democratic variant was the most successful in terms of encouraging group cohesion, superior task results and a high level of individual initiative – all aspects of the cultural changes most actively supported today. That is not to say that an axiomatic link between overall group satisfaction and productivity exists; indeed, there is precious little empirical evidence for any kind of causal connection between satisfaction and productivity (see Grint, 1991; Buchanan and Huczynski, 1985). However, the concern here is not so much with the productivity of the group as with improving the effectiveness of leaders. Of course, it can also be argued that leader effectiveness is itself a prerequisite for group productivity and that interpersonal skills are a crucial aspect of the leader's range of tools for securing the active and constructive compliance of her or his subordinates.

Notwithstanding the theoretical justifications for participative leadership, the empirical reality has been consistently less propitious. Much of the failure of participation in work-based organizations has been laid at the door of worker's lack of interest and, ultimately, of the form of participation on offer. The majority of writers on participation at work have asserted either that employees have only a marginal interest in participation or that their interests are limited to the level of task execution (Hirszowicz, 1981: 229–50; F. Heller, 1979; Wall and Licheron, 1977; Ramsay, 1983; Brannen, 1983: 73–8). Since the execution of tasks is often much constrained by the role of leaders we should expect to see high, rather than low, levels of interest by employees in the assessment of their leaders. Indeed, we can even accommodate the empirical evidence that suggests a very limited interest in participating at work by noting two assumptions: first, if some element of participation is introduced to work it has to be recognized as significant by the individuals and groups involved if they are to sustain or increase their level of involvement (Crittenden, 1987); second, that participation is a skill that can be acquired through experience.

So are leaders those people who devolve responsibility down the organization as far as they dare and let the organization go where it will? Or are they those who merely represent mouthpieces for, rather than representatives of, the followers? This particular debate is reproduced in Plato's *The Republic*, which railed against allowing the mass, 'a large and powerful animal', to control 'a ship' when it was clear (at least to Plato) that only particular forms of expertise would facilitate correct navigation. In effect, allowing the mob to choose its leader would merely ensure that the only criterion for leadership would be a demonstration of sycophancy. Nor would a tyrant provide the solution to the leadership problem since tyrants are apt to lead the mass astray. Only philosophers could fulfil the leadership role because only they had the wisdom to guide the ship through life's many storms (Held, 1987: 28–31). Rousseau's (1968) position was radically different, in that democracy was the only solution but not in its representative variety, since this only made voters free for the moment that they voted, a position Lenin supported in theory (1971), though not in practice (Sirianni, 1982).

If we argue, then, that leaders are those who in some way embody, articulate, channel and construct the values and direction that the followers think they ought to be going in, then we dispense with the leader as isolated hero and return to the leader as the embodiment of the collective. We might, therefore, also dispense with Havelock Wilson's epithet that 'to be a leader of men one must turn one's back on men'. In fact, we might even return to the shop floor to see this kind of leadership in action. Batstone et al. (1978), for example, argued that shop stewards could be divided between 'populists', that is delegates for the mass, and 'leaders', that is opinion leaders, channellers of discontent, who, through a network of relationships, managed to provide what C. Wright Mills called 'vocabularies of motive' for action. In this scenario, leadership is not that activity which develops in isolation from the group, nor is it that which merely represents the (usually inchoate) wishes of the group, but rather it is that which takes the complexities, manages them into a coherent whole and provides a persuasive rhetoric to align the mass with the leader. Abraham Lincoln, perhaps above all, was a master of this – turning the 50,000 casualties of Gettysburg into a eulogy, not about the old American nation but actually a new one: one based on equality and democracy that had not really existed in the minds of American citizens prior to this (Wills, 1992). In effect, an action may occur but whether that action is one given the label 'leadership' or 'suicide' or 'cowardice' derives not from any allegedly inherent qualities of the action but in the interpretation of the act by those involved. Here, for example, is a First World War officer at the point of 'leading' his men over the top for the first time and wondering whether they would follow him:

> Dully I hauled myself out of the mud and gave the signal to advance, which was answered by every man rising and stepping unhesitatingly into the barrage. The effect was so striking that I felt no more that awful dread of the shellfire, but *followed* them calmly into the crashing, spitting hell. (Quoted in Holmes, 1987:353, my emphasis)

In this case, an action occurs which, for the officer involved, is not a manifestation of leadership but an act of consummate contingency: if the soldiers interpret his action as an act of leadership then they will follow him; but if they do not then the act is not one of leadership but folly. The point is that the act in itself requires interpretation before the soldiers can make sense of it – and only after they have interpreted it does it appear that the act *always was* one of leadership.

Clearly, followers act for a whole variety of reasons and will be situated along a continuum of points between what they regard as coercion and normative agreement. These would conventionally range from coercion (economic or physical etc.), through tradition, apathy, pragmatic acquiescence and instrumental acceptance, to normative agreement (see Held, 1987: 182). But it is important to note the limitations on the 'coerced' follower established through Sartre's existentialist doubt about irresponsible behaviour. Since humans can, with very few exceptions, always choose between alternative courses of action, the very notion of coercion as a legitimate excuse for action is necessarily problematized. It may well be that to refuse to act in a particular way will lead to a variety of consequences, perhaps even death, but this does not mean that we have no choice in the matter; certain choices have certain consequences but they are still choices. There are, naturally, situations where decisions taken freely by individuals lead them into increasingly constrained choices, but there are still choices to be made. For example, Sutton (1994) has described how an effective system of slavery exists in some Brazilian mining and forestry areas, where workers are persuaded to join up for promises of easy riches but are rapidly reduced to a state of debt bondage through a systematic policy of overcharging for the costs of transport, tools and food. With threats of injury or even death hanging over those who try to flee the remote camps, the debt slaves are effectively imprisoned. Yet, even here, at the most extreme end of 'free' wage labour, there are choices to be made about fleeing or not fleeing, about organizing resistance and not organizing resistance. This is not to belittle the difficulties facing such workers but it is to state that choices are still available. This is important because it highlights the problem of assuming that power lies in the hands of leaders, and that followers act because of this power. Since followers are (almost) never coerced in any absolute sense (being thrown over a cliff, however, does not give you much choice about whether you will land or not, but dead followers do not make very good supporters of leaders), it follows that being a leader is critically dependent upon the actions of one's followers and cannot be assessed through any kind of evaluation of one's own leadership skills. There are no leaders without followers; but what makes a leader?

Constructing leadership

In the film *Being There*, Peter Sellers plays a simple-minded gardener who, through fortuitous circumstances, finds himself in the home of a wealthy and well-connected business man. Through a series of scenes, Sellers's attempts to explain himself lead his various hosts to assume that 'Chancy Gardener', as he becomes known, is actually an extraordinary man, a philosopher of manifest brilliance. Hence, when Chancy meets the president of the United States and the president asks Chancy's opinion on a current political conundrum, Chancy replies: 'As long as the roots are not severed all will be well in the garden . . . there will be growth in the spring.' Chancy's inability to understand anything that the president is saying does not deter the president from interpreting Chancy's homespun gardening wisdom as a brilliant insight into the seasonal nature of political and economic life. In subsequent scenes Chancy, now a national celebrity, reacts with typical honesty to his questioners who, in turn, read his replies as implying something which Chancy appears incapable of understanding. For example, a financial editor calls Chancy and asks for his opinion on current financial problems, but Chancy gets distracted watching children's TV and puts the phone down. This response leads the editor to assert that Chancy really 'plays his cards close to his chest'. When a TV reporter asks Chancy what he thinks of the newspaper reviews he responds: 'I don't read the newspapers, I watch TV.' Here, Chancy's illiteracy is interpreted as bravery, he is, according to the reporter, one of the 'few men in public life [who] have the courage not to read the newspapers . . . [and] the guts to admit it'. Chancy is not dishonest, indeed he appears to be the embodiment of childlike truth and simplicity, but whatever he does is interpreted as if he were a great leader. When asked if he will write a book describing his philosophy he replies: 'I can't read', to which the book publisher responds, 'No one has the time these days ... but we will provide you with a six figure advance, proof readers, ghost writers.' To which Chancy says, 'I can't write.' Again the editor interprets this as a problem of time not skill: 'Of course you can't [write], no one has the time these days'. And so the story unfolds with Chancy's every movement and word appearing to capture a radical new way of life. The point about this should be clear and is exactly the one Hobbes made at the beginning of this chapter: 'The *Value*, or WORTH of a man, is as of all things, his Price; that is to say, so much as would be given for the use of his Power: and therefore is not absolute; but a thing dependent on the need and judgement of another ... And as in other things, so in men, not the seller, but the buyer determines the Price. For let a man (as most men do) rate themselves at the Highest Value they can; yet their true Value is no more than it is esteemed by others' (Hobbes, 1968: pp. 151–2). In short, leadership is not just intimately involved with, but actively constructed by, followers; it is something which inheres not in the language and practice of leaders but in what others construe.

One does not need to escape to the world of fiction to see this active construction going on. Take, for instance, the comparison of images constructed about the British Labour Party leader, John Smith, who died in May 1994, by Prime Minister John Major. According to Major's tribute in the House of Commons on the day of Smith's death, Smith was: 'a formidable senior member of very rare ability ... He was always master of his brief ... I learned to acknowledge the skill and the wit with which he mastered his arguments ... When I think of John Smith, I think of an opponent, not an enemy: and when I remember him, I shall do so with respect and affection.' Yet in the *Conservative Party Campaign Guide* for 1994, Smith is a leader who 'has failed to live up to his promise ... ineffectual and visionless leadership ... [he] managed to make Mr Kinnock look like a first-rate leader ... [he] has been quick to condemn what he claims are declining standards in public life – setting a new low in double standards' (*Observer*, 15 May 1994). Now one might want to argue here that the latter diatribe is merely for political effect, an inevitable piece of hyperbole that everyone knows is just for the voters; but what about the heartfelt and ringing endorsement? Is this also not an inevitable piece of hyperbole? If so, then one wonders how one might get to the truth about John Smith – or whether there is such a thing.

The constructivist approach to political leadership also highlights a further problem for leadership roles undertaken by women in political and non-political positions, since it is equally clear that apparently identical modes of behaviour are interpreted in radically different ways in women and men. For example, a review of women leaders in American universities noted that: 'Women may face a no-win situation because a democratic style of leadership exercised by them may be seen as "soft" or "indecisive" but then assertive leadership is a definite no-no for women' (Sekaran and Kassner, 1992: 173). In fact, the issue is perhaps not that women are criticized for using assertive leadership – or even not using it – but that, according to some claims (Summers, 1993), men perceive leadership styles differently from women, and vice versa (Rosener, 1990). If, then, business organizations develop models of 'the good leader' which reflect competencies and/or behaviour which they also regard as wholly male in origin and execution, we should hardly be surprised if few women make it onto the boards of such companies. We should, however, be wary of assuming that leadership is a novel issue and problem facing women, for there is considerable evidence that women occupied many positions of leadership in public life even at the height of the Victorian orthodoxy (Shiman, 1992). In chapter 8 I consider the management of gender inequality through technology in rather more detail.

The implication of this is that what counts as leadership cannot be derived from an 'objective' analysis of any particular action but must be contextually read. Such a reading does not imply that, given an 'objective' assessment of a culture, one can 'objectively' assess the form and quality of leadership. Rather, it suggests that what counts as leadership lies in the accounts of those who are assessing the actions of the individual. Nor does this lead on to an assumption that what is a good leader in one account is necessarily contradicted by others to the extent that no consensus prevails over the assessment of leadership. Rather, it implies that some accounts are more powerful than others and that a consensus about leadership is actively constructed. In turn, the construction requires reconstruction and embodies the opposite – deconstruction. Leaders, then, are constructed through the accounts that are provided of their actions, but, in order to resist other accounts which may seek to delegitimize their position, pro-leader accounts must be constantly reproduced. Another implication of this theoretical review is to cast doubt on the essentialist model of leadership in which leaders, whether born or taught, embody leadership qualities that can prevail in (almost) all situations. On the contrary, the argument implies that leadership is a social construction that needs constant action for its effective reproduction. In effect, it casts considerable doubt upon all trait approaches to leadership in so far as they assert that leadership lies within an individual rather than being the product of action by a network. Such essentialist models are, nevertheless, very popular.

Indeed, one could argue that essentialist models of leadership are positively fetishistic in their concern to lay blame and praise for all kinds of event at the feet of individual leaders.

Perhaps the fetish for leadership reflects the desire to legitimate a form of authority which has been eroded in certain other areas of life, at least at some time. In particular, we might consider the inordinate concentration on leadership in politics, the military, and business corporations under dire threat. A great proportion of the heroes and heroines of the leadership texts do appear to be drawn from arenas that are definitively not those associated with peace and tranquillity. We do not seem to be awash with leadership role models from what may be regarded as the less competitive fields of primary education or the domestic sphere. There are, as ever, counter-examples: Mahatma Gandhi, of course, was famed as a leader precisely because of his disavowal of violence in his quest for Indian independence. But his leadership was not over a nation at peace with itself or its ostensible rulers. Might it not be, then, that the frenzied search for leadership qualities that are allegedly unique to a small proportion of the population is something akin to a large-scale rationalization of undemocratic (or at best quasi-democratic) authority? In other words, leadership qualities might be construed as those that are attributed to individuals *after* a particular event in order to account for that event. For example, organizations which are structured along hierarchical lines are more likely to explain success or failure through the leadership qualities of incumbents of power roles. In civilian life this may take the form of attributing leadership qualities to individuals who are seen to embody the particular qualities valued by the group, rather than those required by some form of abstract leadership. For instance, Whyte's (1955) street-corner society invested those members most closely resembling the 'ideal' of the gang with leadership qualities. In its military guise, the effect of this attribution is to ensure that only 'militaristic' individuals are regarded as leaders. In effect, military success or failure are more likely to end up being attributed to generals than the success or failure of gardening club fetes are to the club president. The result is that military defeats can then be explained by the absence of leadership on the part of those responsible, and victories by the presence of such qualities. Are there many (any) battles where victory has been attributed to the actions of troops in spite of their commanders? Wellington himself appears to have been dubious about trying to attribute causality in battle, and is said to have told a correspondent seeking verification of 'what actually happened' to 'leave the battle of Waterloo as it is ... some individuals may recollect all the little events of which the great result is the battle lost or won; but no individual can recollect the order in which, or the exact moment at which, they occurred, which makes all the difference as to their value or importance' (quoted in Keegan, 1976: 117). The upshot of this form of assumption is that causal agency is located within the body of the individual leader; it is leaders, not ourselves, who control our destinies, and hence leaders are personally responsible. (The issue of personal freedom and responsibility is covered in detail in chapter 9). But what do leaders actually do?

This question, in itself, requires an analysis of power in organizations. Conventional perspectives on organizational power imply that where it is in the hands of an individual or a small elite, then power emanates from the centre to the periphery, with the causal influence similarly centrifugal (see Handy, 1985). In short, a leader's power causes others to act. Where organizations are controlled by people who do not see employee empowerment as a significant part of their responsibilities, we can expect the conventional pattern of agenda setting and decision making to ensure little progress (McGrew and Wilson, 1982). As Yukl notes: 'Much of the research coming under the power-influence approach attempts to explain leadership effectiveness in terms of the *amount of power possessed by a leader* . . .' (1989: 254, my emphasis).

Yet when such a leader does 'exert power' it is subordinate others, not him or herself, that actually engage in action. If the subordinates do not act then the leader has no power; only as a *consequence* of subordinate actions can leaders be deemed to have power. The political demise of Mrs Thatcher is a good example of the fallacy that locates power within individual leaders rather than within the social relations that support and underpin them: when the subordinates refuse to comply, the superordinates' power literally disappears over night.

Yukl (1989) almost accedes to the interpretivist line in his acceptance that 'potential influence is largely a matter of perception. Power depends on the target person's perceptions of the agent's attributed resources and credibility' (1989: 255). However, this subjectivist line is rejected when Yukl moves to distinguish between 'real' and 'potential' power – as if the two are clearly separable. When an individual thrusts an implement that appears to be a real gun in your face and demands money, does it matter whether the gun 'may' be real or an imitation? Or is there really little difference between the power with which we endow such a technology whether it's 'real' or not? The result of this concern to strip out the subjective from the objective leads not to a more 'scientific' approach to leadership but to a form of epistemological immobilization: the fear of the subjective immobilizes research or sends it in spurious directions rather than acts as a reflexive disciplining device.

Power, therefore, is contingent upon the production and reproduction of a network of associations that facilitates 'acting at a distance' (Latour, 1987). Thus, power is a consequence of action, rather than a cause of action. Perhaps the difference is best appreciated by comparing the cause of a 'domino collapse', where the action requires just one human action to initiate it with the cause of a 'human wave', where every member of the wave is involved in reproducing the effect.

This shift from the 'principle' of power to the 'practice' of power, as Latour (1986) calls it, also implies that subordinate action only occurs through the interpretation of self-advantage by the subordinate: subordinates obey because they consider it to be in their own interest to do so. In turn, it is likely that the command of the leader will become distorted through what Latour calls the 'translation' process: not only are leaders dependent upon their subordinates but a subordinate's translation of the edict may well prove to be a distortion of the leader's intention. The implication of this is that rather than the rays of power spreading out from the centre to the periphery in a determinate and unmediated fashion they are both highly contingent and the subject of constant interpretation and renegotiation. Such a revision in this context implies that the existence of corporate policies that stress the team-like nature of the organization, or even overtly 'democratic' leaders, does not ensure the enaction of such policies or commands at the level of the workplace. Thus the chain of command from CEO to department or line manager does not, in and of itself, secure the execution of the policy. Indeed, the critical deduction to be made from this is that to concentrate upon the personal characteristics or charisma or power of an individual is to miss the point: actions are generally achieved through an alliance of actors (human and non-human) rather than through such individuals.

The attempt to distinguish and measure different forms of leadership power has often led to what may appear as a liberal analysis of power tactics: the greater the level of coercion the greater the level of resistance. Yet a glance at the action of systems of power such as the Nazis', suggests that there are many situations where extreme coercion can eliminate resistance (see M. Gilbert's (1986) harrowing account of Jewish resistance and fatalism). This does not mean that coercion always works nor is it to support authoritarian management but the point is that coercion does not axiomatically or mechanically generate resistance. The related but opposite form of management control – participative management – is similarly problematic: there is little evidence that participative management necessarily leads to optimum efficiency, however defined. On the contrary, as Yukl notes: 'after 35 years of research on participative leadership, we are left with the conclusion that it sometimes results in performance, and other times does not' (1989: 259).

Relatedly, the development of human resource management guidelines and policies which strive to promote the new approach is also inadequate, in and through itself, to ensure the elimination of traditional management practices. In theory, once we know the rule the action is determined by it. However, rules are inherently ambiguous: there can never be enough rules to cover every contingency, nor are rules self-explanatory – we need rules to explain which rule to apply and to interpret the meaning of each one *ad infinitum*. It is for just this reason that 'working to rule' – which should mean working as effectively as possible – leads to the development of grossly inefficient working practices. Rules, then, may be conceived of not as determinants of action but as *post hoc* rationalizations, as resources to justify action already taken, or as measures by which organizations can defend themselves against their employees. Again, the implications of this interpretative approach are profoundly disturbing to any assumption that a sufficient level of rules provides for rule-bound behaviour (Zimmerman, 1973; Salaman, 1980a). The principle of participation relates directly to this distinction between words and deeds: to rely upon the policies is to fall into the trap of assuming action follows directly from rules; it does not. Because it does not, CEOs need to ensure that ostensive actions become performative actions: that policies become practices. But even putting a policy into practice does not resolve all the problems. The *post hoc* interpretation of individuals as 'great leaders' also incorporates the opposite: 'great leaders' who fail suddenly seem to lose their leadership qualities. Keegan's trio of failed army commanders is an appropriate example here:

> when the germ of defeat takes a hold, even very large armies can fall apart with epidemic rapidity. Such was the fate of the Italian army at Caporetto in November 1917, of the bulk of the French army of the north-east in May 1940, of the German Army Group Centre in 1944. The resulting humiliation of their commanders was pitiable. Cadorna, Georges, Busch had all been paladins; the first a general whose unapproachability struck fear into his subordinates, the second an Olympian of the generation of Foch, the third a victor of the French and Russian Blitzkriegs. Overnight they dwindled into despised nonentities. Cardona was hurried into obscurity, Georges left weeping at his map table, Busch consigned to the pool of rejects unemployable even in the backwaters of Hitler's regime. (Keegan, 1991: 44)

Do people who exhibit great leadership one moment (when they are successful) suddenly lose these qualities when they fail? Does the failure lead to the loss or the loss to the failure? What happens when a renowned leader faces impossible odds and loses – does she or he remain a great leader who lost or does her or his failure demonstrate a lack of leadership? The point really is that if we cling stubbornly to the notion of leadership as some form of essentialist phenomenon, some-thing which individuals 'have', then the loss of leadership is difficult to explain and the predictive qualities of the theory are negligible. To assert that individuals have leadership qualities that exist and persist irrespective of the social situation leaves us to ponder how great leaders can weep at their own 'failure'. The alternative – to assume that leadership is a construction developed in and through the rhetoric and practice of those whom we take to be leaders, in relation to the rhetoric and practices of those whom we take to be followers – allows us to grasp the leadership nettle: Georges with an army of followers is a leader, without an army he is not. Attempts to replicate the point that leaders are highly dependent upon followers tend to suggest that followerless 'leaders' do indeed exhibit the kind of confused behaviour one might expect (Mmobuosi, 1991). They may be leaders in rhetoric but not in practice.

So is the division between rhetoric and practice a critical element in the construction of leadership? Knights and Willmott (1992) certainly make an important claim in the problem of leadership in their assertion that the critical issue is not so much the attribution of leadership qualities to individuals as the *practices*, 'the (social) process through which dominant, commonsense identifications of leadership behaviour are sustained (or transformed)' (1992: 765). They go on to argue 'that if the practices of leadership, as opposed to the accounts of these practices, are to be a central focus of research, then the study of how leadership is reflexively attributed to action or data must be complemented with analyses that seek to illuminate how processes usually identified as leadership are practically accomplished' (1992: 777). I take this to mean that concentrating on attribution and accounts of leadership is only one part of the issue and that practices are the other, hitherto missing, part. How do they suggest we do this? By providing 'actual leadership practices' to 'generate fresh insights into their dynamics' (1992: 761). Now the problem here lies in the distinction drawn between accounts and practices. On the one hand Knights and Willmott note the import-ance of the latter but on the other hand they can only provide an example of the latter by creating an account of it. This assumption that 'practices' can be transparently reproduced but 'accounts' are somehow distorted is precisely the problem with the division between 'rhetoric' and 'reality' that transfixes so much writing in the area. How can an account of 'reality' be provided except through rhetorical practices? If it cannot, then the practices pursued by Knights and Willmott are no different in principle from the accounts (of practices) provided by others.

Rather more valuable is the work of Lilley and Platt (1994), whose account of the civil rights movement and the leadership of Martin Luther King suggests that he represented a markedly heterogeneous figure to the followers of the movement. For instance, using 621 letters sent by correspondents to King, Lilley and Platt claim that writers regarded him as one of (at least) four different characters – as a black leader, as a Christian leader, as a non-violent leader or as a democratic leader. Nor does this division map 'naturally' onto the backgrounds of the writers – for example, not all black writers regarded him as first and foremost a black leader. As they argue:

> he bore several meanings simultaneously for both black and white partici-
> pants in the movement ... Correspondents saw in King and his efforts
> multiple conceptions of his leadership and performances ... King seems
> aware of his multiple public meanings for he once confided, 'I am conscious
> of two Martin Luther Kings ... The Martin Luther King that the people
> talk about seems to be somebody foreign to me.' (1994: 75)

One critical implication of this is that a social movement need not be rooted in a consensus to achieve an effective solidarity – there was no consensus about what King represented, but there did appear to be an effective solidarity within the civil rights movement. In Kertzer's (1988) words, rituals can construct 'solidarity without consensus ... since what often underlies people's political allegiances is their social identification with a group rather than their sharing of beliefs with other members' (quoted in Lilley and Platt, 1994: 77).

One need not assume that leaders are merely the prisoners of the webs spun by their followers here. On the contrary, it may well be that intentional ambiguity on the part of leaders is precisely what facilitates the incorporation of a large body of followers, who are freely able to interpret the meaning of leadership courtesy of its ambiguity. One might usefully borrow here from Barthes's (1990) distinction between 'writerly' and 'readerly' texts, discussed in chapter 3. The point here is twofold. First, one might argue that the more ambiguous the text (speech, action, practice and so on) the more likely leaders are to facilitate the multiple interpretation (reading) that encourages heterogenous followers to combine. Second, this still denotes an 'author-itarian' model in which it is the writer/leader rather than the reader/follower who denotes what counts as an ambiguous text/speech/practice. In effect, the ambiguous readings by followers may well serve to corral or coerce a heterogenous body of followers, but what counts as an ambiguous text/speech/practice does not essentially lie in the hands of the writer/leader.

A related problem, and one very much concerned with the constructivist approach, is that of what counts as coercive anyway. How do we know that when soldiers go over the top behind their officers they are doing so wholly out of loyalty to the individual leader? Might it not be that soldiers go over the top for a whole variety of reasons, including faith in their leader, fear of 'cowardice', fear of the results of 'cowardice', a desire to protect their colleagues, a desire to fulfil their 'duty' to a country or an ideal, drug-induced insanity or whatever? Once we start to ask the question 'What counts as coercion?' we begin an immediate descent into the quagmire of uncertainty and contending interpretations. In effect, to construct a leadership criterion around an ostensibly objective phenomenon like coercion is plainly problematic. This does not mean that we must replace the apparently objective consent–coercion polarity with a subjective free-for-all. The point is that ordinary soldiers, in this example, do not have the same resources for imposing their own definition or explanation of their actions upon others; what appears as consent to an officer may appear to the soldier to be coercion. If, then, we continue to maintain that leadership must be distinguished by reference to the consenting behaviour of the led, we are likely to develop severe indigestion when establishing the 'truth' of the example at hand.

Conclusion

If leadership is not a trait which people 'have', that is something which forms an inherent part of their character, but rather something which is created through the social process which we call leadership and then attribute to individuals either during, or more likely after, the event, does not mean that leadership is irrelevant. If not, does it mean that leadership is something which we can easily teach through leadership courses? The first point is that to regard something as socially constructed as the result of a complex social process which interprets an action as leadership, rather than the action being axiomatically one of leadership without any interpretative process, does not mean that leadership is irrelevant. To distinguish between a leader and a non-leader on the basis of the interpretative process is to argue that the nature of that relationship is not determined by the 'objective' actions involved. For example, a leader's call for self-sacrifice is probably more likely to succeed where the followers interpret the situation as being one where self-sacrifice is crucial for organizational success. Whether such sacrifice is either necessary or sufficient to achieve the aim may never be known in any objective sense; so self-sacrifice depends upon interpretation and persuasion, not upon 'the facts'. But it is because the 'appropriate' interpretation and action of subordinates is partly dependent upon the persuasive powers of their superordinate that leadership *is* important. Those leaders who 'fail', then, fail not because they have somehow lost the magical qualities that they originally embodied; this embodiment has already been criticized as extremely dubious. Rather, they fail because the interpretation of those followers who are required to act is no longer commensurate with that of their leader. This incommensurability may occur for a whole variety of reasons that are probably beyond objective measurement, but it is ultimately rooted in the interpretative processes involved. Once the Romanian population interpreted their situation differently, and began to act on these alternative interpretations, the rule of Ceauşescu turned from the autocracy of a dictator to that of the emperor with no clothes in just 48 hours.

One might want to deduce from this that leaders are false gods whose talent lies in manipulating others rather than in demonstrating their own abilities. But, since leadership rarely involves personal actions that are complete in themselves, and more often invokes action by others, the falsity only lies in the misplaced belief that subordinate actions are the consequence of superordinate power, whereas, as we saw above, superordinate power is actually the consequence of subordinate action. The question of whether leadership is actually necessary, then, is not something that can be answered through a universal response. Where cultures develop that impute mystical talents to a restricted number of individuals (through such devices as 'normal distributions of talent') then it would be surprising if leaders were not regarded as essential, and unsurprising if leaderless organizations atrophied rapidly. If, on the other hand, cultures developed where leadership was regarded more as an administrative duty than as a special 'calling' then the opposite would be appropriate: organizations would persist and succeed despite the rapid turnover of leaders, whose qualities would be interpreted as variable but generally irrelevant. For example, the Ancient Athenian state's sovereign body, the Assembly, authorized a council of 500 to run the administrative business, which in turn was organized through a committee of 50. All these officials held office for just a year while the president of the committee 'led' for just a day (Held, 1987: 21).

Whether leadership can be taught (or at least one's minimal talent can be honed), therefore, depends upon how leadership is construed.

For those who believe that leadership is an inherent talent the best that can be achieved is to make some marginal improvements through best practice; but there will still be some people who are naturally better than others at leading. And, more importantly, this innate talent occurs in all situations and at all times – otherwise it cannot be innate. Such internalist accounts have particular problems in explaining the fall of leaders in the absence of extreme extenuating circumstances (like falling asleep at dinner and drowning in your custard).

On the other hand, if leadership is regarded as an interpretative process, that is dependent upon 'appropriate' subordinate action, itself rooted in 'appropriate' interpretation, then the skills of persuasive rhetoric are essential. Assuming that persuasive rhetoric is something that can be acquired, or at least improved, then leadership can be 'taught'. But what is taught focuses less on the completion of leadership tasks than on the social construction of 'leadership'. To take the example of Nelson: it's not enough to be brave and successful in battle; there are probably thousands of such individuals who have been obliterated from history and are consequently not endowed with leadership qualities. No, to be a good leader one has to make sure that everyone who is significant in the development of one's own image is thoroughly conversant with the 'appropriate' version of events. Even those who don't have a propaganda machine of the style that most military, political and business 'leaders' have still need to have the good fortune to engage with someone who has. Spartacus has a reputation as a great leader not because he led a slave revolt but because he led a slave revolt against the Romans, whose information and propaganda machine was, at the time, second to none.

Moreover, a Foucauldian perspective would support the way certain forms of leadership are held to remain 'true' only in certain points of time and space. Thus, we would expect Woods's (1913) theory of inherited leadership qualities to prevail only during a period when scientific and popular support for 'the truth' of inherited behaviour persisted. The First World War may well have persuaded many that if leadership was an inherited skill the sooner the existing leaders were removed from office the better for everyone else. That Woods's account was the last of a dying breed can also be judged by the far more pessimistic account provided by Veblen just a year later, with the war a mere five months away: 'History records more frequent and more spectacular instances of the triumph of imbecile institutions over life and culture, than of peoples who have by the force of instinctive insight saved themselves alive out of a desperately precarious institutional situation, such, for instance, as now faces the people of Christendom' (Veblen, 1914: 24–5).

7

The Culture of Management and the Management of Culture

Introduction

This chapter is concerned with the significance of culture for management. Culture is rather like a black hole: the closer you get to it the less
light is thrown upon the topic and the less chance you have of surviving
the experience. This is partly because there is very little consensus
about what culture is (Kroeber and Kluckhohn (1963) note 164 definitions), and even less about whether culture is something that managers
can ever change. In what follows, the idea of culture is subjected to a
critical review that highlights the major differences between orientations
towards culture and considers the way the philosophical underpinnings
of the understanding impose different evaluations of the utility of
culture for management. Although there are numerous versions of
culture, I want to simplify the debate by reducing them to four basic
approaches. This division is based upon a double axis: the first distinguishes between culture as meaning (a set of ideas) and culture as
practice; the second distinguishes between culture as a phenomenon
restricted wholly to humans and culture as a phenomenon that includes
human and non-human.

I begin by considering the origins of the word culture in the
development of 'horticulture' and 'agriculture'. Here, culture can be
configured as *heterogeneous practice*. By this I simply mean that culture
is not restricted to the world of ideas but encompasses a material
practice that involves humans and non-humans (soil, tools, animals,

seeds and the like). In effect, this kind of approach is inclusive – it draws things together through a network of otherwise unrelated phenomenon. The second form considers culture as *homogeneous practice*. Here the emphasis moves from inclusive to exclusive and from an alloy of humans and non-humans towards humans on their own. This shift has its origins in the Enlightenment which, amongst many things, sought to distinguish humans from everything else, based on what the leading lights in the Enlightenment (the *philosophes*) claimed to be the exclusively human attribute of reason. There is clearly still a place for artefacts in here – human reason makes itself visible through the development of machinery, for instance – but the trend is away from artefacts and towards boundary-constructing practices. In the first place these distinguish humans from non-humans, but in the second place we can see the development of class cultures that mark off social classes and status groups from each other. The third approach to culture, culture as *homogeneous meaning*, brings us directly to the more conventional managerial approach to culture, clearly present in the organizational and corporate culture literature that has proliferated throughout the 1980s and 1990s. Here culture reacquires an inclusivist colouring, as the organization is deemed to be glued together through a consensual and unitarist culture. There is also a perceptible shift from practice to meaning as analysts seek to identify the 'meaning systems' and 'the ways we do things round here' that, they argue, facilitate the uniting of organizational members around a core set of cultural principles. Finally, we appear to come full circle in the last approach considered, in which culture is constructed as *heterogeneous discursive practice*. This rather longwinded title embodies four important elements. First, culture takes on again the heterogeneous garments that it wore under the horticultural approach. That is, culture reappears as a network of human and non-human phenomena. Second, culture is not 'just' about a body of ideas that float around in people's heads but actually involves people doing things – a set of practices. Third, the practices are not separate from the meaning systems; we do not have a set of practices that we attach various meanings to. This would imply that we could have a set of practices that are neutral, raw, untainted, and the like, whereas the argument in this perspective is that we only understand what is going on through meaning systems. Everything, then, comes 'cooked'; all practices are discursive practices. Fourth, culture is a constructed phenomenon not a 'natural' one. In effect, culture has to be created and recreated all the time for it to persist, but precisely what 'it' is depends upon who manages to construct the most powerful – that is persuasive – representation of it.

Although there is some form of historical development involved in the difference between these approaches, I want to concentrate on the theoretical rather than the historical differences here. I also intend to spend more time on the issues that are probably more important to the student of management – which means that less time will be spent on the first two approaches. Let me, however, begin with the beginning and delve into the origins of culture.

Horticulture: culture as heterogeneous practice.

The very word 'culture' has its origin in the Latin *cultura*, which comes from *colere*, meaning to tend or care for something: hence 'agriculture' – working on the land, 'the tending of natural growth' (Williams, 1958). Culture, here, is not something that just sits outside waiting to be garnered without effort, but something that needs to be worked on – to be constructed in the first instance and then subsequently to be permanently reconstructed. In short, culture, here, is a practice, not just an ideology; it is a constructed rather than a natural phenomenon. A second aspect of culture that needs to be highlighted can be 'gleaned' from the term 'horticulture' – the construction of a garden. Gardening is not simply the production of food and/or flowers from the soil, it is also the separation of certain kinds of plant from others. 'Weeds' are not welcomed by most gardeners and the 'weeding out' of unwelcome elements (human or non-human) is an important process in gardening and organizational life. But what are 'weeds'? Are they a category of plant which we can assess by referring to a catalogue of weeds? Or are they merely plants out of place, transgressors of boundaries imposed by the human gardener? For some gardeners, poppies and daisies are 'weeds', but for others they are 'wild flowers'. The point here is that the development of horticulture requires the imposition of a boundary so that the cultured and the uncultured can remain separated.

We can see how important the development of boundaries is, particularly in social anthropology, keeping the sacred free from the profane (Durkheim, 1961) or the cooked from the raw (Levi-Strauss, 1966) or the clean from the polluted (Douglas, 1966). But we can also see its significance in everyday speech, especially in terms of remarking the boundaries between high-status and low-status occupations. Since the days of the Ancient Greeks most Western societies have considered intellectual activity, which maintains a distance between itself and the material world, as superior to manual activity, which is in direct physical contact with the material world (Applebaum, 1992). This even appears in relation to money and wealth, where a direct and visible tie between work and money has traditionally been regarded as rather crude, whether for Japanese samurai (Cook, 1993) or English aristocrats (Wiener, 1981; Cain and Hopkins, 1993a, 1993b; Rubinstein, 1993). It was precisely this overt disdain for money (though of course the disdain was premised upon the possibility of surviving through 'unearned' money that could be secured at a distance) which Veblen (1953) captured in his attack upon the 'conspicuous consumption' of the American *nouveaux riches*. Having overt forms of wealth came to be regarded as being 'filthy rich' or 'stinking rich' or 'rolling in it' or 'flush with money', or in Chaucerian terms, having 'filthy lucre'. One need not be too imaginative to note the relationship between money and excrement. Indeed, it is clear from Francis Bacon's Enlightenment concern that we should be endeavouring to facilitate 'the culture and *manurance* of the mind' (my emphasis). This is also reproduced in the opposite: having no money is considered as being 'clean broke', 'cleaned out', 'washed up' and so on.

Most of the managerial writings on culture make a passing reference to these origins of culture (see Pheysey, 1993) but then rapidly move on to narrow the topic to either a set of collective norms or a collective way of seeing, the latter being most forcefully put by Hofstede (1980). But is there anything other than a root which should be highlighted here? Two things are important. One, the word starts out by reflecting the concern that culture is a common practice rather than a common attitude. Indeed, one might be tempted to say here that it is the repetition of the practice that ensures the reproduction of the 'culture', which, in turn, makes the practice 'sensible'. Two, the practice itself is not merely concerned with, or limited to, human repetition. Instead, the practice of culture required humans to construct gardens using technologies within an institutionalized framework of rules, regulations and traditions. This is well documented in Malinowski's (1921) description of yam growing amongst the Trobrian Islanders, in which magical rites, fencing posts, yams and the Trobrianders themselves were bound together in a *practice* that involved human and non-human, and which was made sense of in and through the Trobrianders' cultural traditions. In effect, we might reconsider the extent to which our popular contemporary assumptions about the nature of culture are more or less effective, in accounting for organizational life, than the myths, computers, products and people that the medieval horticulturist might regard as making up contemporary work. So how did we get from the rather rich and earthy picture of horticulture to the rather fragile and ideologically based assumptions of today? In two words: the Enlightenment.

Enlightened culture: culture as homogeneous practice

The second development of the term 'culture' can be located in the general movement towards the Enlightenment, the intellectual movement of the eighteenth century, centred in France, which replaced the church with human reason as the font of all valuable knowledge. Here, culture was still a form of cultivation, but now it was associated with a cultivated mind, a specifically human attribute, separated from, and superior to, the cultivation of plants or animals. This is not the place for a lengthy discussion of the Enlightenment (see Gay, 1973; Hawthorn, 1976; R. Porter, 1990; Hamilton, 1992), but there are several issues that need to be raised if we are to understand the move away from culture as a practice with things to culture as a practice which distinguished people first from things, and then from each other. The two forms of separation, from non-humans and then from other humans, are represented in the words of one Mary Pettibone Poole, who is alleged to have said that, 'Culture is what your butcher would have if he were a surgeon.' (Peter 1978). Note how the association of practice with non-humans leads to a subordinate status, and this becomes clear in the form of division between the 'lowly' butcher and the 'superior' surgeon. A contemporary piece of research into similar 'butchers', by Ackroyd and Crowdy (1990), confirms the relationship between a (disassembly) practice that involves animals and generally low social esteem, though the slaughterers in the research tended to respond by undertaking 'cultural' pursuits (hunting, shooting and fishing) that exacerbated the 'moral ambiguity' of their image (see also Searle-Chatterjee, 1979). The research is also a good demonstration of the difficulties of changing cultures where occupational cultures are strong and become very much interlinked with class-based cultures.

The difference between butchery and surgery is important too in terms of the striving for perfection which is often associated with the development of 'culture' in this second sense. 'Perfect' surgery may be configured as slicing up flesh in a way apparently little different from 'perfect' butchery, but the former will generally remain regarded as a higher form of skill and the latter, 'butchery', is often associated with indiscriminate killing, not the perfection of a craft skill.

The development of the term 'culture' as a manifestation of perfection is also associated with the writings of Enlightenment *philosophes* like Adam Ferguson (1723–1816), who considered Scottish society to be the pinnacle of human achievement, and the future destiny of all other 'civilized' societies. In a different approach, Coleridge contrasted 'civilization', which he regarded as a 'mixed good', with culture, which he regarded as perfection. It was not that much of a leap of imagination to develop the idea that culture was a means of discriminating between 'perfect' and 'imperfect' human practices, and then to assume that social class was the manifestation of this boundary between good and bad taste. For some, like Matthew Arnold, there was no existing (English) social class that embodied 'culture'. The 'barbarian' aristocracy merely wanted to maintain the privileges associated with the *status quo* the 'philistine' middle class were intent on mechanizing everything in sight, and the 'degraded' mass of the population were closer to anarchy than culture; hence the need, in Arnold's eyes, for an elite of 'aliens' to administer culture on behalf of the population (Hartley and Hawkes, 1977).

Such theoretical claims to cultural superiority also received support following the 1859 publication of Darwin's *On the Origin of Species*, in which cultural superiority seemed coterminous with the 'survival of the fittest'. Subsequent claims by anthropologists like Lewis Henry Morgan (1818–81) and Edward Burnett Tylor (1832–1917) paralleled the claim that a hierarchy of civilizations could be seen from the 'evidence' of human evolution (Jenks, 1993). It requires even less of a leap of imagination to consider the way this kind of elitist concern became transformed into the notion of culture as the repository of all that was of high value – that is, all that the mass did not have and could not expect to secure. In short, whatever could act as a boundary device to discriminate between the elite and the mass could take on the guise of 'high' culture. As a contemporary British example, what many might regard as a rather boring spectacle – two long and narrow boats racing along a river in the 'Varsity boat race' – becomes a (high) cultural form when it acts to remind the population as a whole that certain forms of messing about on the river are culturally superior to others. This does not mean that those members of the population who do not frequent the likes of the Henley Regatta or 'Royal' Ascot are enamoured of such cultural forms. Indeed, one might read activities like football, pigeon-racing and bingo as the counter-cultural pursuits of those without access to (or interest in) 'high culture'. Quite what marks the boundary between working-class culture and popular culture is unclear and not especially important here: whether horse racing at Royal Ascot is intrinsically superior to sports races at school, or whether gambling on dog racing is intrinsically inferior to 'playing the stock market', is not the critical issue (though I have my doubts). What is important is the way culture is constructed as a boundary device to mark off insiders from outsiders: the privileged from the unprivileged; men from women; and 'them' from 'us'. Culture, in this sense, is largely, if not mainly, about distinguishing one group from another on the basis of where the boundary lies: in effect, culture is an exclusionary mechanism as well as an inclusive one.

Besides its origins in the Enlightenment, and its 'refinement' by anthropologists, this kind of approach to culture has at least two sources in classic works of sociology from Durkheim and Weber.

From Durkheim it is derived from the distinction between 'primitive' and 'modern' societies; the social glue – or culture – of the former, which Durkheim called 'mechanical solidarity', lay in the similarities between people; but the social glue or cultural bonding of the latter, 'organic societies', was rooted in the dissimilarities between people. Solidarity in so-called 'primitive' society rested on the principle of replication: everyone did the same or very similar things and the division of labour was low, so that each person and community was essentially self-sufficient. In what Durkheim took to be the future model of society, organic society, the extended division of labour led to solidarity through the mutual interdependence that the differences between people generated. Durkheim unnecessarily restricted the different forms of solidarity to different evolutionary stages in society, and sometimes implies that a high level of labour division automatically creates the conditions for solidarity through the dependencies formed. However, it is clear that some forms of dependence do not lead to an automatic bonding. Slavery, for example, generates a system through which slave owners become dependent upon the actions of their slaves, but this does not usually lead to any form of mutual or cultural solidarity. However, the important thing here is to note that cultures that promote solidarity through difference can be read as supporting individualism and resisting the rights of corporate bodies, including the state, to interfere with the 'rights' of the individual. Those cultures considered to promote solidarity through similarity can be read as establishing a preference for the rights of the collective over the individual.

From Weber this kind of approach has its roots in his ideas about social closure, in which groups differentiated themselves from others on the basis of some attribute or other which they possessed, whether nationality, wealth, social class, status, skin colour, gender or, more recently, educational or professional qualifications (Weber, 1978: 999–1001; Parkin, 1979). The significance of this is Weber's concern that the attribute which distinguishes those within the group from those without is essentially contingent – it is chosen to ensure the maintenance of a boundary; it is not there because it represents a 'real' boundary; it is the constructed boundary that operates to distinguish. It is this idea of construction, clearly demarcated and heavily monitored, that Geertz took to be the most valuable approach to culture: 'Believing, with Max

Weber, that man is an animal suspended in webs of significance he himself has spun, I take culture to be those webs, and the analysis of it to be therefore not an experimental science in search of a law but an interpretive one in search of meaning' (Geertz, 1973: 5).

This kind of approach can also be seen in elements of the grid/group analysis of Mary Douglas (Douglas and Douglas, 1989), itself influenced by Durkheim, in which the distinguishing feature is the way boundaries are drawn around individuals or around groups (and in Alan Fox's (1974) distinction between high- and low-trust cultures: see also Grint and Choi (1993)). The differentiating forms that are central to the cultural model developed here, then, tend to be individualism and corporatism. The former implies a culture where the rights of the individual are regarded as paramount under most, but not all, circumstances. Within the corporatist form, the group or team or nation is regarded as paramount. Adopting a Weberian ideal-type approach, individualist cultures have a strongly delimited role for state and quasi-state agencies, while corporatist cultures have interventionist states. This manifests itself in the adoption of laissez faire attitudes (towards the economy at least) for the individualist culture or 'managed' capitalism for the corporatist.

It is worth pointing out here that Durkheim's materialist explanation of cultures is problematic. For example, it has been argued that the shift through the period of industrialization in England did not, in and of itself, generate a new individualist culture; rather, the individualist culture appears to predate the industrial revolution and the extended division of labour by several centuries at least. As Macfarlane (1978) asserts, the effective elimination of the peasantry and the establishment of common law, which emphasized individual rights and land ownership, undermined the kinds of peasant culture that Durkheim's mechanical solidarity was modelled on. The precise timing of the transition from collective to individual culture is both contentious and, for our purposes, irrelevant. The point is that, according to this model, before industrialization England was an individualist more than a collectivist society. One might also note in passing here that the avoidance of a legal system rooted in abstract theory and a formal legal code, in favour of a system based on precedent, may itself support an approach to other areas of social life based on the same principle. For example, the British manager's historical lack of interest in formal education is as clear as the support for experience and apprenticeships as the route to success. This point was covered in more detail in chapter 3.

Within employment, individualist cultures tend to be associated with weakly institutionalized employer–employee collaboration – that is confrontational industrial relations and voluntarism. They also tend to focus on short-distance control, that is a relatively limited span of discretion, and external and individual forms of motivation: money and individual pay. Corporatist cultures have longer-distance control systems, and rely much more upon team disciplines, team payment systems and internalized mechanisms of control. The team orientation of the corporatist approach also encourages a reliance upon internal labour markets for promotion and a leadership style that can be described as 'consensualized'; that is, a leadership where subordinates are encouraged to have some say in the decision-making process, and where, even if this contribution is negligible, the process of participation binds the subordinates tightly into the system, so that the leadership style, while not necessarily based on consensus, has a consensualizing process built into it.

Individualist cultures adopt external labour markets for promotional purposes, and have a leadership style that is authoritative, if not necessarily authoritarian. It takes the gap that exists between subordinate and superordinate as crucial to the maintenance of the entire system and rejects participatory developments by the subordinates. The 'low-trust' system which this form represents also impedes a consideration of the long-term performance of an organization, since this would require longer spans of control and limit the role of the market in determining the future success of a firm.

If one adopts the boundary approach to culture, then its utility in explaining – that is providing persuasive accounts of – culture can be quite large. For instance, it is not restricted to alleged national differences between cultures, but it can be used to model the subcultures of organizations where boundary devices are constructed to keep the 'other' out, and through this exclusionary practice to formulate the identity of those within. This might be through the wearing of different uniforms, typical of most Western companies, where blue-collar workers wear overalls and executives wear suits, so that status symbols are permanently displayed. Or, conversely, it may be that uniformity of clothing is adopted to construct a culture of homogeneous interests. This was historically associated with Japanese manufacturing companies, though Western companies such as Rover in the UK have also adopted it. At a lower level still, one can consider the boundary device in operation as certain categories of people consistently sit in certain areas of the collective canteen – and woe befall those people who have the temerity to sit in the 'wrong' place; that is a place on the other side of the (invisible) boundary.

One might also consider the utility of boundary construction in terms of various levels of 'wrapping', with firm boundaries around things, words and people. Hendry (1993) has argued that wrapping, far from being a metaphorical representation, is itself a critical aspect of culture. Hence Japanese language is wrapped in distinct levels of politeness, which are only removed under certain conditions and in certain forms. This is especially important where Anglo-Saxon approaches tend to consider external decoration to be just that – decoration – a veneer covering, indeed concealing, the important core, a true essence. The wrapped nature of Japanese culture is also 'revealed' in the distinction often drawn between *honne* (true feeling) and *tatemae* (formal front). *Tatemae* is a critical boundary device through which outsiders are excluded from the inner thoughts of the individual and deprived of access to the group (Yoshino, 1993). It is also important to note the role that *tatemae* plays in the construction of 'harmony' in Japanese corporations. That Japanese employees do not voice dissent from their managers may be seen by Westerners as overt compliance, but it may be perceived by themselves as the necessary maintenance of harmony in the face of an outsider. Similarly, the absence of overt dissent, conflict or even decision making in business meetings in Japan may be less the outward display of consensus than the result of *nemawashi* – the 'tending of the roots', or prior meetings, that ensure that the formal meeting is one that displays harmony to the outside. Small wonder, then, that so much cultural confusion reigns over the difference between (typically) American frankness, which may appear extraordinarily inept and tactless to the Japanese, and (typically) Japanese tactfulness, which may appear incredibly obscure and even two-faced to the Americans. Loyalty to the group, demarcated by a rigid boundary which separates actions taken towards the group and those taken towards all outsiders, becomes a very powerful device in Japan; whereas in Anglo-Saxon countries, the boundary is much more likely to be drawn around the self and much less likely to be drawn around a work group.

The significance of considering culture as a boundary device can also be seen in the debates surrounding cultural competence. Cultural competence often seems to imply an ability to 'pass' as a local. If one is unable to speak the local language, understand the local traditions, and act appropriately in the situation, one might rightly be regarded as culturally incompetent. 'Foreigners' in Britain who do not wait in bus queues properly but rush for the front are regarded as incompetent if not downright rude. Yet there is a paradox here, because elements of culture seem also to require people to act as if they were indeed 'foreigners'. For example, little can be more embarrassing for teenagers than having their parents attend the local night-club, wearing clothes that are fashionable for teenagers but not for them. In this case parents are regarded as culturally incompetent if they attempt to 'pass' as teenagers. Similarly, although Japanese bow to each other on meeting, it is not regarded as necessary for Westerners to bow to Japanese. This, like the 'discoing' parents, is a manifestation of incompetence, an attempt by 'the other' to ingratiate him or herself, to cross a cultural boundary that is constructed specifically to provide protection from the 'other'.

Cultural competence, therefore, is more than the ability to pass as a local; it is the ability to recognize and accept cultural boundaries that include not passing as a local. One could go further to consider the extent to which the status of the 'other' provides not just constraints but freedom from constraints too. For example, if you are approached in the street and are asked in an almost incomprehensible way about the whereabouts of the bus station, you can either assume that the questioner is drunk or incompetent, and simply ignore her or him or threaten to call the police, or you can assume that the questioner is foreign and has a poor understanding of English. In the latter case one might develop an empathetic response and, following traditional British procedures, speak slowly and loudly. Again, the point is that one does not have to be fluent in the language and customs of a country to be successful at negotiating one's way around, but one must appear to reproduce the required characteristics if one is to elicit local support. In short, it may be that it is culturally acceptable to appear culturally incompetent providing the incompetence can be legitimated. To appear an incompetent speaker of French with a strong English accent is much more acceptable to the French – and more likely to elicit sympathy and help – than to assume that, when in France, English will suffice.

The upshot of this is that the provision of a potted guide to the mores, language and customs of a foreign country is likely to be insufficient as a guide to successful business. We need to know not just what the 'other' is like but how the 'other' views us and expects us to act properly. In effect, we need to construct a series of empathetic competencies, an array of dual liaisons, or mirrored mores, in which we can view both the other and the other's view of ourselves. We need, in short, to be able to recognize the existence of all these cultural boundaries.

What are the practical consequences of this approach? First, one constructs a mechanism through which the relevance of the other's interpretation of self is revealed. For example, an individual might regard him or herself as extremely competent to operate in a particular country on the grounds that his or her own attitude towards leadership and that of the other country are very similar. In this instance one could construct a system that compared the self-review of the individual with the review provided by others (peers, subordinates and superordinates, if necessary and the expense can be justified). Second, this composite, and probably contradictory, evidence provides the basis for an evaluation of the individual's competence in the light of the models of the other culture with which the organization is familiar. If the other culture appears to place a lot of emphasis on strong individual leadership style, and the individual believes him or herself to mirror this, but his or her peers, subordinates and superordinates do not, then there may well be an opportunity to reconsider the move or develop some form of leadership training. This system of competence assessment does not rest on dubiously objective grounds but on the importance of interpretation. Achieving a 100 per cent rating on a psychometric test by the popular method of double guessing the point of the question or task is going to be less useful once you are exposed to the other culture than having your colleagues tell you, as honestly as they can, that you are not perceived by them to be this person, at one with the culture of the 'other'.

Organizational culture: culture as homogeneous meaning

While the notion of class cultures, and indeed national cultures, draws its power from the exclusionary boundaries that mark 'us' off from 'them', the concern for culture as an attribute of an organization, and as an inclusionary system, is rather newer. Certainly, writers had covered organizational culture in the early 1950s (Jaques, 1951), and subsequently the 1970s (Pettigrew, 1973), but the headlong rush into culture is usually tied more closely to the rise of the Japanese threat to Western industry. Under the initial influence of Abeggelen (1958) and Dore (1973), but probably more importantly of the 1977 OECD report on Japanese industrial relations, and the subsequent works of Ouchi (1981) and Pascale and Athos (1982), Japanese business success was explained through the competitive advantage secured through Japanese national and corporate culture.

The assumption that culture operates to include rather than to exclude, and that it is associated with the development of collective harmony, has its roots in the kind of cultural analysis originally developed by social anthropologists, notably those of structural-functionalist attachment, for whom the function of a culture was to maintain the social structure. As Meek (1988) argues, not only do the ideas of organizational culture have their theoretical origins in this kind of approach, developed originally by Levi-Strauss, but the problems pertaining to structural-functionalism also remain at the heart of many contemporary corporate cultures' approaches. In particular, these include the tendencies to ignore counter-cultural movements; to regard culture as a unifying force; and to relate conflicts of interest – where they are recognized as such – to 'communication problems' or 'inadequate understanding' on the part of those who appear to dispute the unifying nature of culture. On the other hand, anthropologists do not normally consider culture to be something which is the result of a particular leader's actions, or that culture can be manipulated in the way some managerial theorists claim (Helmers, 1991). Culture for anthropologists tends to be something which an organization is, rather than something which an organization has (Smircich, 1983). In traditional Durkheimian fashion, these kinds of approach are littered with 'internalized norms' and 'collective wills' of the kind that *might* be useful in explaining the culture of a particularly homogeneous group in the middle of the Brazilian jungle, but do not necessarily provide any valuable insights into the world of big business – except in revealing how inadequate such approaches are.

Perhaps the approach is best captured in Kilman et al.'s (1985: ix) phrase, that 'Culture is to the organization what personality is to the individual' (quoted by Meek, 1988: 457). The problems of assuming that individual personality is unitary in itself were addressed in chapter 4, but suffice it to say here that the kind of 'norm-knitting' this assumption embodies, in which organizations construct social norms that individuals 'fit into', appears beyond the capacity of all but the kind of total institutions that make up the world of fundamentalist religious cults.

Culture now becomes configured not as a practice, whose execution determines the identity of a group by excluding 'others', but as a system of 'shared meanings', a pattern of internalized norms and attitudes; 'a complex set of values, beliefs, assumptions and symbols that define the way a firm conducts its business' (Barney, 1986: 657), or a 'shared mindset' (B. L. Porter and Parker, 1993: 48). In effect, culture becomes divorced from practice and resides wholly within the minds of the organization's members. This kind of model is used by the most recent attempt to explain competitive advantage through 'national cultures' (Hampden-Turner and Trompenaars, 1994). As Sathe (1983: 6) asserts, about a similar definition, 'this definition limits the concept of culture to what is shared in the minds of community members.' Yet, Sathe goes on, this does not mean that we can 'simply rely upon what people say about it. Other evidence, both historical and current, must be taken into account to infer what culture is.' This, of course, raises the problem of what the historical or current evidence could be that does not involve, at some level, 'what people say about it'. We shall return to the problem of the non-articulated evidence below.

A related problem is raised when considering the extent to which cultures can be effectively manipulated by managers. If cultures are often subconsciously held, and if they are deeply ingrained, then one of the conventional responses suggested to managers is to seek to alter the behaviour of their staff as a first step in encouraging a change of culture (see Sathe, 1986). Hence, people can be more easily persuaded to undertake different kinds of action – behavioural change – than they can to believe in different things – cultural change. A large stick is often sufficient to persuade people to move away but they may not believe that they ought to move away for long, and may return as soon as you drop the stick.

On the other hand, the division between behaviour and culture is only valid in so far as the term 'culture' is restricted to the realm of ideas. One might want to argue that an organization encouraging forms of behaviour that contradict the culture of the staff itself demonstrates something about the culture of the organization. In this instance, it may be that the organizational elite has an authoritarian culture, but pretends that it is merely attempting to alter the behaviour of its employees, and manages to persuade itself that such actions are not affected by, or manifestations of, its own culture. The upshot is that it becomes more and more difficult to hold a boundary between thoughts and actions, because actions only make sense through thoughts. Furthermore, this has implications for the idea that managers should concentrate upon behavioural change as a prerequisite of cultural change, because behavioural change *is* cultural change.

This can be illustrated by considering the response of organizational elites to those who do not accept the official party line on the new culture. We do not have to accept Willmott's (1993) *1984* parallel between the 'culturalist' approaches deployed by managers and the systems of domination utilized by fictional and historical totalitarian regimes to note that strong cultures premised upon unitarist philosophies do not tolerate dissent – whatever Peters may claim. On the contrary, the logical end product of totalizing cultures is to solder the behaviour of employees to the culture of the employers so that, in direct contradiction of the claims, no personal autonomy remains (Rose, 1990; du Gay and Salaman, 1992); to further the Orwellian analogy, it becomes impossible to distinguish the pigs from the people.

If the culture did not reside in the minds of members then the implication was that it should do, since this was the alleged source of Japanese competitive advantage in the first place. Whether it is, or was, the source of Japanese competitive advantage is another issue (see Grint, 1993a); however, its significance here lies in the way culture came to be construed.

Of particular import is the movement from exclusionary to inclusive developments, since the point of culture now was not so much to demonstrate membership by marking and remarking the boundary lines as to persuade everyone within the organizational boundary that they were all members of the same culture. In short, the process was one that mirrored the transcendence of class cultures by national cultures. It may well be regarded as important for elites to resist popular encroachment upon their own culture, but to cling on to an overtly exclusionary culture is to risk alienating, rather than merely excluding, the popular mass. In this perspective national cultural rites, such as Bastille Day in France, the Trooping of the Colour in Britain, and the 4th of July in the USA are attempts to cement the population as a whole into an alliance, an 'imaginary community' but none of these rituals undermines elite cultural rituals practised by the elite to reinforce the boundaries between it and the mass. The equivalent in corporate culture is to persuade all the members of the organization that they inhabit the same world, whilst retaining the differentiating mechanisms that exclude most employers from certain car parks, restaurants, executive toilets or forms of dress.

Of course, there are attempts to overcome the 'multiple culture' problem, as there are to overcome it at national level. The most popular attempts involve doing away with the forms that reproduce the boundaries: 'free-for-all' parking, the abolition of the executive restaurant – though note how subcultures still prefer to dine together rather than to mix with 'others' – and the requirement for all members to wear the same uniform, most visible in car manufacturer plants. Yet some are always more equal than others: monetary rewards and conditions of service are seldom, if ever, levelled; indeed, the trend in Britain and the USA over the 1980s and 1990s has been the opposite, as executive income and rewards have risen sharply above those received by blue- and white-collar workers. As a result, high levels of material inequality are juxtaposed with ritual genuflections towards status equality and the result is, purportedly, the development of corporate culture and the kind of organizational commitment and flexibility that Deal and Kennedy (1982), and more influentially Peters and Waterman (1982), assured their readers would follow all 'excellent' companies.

There is another problem in this approach since, as Barney (1986) argues, a particular culture can only be a source of *sustained* competitive advantage if it has positive economic consequences, if it is rare, and if it is imperfectly imitable. If everyone has it then it serves no one and it clearly cannot be a source of competitive advantage – even if it might serve to narrow the gap in performance between competitors. One could go further and take one of Barney's examples to consider the consequences of firms imitating market leaders. Since IBM was a market leader at the time both Peters and Waterman and Barney wrote, presumably firms looking to end up where IBM is today should have copied IBM's corporate culture. Perhaps this explains the consummate failure of so many culture copiers.

Also of concern is the notion that strong corporate cultures, which means cultures that are homogeneous, thrive better than weak ones, which are heterogeneous (Gordon and DiTomaso, 1992; cf. Denison, 1990). Yet, simultaneously, Peters (1993) argues that the dynamic nature of the world requires organizations not just to tolerate eccentrics and individuals who are organizational irritants but to facilitate them positively, to celebrate them even. Hence the successful organization of the day is one which has a strongly homogeneous and a strongly heterogeneous culture; it must be centrifugal and centripetal simultaneously. Seldom, it might seem, has there been a more apt title than that of Peters' 1993 seminar series 'Crazy Times Call for Crazy Organizations'. There are organizations that appear to have experienced both centralized and decentralized cultures, but these tend to occur at different times; in effect, a core culture is promoted through a centralized system and, at a point when the culture seems to be accepted, individuals are restructured to manage this same culture in a decentralized fashion (Selznick, 1957; Weick, 1987). In a political analogy one might compare the way the ex-Soviet Union adopted the decentralized market economy and the decentralized political democracy on the basis of a very limited quasi-experiment in centralized change. The results of decentralizing without first establishing a core set of values through centralized control (the core set of Soviet values having been unceremoniously dumped) have been less than auspicious. In contrast, the Chinese Communist Party has maintained a firm, indeed, an authoritarian, control over the political system of China whilst decentralizing the economic system (Overholt, 1993).

Where overt authoritarian approaches may be of limited significance in most democratic capitalist countries, the move to crank up productivity through culturally inspired commitment to a single corporate ideal conflicts with the pluralist ideals of a democratic society. Unitary-oriented political theorists (like Rousseau (1968) and Madison (1966)) have attempted to overcome the fragmentary desires of the population by encouraging the plurality of interest groups in the hope of preventing domination by one powerful group. However, management theorists have tended to avoid rather than confront the dilemma raised by the strong-culture approach, in the same way as Dahl originally restricted the applicability of democracy to the political sphere – though he subsequently changed his mind (Dahl, 1985) and suggested the extension of the 'franchise' to economic organizations too (see Held, 1987). One might go further to suggest that managing cultural conflict is a critical issue for organizations attempting to utilize corporate culture as a source of competitive advantage to overcome, if they are to develop long-term change rather than short-term compliance. Just as dominant class cultures represent themselves as *the* culture by first undermining subordinate or counter-cultures, and then parading themselves as neutral or even natural, so corporations may follow a similar strategy. This might involve the official corporate culture – as envisaged by the directors – confronting all subordinate cultures, in particular those supported by trade unions, and developing procedures and processes that bypass trade union channels (semi-autonomous work groups, teams, communication groups, quality circles and the like). The long-term aim is first to eliminate the institutional mechanisms that embody alternative cultures and then, once these have been removed, to represent the official culture not just as the only culture but actually as a perfectly normal way of seeing the world. Thus, stripped of its sectional heritage, the elite corporate culture can, eventually, wither away in this guise to leave not culture but nature, not bias but the truth, not 'the way we do things round here' but 'the only way things can be done'. The images of scientific management can be seen reappearing afresh; just as Taylor argued that there was just one way (as determined by science), here there is also just one way, as determined by common sense. It was just this kind of control through a monopoly on claims to rationality that Barthes (1973) called the process of 'silent domination'.

It is worth considering here that domination need not require some form of cultural or ideological hegemony that controls a subordinate population by inhibiting subversive ideas. Such a control system may be very effective but it is not at all clear that dominant groups have historically maintained control by this process. Hence, although traditionally Marxists have considered capitalist and ruling class ideological control as the capstone of domination, Abercrombie et al. (1980) suggest that there is little evidence to support the claim historically. Their counter-argument rests primarily on what Marx called 'the dull compulsion of economic relations' (1970: 737). In effect, the implication is that where material conditions are such that subordinate populations do not have the wherewithal to resist dominant groups, then the elite will remain dominant irrespective of the ideological persuasion of the mass.

The parallel in organizational culture would be to consider the extent to which the 'new working practices' that are becoming more common in the West, and the spread of corporate cultures that go with them, are premised upon the 'dull economic compulsion' of mass unemployment or the threat of it. In other words, employees may be prepared to wear the corporate uniform and articulate the 'company-speak' as long as they feel economically vulnerable, but should economic prosperity return we might well see a return to older subordinate traditions of scepticism, instrumentalism and lack of interest in the machinations of the corporation.

This does not mean that the methods open to managers to control their subordinates are limited to the indoctrination school of corporate culture or the 'big-stick' school of economic compulsion. It may be that fatalism – acquiescence in the face of an apparent inability to configure or construct an alternative – plays an important part here, though we shall leave that discussion to chapter 9.

A further parallel between dominant political and corporate cultural development rests in the extent to which these are constructed rather than emanate naturally from the population as a whole. Though it may appear, for instance, that much of a country's culture is the result of ancient secretions, embedded in the amber of time, many facets of national culture can also appear as the result of purposive activity. For example, many of the British royal traditions do not stem from the monarchical mists of millennia but can be traced to the desires of late Victorian politicians to create an array of formal procedures that would, over time and with constant reaffirmation through repetition, create traditions. Just as Dimbleby's description of the crowning of Elizabeth II in 1953 as 'a thousand-year tradition' of 'pageantry and grandeur' turns out to be a tradition based on barely one hundred years, so we should note that many of our national and corporate traditions are 'invented' (Cannadine, 1994: 102). During the Second World War, Winston Churchill constructed an image of the British as 'a famous island race', though the very notion of an impermeable boundary around the population, through which the differentiation between British and non-British could be made, was very suspect for a nation soaked in its colonial traditions (Warner, 1994). Similarly, many of the Japanese traditions of group loyalty and dedication were constructed during the 1890s through a system of national education that systematically spread the code of National Shinto – the unique and superior spirit of the Japanese nation and devotion to the emperor (Cook, 1993; R. J. Smith, 1983; J. E. Hunter, 1989). Likewise, many American traditions, indeed the very concept of an American nation itself, has been located in the imaginative activities of early Puritan colonialists (Bercovitch, 1993). Even the heroic battle of the Alamo in 1836 appears as a conflict between imaginations, with John Wayne and the 'American Thermopylae' version now being undermined by revisionist historians eager to demonstrate that Travis, the American commander, was 'high' on mercury at the time, that Davy Crockett was incapacitated through alcohol, and that Jim Bowie only remained at the fort because he had buried some stolen Apache gold there (Tisdall, 1994). For our purposes it does not matter whose representation of events is the most accurate, but it is important to note how history, and culture, are constructed and reconstructed rather than merely 'emerge'. One implication of this is that management theories and practices developed in one culture simply may not operate in another (Hofstede, 1993).

A similar pattern is evident at the corporate level. Recognizing that the life span of many organizations is often considerably less than a human one, let alone that of a nation, there are many who argue that cultures have, indeed, to be constructed from the beginning through the vision and goal setting of the leader or leaders, who then must persuade others to accept the new culture and work to develop rites and rituals that support it and undermine any contenders (Schein, 1983; Payne, 1991). A typical example might be that of Cadbury's, the British chocolate manufacturer, whose Quaker origins have often been deployed to demonstrate the significance of particular, and in this case religious and philanthropic, cultures for corporate success. Yet Cadbury's appears to have spent considerable effort on constructing this very image by reconstructing its own past, so that the insignificant differences between eighteenth- and nineteenth-century Quaker capitalists and non-Quaker capitalists were construed as revealing the moral superiority of the former, and the early period of Cadbury's was configured as laying the basis for all subsequent cultural developments (Rowlinson and Hassard, 1993). In the event, Cadbury's invented its past to fit its future. Or, as Jeanette Winterson put it, considerably more elegantly: 'Everyone remembers things that never happened. And it is common knowledge that people often forget things which did. Either we are all fantasists and liars or the past has nothing definite in it' (Winterson, 1990: 92, quoted by Rowlinson and Hassard, 1993: 299). This is an important theoretical point and it cuts right to the heart of the corporate culture approach with its recognition that meanings are imposed upon events and that, potentially at least, an infinite number of meanings are available. It is, then, from the potentially infinite number of accounts of organizational culture that the organizational elite draw, develop and deploy the official version, and in doing so arrange a cull of all those that protest too much. The result is a culture that operates in an 'authoritarian' way: it is a narrative that secures a purchase on 'reality' only by repressing all other accounts. This is not so much Barthes's (1973) 'silent domination' as the domination over the silenced. When this rather bloodstained result is contrasted with the single, coherent and universal culture that lies at the heart of the corporate model, we should be reaching for a scalpel too. Might it be that organizations are *never* the kind of united fellowship of clones that is purported to stalk the corridors of big business? Might it be that organizations are typically riven by political intrigue at all levels and amongst all kinds of formal and informal groups, and that whatever is produced by the organization gets produced despite, not because of, the cultures that seep out of every pore and every drawer?

Culture, in this context, therefore, is not a set of free-floating ideas that by some magical mechanism appears to be pervasive within a group and to be reproduced by or for it. But neither is culture regarded as a set of material processes that generate self-supporting ideologies. Rather, culture is closer to what B. Anderson (1983), in a different context, has called 'an imagined community'. That is, since the members of any sizeable group, and especially a national or ethnic group, will never be able to meet, let alone understand, all the other members of their group, the development of, and allegiance to, a particular cultural identity has to be undertaken through a leap of faith and imagination. For an individual to feel that she or he 'belongs' requires her or him to imagine that her or his ideas and values are both similar to those of the group as a whole and, equally important and a necessary aspect of the same process, different from those of other individuals in other groups. Of course, this leap of imagination, this assumption of cultural homogeneity, can be 'facilitated' by those wishing to encourage such 'imagining', and this is precisely the role of management in the generation of corporate culture.

Constructed cultures: culture as heterogeneous discursive practice

The final model of culture here takes us back to the beginning of the story. Just as the original term 'culture' implies a practice in which humans and non-humans interacted in an homogeneous network, so too some contemporary accounts of culture suggest that we should abandon the division between nature and culture, between non-human and human, on the epistemological grounds that the two should be examined using the same approach, and on the practical grounds that humans only operate with non-humans. The human stripped of all that is 'artificial' (that is not 'naturally' occurring, and therefore made by human hand) is a naked human in an environment that has long since disappeared from almost all corners of the earth. To all intents and purposes, therefore, to consider humans separately from the world they have created is to rely upon a 'state-of-nature' argument that simply cannot be upheld: there never were individual humans alone against the world. Yet, despite this, our general approach is to deny the interconnectedness of life and to impose boundaries around academic disciplines and around human activities. Thus we can 'analyse' (break down into its constituent parts) human society, amongst other things, into 'technology' and 'culture', considering the first through 'science' and the second through 'social' science. Yet neither technology nor culture exists in isolation from the other, as social anthropologists rightly remind us. The paradox is twofold. First, social science only seems to enter the equation when technology failure or error needs to be explained; the truth appears to be self-explanatory and therefore beyond human interpretation. Second, social anthropologists themselves have, at least until relatively recently, tended to limit their concerns to 'marginal' and often 'non-literate' groups encamped at a considerable distance from their own homes (cf. Silverstone and Hirsch, 1992).

In contrast, Latour (1993) (following Bloor, 1991) argues for a 'generalized principle of symmetry' in which there are no *a priori* epistemological breaks between the study of science and the study of nature, and in which explanation is firmly focused upon the 'quasi-objects' that make up the world, that is the networks of humans and non-humans. If we take this approach to its logical extreme then 'the very notion of culture is an artefact created by bracketing Nature off ... Cultures – different or universal – do not exist, any more than Nature does. There are only Nature-Cultures – "collectives"' (Latour, 1993: 104–7). The result of this radical claim should be the suspension of this chapter, since clearly we cannot isolate culture from nature. The usual response is to argue that, for the sake of simplicity – and in order to analyse the issues better – we should nevertheless maintain a division between nature and culture. Note here the word 'analyse' again, with all its attendant ramifications of (re)splitting the natural from the cultural. I have some sympathy with Latour's claims to holistic synthesis rather than analysis, and the desire to avoid examining social phenomena in a way substantially different from the way we examine 'natural' phenomena. This does not mean that we should abandon an examination of culture, but it does mean we should stop pretending that cultures exist in a pristine form untouched by artifice. Nor does it mean that we should abandon the constructivist ship and settle back into the comfortable world of contingency theory where, a decent sweep of all the variables, human and non-human, will suffice to explain the world. On the contrary, contingency theory is itself modelled on the divide between human and non-human, between the cultural and the technical, so that we can measure the objective variables of technology and economic environment and then worry about where the cultural variables fit, or how they can explain the residual results that the more 'objective' analysis so often seems to stop at.

As Mary and James Douglas have argued, in many contemporary accounts: 'culture becomes an extra resource to be wheeled in after other explanations are defeated. It is the flexible, powerful residual factor after other explanations are defeated' (1989: 34). Their example of this residual status, which leads to a cultural explanation being tautologous, is particularly appropriate in the context of this chapter: enthusiasm for work is explained by the attachment of the workers to a powerful work ethic. The culture in this example is not the *explanans* but the *explanandum*: the thing to be explained not the thing which does the explaining. Since the peculiarities of different countries are unlikely to be explained by reference to different attitudes towards issues like freedom (that is, it is unlikely that one group wants freedom and the other does not), then the interesting question is why different groups go about achieving a related aim in very different ways. Or, more specifically in their case, why do the Swedes appear to adopt a more consensual approach to industrial relations than the British, when presumably everyone involved seeks relatively similar goals (especially when the consensual account of the empirical evidence seems to suggest that the consensual approach is economically more viable)?

Further, and in contrast to conventional accounts, culture in this approach is constructed through accounts of cultural practices rather than merely through a neutral, and thus inactive, observation of cultural practices. The implication of this is that those accounts which hold culture to be 'the thing which lies beneath the surface', the raft of norms that are subconsciously held and ritually displayed by all, become a deeper source of confusion. If culture is invisible, because of its very nature as a taken-for-granted series of practices and thoughts, then we are left with nothing but different accounts of it. There can be no yardstick to measure the invisible, so we are left with relying upon the accounts. Of course, we can observe and possibly measure the behaviour that is allegedly the result of the unconscious culture but the allocation of causal agency to behaviour is notoriously confused and confusing. Moreover, can we step outside our own culture to secure some kind of purchase on the behaviour of others? Hofstede (1991: 14, 19), for instance, considers culture to be 'mental programming', or 'the collective programming of the mind which distinguishes the members of one category of people from another'. In so far as cultural constructions are organized around the construction of boundaries, to differentiate those within the boundary from those without, I would agree. The issue is not whether the boundary is 'real' but whether it is made 'real' by its adherents' discourse. Discourse, here, is the form and content of representing: the discourse acts as a conduit so that the way culture, in this instance, is represented is made possible through the particular discourse. As parts of a jigsaw only make sense when fitted together to make the right picture, so too elements of discourse only make sense as a result of the total picture. Further, discourse does not rest wholly in the realm of language but also in the realm of social practice, which produces meaning. This social practice will itself usually combine thought and action, as S. Hall (1992) argues, but it will involve representations of technology too. Thus culture can be considered as a way of understanding rooted in social practice; it is not just a body of mental ideas held by individuals, but a raft of social practices that involve the interpretation and application of technology, which produce social meanings.

If this is so then how do we measure culture? Let us take, for example, the question of whether the Japanese are committed workaholics and whether this is a cultural issue. The first point is that this is not something for which we can develop a device to measure the truth content of the statement or observation: workers may be *at* work for a considerable amount of time but doing precious little that the management might regard as *work*. Traditionally, British workers have worked very long hours (43.7 hours on average) in comparison to the European average (40.4) (Employment Policy Institute, 1993), but since British productivity is also comparatively low it ought to be clear that being at work and working are different activities. Second, this does not mean that whether or not the Japanese are workaholics is merely a matter of opinion; that workaholism lies wholly in the eye of the beholder. The point is that some beholders are more powerful than others and the taken-for-granted 'truth' of the issue will depend upon the network of forces that support or deny the claim. In pragmatic management terms this does not mean that the issue is irrelevant, because if people act as if the Japanese are workaholics then their actions are informed by these beliefs and will have particular consequences. But nor does it mean that we should expend great energy trying to measure the unmeasurable – unless, of course, the measurement process is the device through which contending truth claims are (contingently) resolved in favour of one interpretation or the other. In short, the truth claims upon which we act do not have to be true to have consequences (though what these consequences are is again a matter of representation and interpretation). Third, there are many mechanisms in Japanese management systems that operate to 'encourage' the view that dedication to the corporation is a normal, that is a cultural, thing. For instance, long-term employment, seniority pay and promotion systems, and the constant mobility required of all employees operate to discourage affiliations to anything other than the corporation. Whether, therefore, it is cultural or 'material' forces that encourage dedication is really irrelevant, because the so-called 'material' issues – the pay and conditions – still require representation and interpretation; they are also, then, culturally constructed. At the very heart of the issue is the case that what counts as a 'good' reward package is itself a cultural issue.

The critical point is not that we may be able to prove the Japanese culture to be one that encourages workaholism but that the 'imaginary' place which we know as Japan has its culture actively constructed through the telling and retelling of stories and myths. Thus, the issue is not that there is a culture 'out there' which we can apprehend through the correct methodology, or that we can simply compare interpretations of culture against the real thing. This is the familiar claim about the division between rhetoric and reality again. In this sense, culture is not so much a matter of interpretation as one of representation. Interpretation implies a distancing between the 'real' world and the interpretation, and it is on the extent of the distance between the two that we can assess the validity of the interpretation: when there is no gap between the interpretation and reality then the interpretation is adjudged valid. But, since each interpretation is a representation, there is no way to differentiate between rhetoric and reality.

Does this mean that we are left meandering around the cultural pool in an aimless and irrelevant way? Well, it might seem like that – and yet people act as if this were not the case, as if there were a gap between reality and rhetoric that we could measure. And this is the point: because the conventional mode of operating is itself a realist one, actions are taken on the basis of realist epistemologies. For the non-realist the result is not that the constructivist approach is demonstrably false and therefore unusable but that we should concentrate on the mechanism through which reality is represented in persuasive or non-persuasive ways. In short, what managers do is provide accounts of corporate or national culture that are deemed to be more or less persuasive. If culture is itself produced in and through various forms of representation, then what are these forms?

In the context of today we can see a similar attempt by many corporations to instigate rituals and traditions which can be perceived, in a modernist form, as surface symbols of a deeply held system of collective ideas or, in a postmodernist form, as the processes by which belief in a set of deeply held ideas is actually constructed in and through the representation, the performance. If the culture is deeply imprinted upon the minds of the population then the cessation of such rituals will do little to weaken the culture, since they are merely the epiphenomenal and spontaneous form of deeply held beliefs. But if the outward manifestations are the processes through which belief systems are created and reproduced, then the removal of such rituals will undermine the belief in a collective identity. I assume that arguing that culture exists only in and through its representation does not imply that any particular form of representation is more valid than any other, though I accept that some forms of representation are taken to be more valid than others.

The models of culture adopted all assume a set of institutional and organizational frameworks, rituals and processes, but it is not assumed that cultural identity flows mechanically from the material processes, since all such processes require interpretation: the Trooping of the Colour does not reflect the homogeneous thing called English or British culture, first, because it is not clear that such a thing exists, and second, because what the ritual means will depend upon who is doing the interpreting – there are many in Northern Ireland for whom such a ritual embodies contradictory meanings: liberty or tyranny. Ultimately, then, culture is important not just because it is epistemologically dubious to separate its examination from the method used to examine it, and not just because it is always practically entwined with technology. Rather, culture is important because it is through culture that the separation between the human and the non-human occurs. Hence, some cultures do not separate human from non-human in the way that Western culture generally has done since the Enlightenment. The issue is not so much that we should not separate culture from nature, human from non-human, the social from the technical, but that we examine the consequences of cultures that do.

If, then, we (re)consider culture as a heterogeneous discursive practice, in which language and practice, people and things, are essentially and necessarily conflated, then we get a rather different picture of culture from the one provided by those writing in the organizational culture school discussed above. The culture of an organization now becomes manifest as a contingently successful representation of a web of significance. In effect, this means that what counts as the organizational culture requires constant reproduction and is subject to possible change, radical or revisionist. However, if culture is also considered holistically then perhaps this gives us the clue as to why culture change is so difficult. If culture pervades an organization and predisposes its inhabitants to represent the world in certain ways then minor incursions into that world are likely to fall beneath the onslaught of the traditional culture: common sense. However, where the entire culture is subject to doubt then the conventional resources which predispose people to resist change are subject to radical doubt and become severely weakened. For example, if an attempt to change the culture of a traditional manufacturing plant starts from the premise that declining profitability means that overtime will no longer be considered the 'norm', but the 'normal' bonuses to the chief executive are maintained irrespective of the same decline in profitability, then there is likely to be considerable resistance as workers utilize their representation of organizational culture as a resource for resistance: 'This is another example of the "them and us" that this company has adopted for years, and we will not be made the scapegoat for economic failure.' On the other hand, if we assume the holistic approach we might argue that only a total and radical transformation at all levels is going to succeed in persuading people to change. Thus, for example, we might see the end of overtime, the end of executive bonuses, a fairer distribution of whatever profits are eventually secured and so on, as the alternative to economic catastrophe. In sum, the network of webs that sustain an organization implies that sustaining and changing cultures is problematic if only part of the network is mobilized and if managers think that organizations and their cultures speak for, or represent, themselves. Waiting for organizations to represent themselves is a bit like waiting for the lottery win to arrive: it is not a good practice to hold one's breath.

Conclusion

This chapter has argued that models of culture are heuristic in intent. That is, they are not necessarily best understood as attempts to *describe* a particular form of culture but might be better utilized to develop ways of *interpreting* culture. If the models facilitate ways of understanding culture then they can be regarded as valuable. However, two issues should be remembered: first, to argue that the patterning of culture is produced through the representation of the pattern itself, rather than to assume that the pattern merely reflects the culture that is really 'out there', does not mean that patterns are only in the heads of their authors and therefore irrelevant. If the pattern is persuasive then it may act to encourage others to articulate it in the same or a similar way, and this may, in turn, act to ensure the reproduction of the very culture these actors appear to be merely modelling. If, for example, I am persuaded that shop assistants in the USA are much more polite than the equivalent in the UK, then I may 'read' their 'Have a good day' as implying great sincerity. Thus I respond with a sincere 'Thank you, and you too', which generates a further token of concern from the shop assistant. The upshot of the exchange is 'confirmation' to me that the culture of American shop workers leads them to be more polite than the British shop assistants. On the other hand, if I read an account of

American shop assistants that persuades me they are all cynical, and merely repeat the words in line with a robotic stimulus derived from Pavlovian training, then I 'read' the words along these lines and have my suspicions of cynicism confirmed. In short, it is I who 'create' the culture of American shop assistants through 'reading' various accounts; it does not lie in American shops waiting to be grasped by the shopper. A pattern of understanding is imposed upon the utterances; it does not lie within them. This, of course, is also the reason that irony and sarcasm so often 'fail' – because they are understood in a literal fashion and not in the way intended by the speaker. As generations of students will have discovered, the words 'quite good' or 'not bad' at the end of an essay can be read in an infinite number of ways: 'quite good' given the terribly difficult question, or 'quite good' in comparison to your last terrible essay, or 'quite good' given that I know you put no work into this, and so on. As one unconsciously ironic English participant at an international management conference put it: 'In the USA the word "quite" means "very", but in England the word "quite" means . . . well "quite".'

The second point of the models is to note how each one attempts to channel one's thoughts in particular ways. Thus a model which stresses boundary construction attempts to strip out all the complex issues of the debate and retain only those relevant to the model. It then tries to persuade us not that this is just a heuristic model – and that it is merely one among many – but that it is the most appropriate way of considering the issues. Hence what starts out, in Weber's terms, as an 'ideal' model, in the sense of being the author's 'ideal' for a particular and limited intellectual purpose, ends up being an 'ideal' model in the sense of perfection, for a universal explanation of the material.

Which model is the most appropriate thus depends as much on the reader as on the writer – or at least that's what postmodernist cultures would have us believe.

8

Managing Gender Inequality through Technology

Introduction

This chapter (originally written with Steve Woolgar: see acknowledgements for references) is concerned with exploring the relationship between gender, gender inequality and technology. It is not an attempt to document in any detail the current situation facing women managers – there are already many accounts of this, the so-called 'glass ceiling', which appears to inhibit the rise of most women through the ranks of most organizations (see the special edition of *Human Relations*, Vol. 47, No. 6, 1994; Hantrais and Walters, 1994; Coe, 1992; Maguire and Kleiner, 1993; Aitkenhead and Liff, 1990; Davidson and Cooper, 1992; Purcell, 1990; R. M. Kelly, 1991; Morrison et al., 1987; Lam, 1992; Sekaran and Leong, 1992; Walby, 1986; B. White et al., 1992; Mills and Tancred, 1992; Van Nostrand, 1993; McLoughlin, 1992; Grint, 1991). Instead, this chapter will seek to advance the theoretical issues raised in the previous chapters by posing them against a background of two particularly complex areas: technology and gender. Technology is complex in the sense that it appears, at first sight, to be impervious to the kinds of theoretical criticism and analysis that have been deployed so far; I shall seek to cast doubt on this. Gender is complex in a rather different way: it appears, perhaps, less impervious to the constructivist approach than technology seems to be, but the prescriptive and moral implications of considering it in this way are controversial. What particularly intrigues me here is the way that technology can be considered not as having direct effects upon women but as *managed* in such a way that it appears to have these effects. In other words, this chapter concerns the use of technology as a rhetorical resource by managers (men and women), amongst others, in furtherance of, or in resistance to, gender equality.

The emphasis here lies on the theoretical analysis of technology rather than of particular equal opportunities policies, because the existing accounts appear to be heavily biased in the other direction. In short, there is no end of prescriptive accounts for those seeking to advance equal opportunities at work, but there are precious few which consider the way an analysis of technology can provide further insight into the relationship between inequality and technology, and throw some necessary cold water on some explanations of, and prescriptions for, gender equality. In particular, this chapter is aimed at provoking the reader to consider the extent to which we take for granted what technology is, what it does and what its effects are. If the reader is persuaded that we should be rather more sanguine about technological solutions to inequality or even technologically oriented causal explanations of gender inequality then, *a fortiori*, she or he might ponder the way we often generate causal explanations of inequality that rely on allegedly less robust phenomena, like people. For example, Callon's (1986) account of the relationship between French fishermen and their catch – scallops – talks about the scallops in terms of their 'interests'. Many readers might recoil at this approach, since it imputes all kinds of things to non-human creatures that we have traditionally regarded as beyond such reasoning. Whatever one feels about this with regard to the scallops, the significant point for this chapter is that it should alert us to the way we often impute interests to other human groups in an extraordinarily cavalier way. Thus we often appear to explain the causal factors behind a woman manager's action on the basis of wafer-thin assumptions about the determining effects of her gender or class or ethnicity, with hardly a shred of evidence and even less reflexive concern for our own part in the construction of others' interests and a causal explanation of their behaviour. The relationship between technology and gender is important, then, both because it is often regarded as a significant element in and of itself in the continuing patterns of inequality that prevail at work, and, moreover, because the way that we analyse technology may be illuminating in any attempt to account for the persistence or decline of gender inequality. If we should be rather more wary of technology as a determining factor in unequal opportunities, perhaps we might also reconsider other, non-technical, explanations.

One of the main reasons often given for the unequal opportunities that appear to prevail at work, especially within the ranks of management, is the different relationship that prevails between the genders and technology (see Grint and Gill, 1995). Women are often held to be absent from, or remain at the lower managerial levels within, manufacturing industry because of their alleged antipathy to technology or because much technology is essentially masculine in origin and/or use. Hence, only when there are women directly involved in the design and use of work technologies will the proportion of women managers rise. Similarly, only when there are more women engineers and scientists will there be sufficient role models to encourage younger women to enter such professions and begin to break down the brick and electrical ceilings that seem to be a major mechanism for ensuring male exclusivity. It follows that once women have secured access to such knowledge they will secure access to the social networks that men use to keep women out of the executive offices and the boardroom. Although by no means the only key to the 'men's club', as Coe (1992) calls the patriarchal domination of management, technology does appear as more intransigent than many other issues: legislation can be rewritten and education reconstructed, but how can we rebuild all our technology? Is this more like a Weberian ferric cage than a glass ceiling? Glass may, after all, be cracked but metals appear to be altogether harder and less brittle. This chapter, then, is concerned with the extent to which constructivist and feminist analyses of technology may be a wedge that, in theory at least, may prise open the door to the men's club just a little more.

Determinism and beyond

For the sake of clarity, two main kinds of approach to technology can be distinguished. First, a traditional approach is based on an acceptance of one or other statement of the technical capabilities of technology. This view accepts that there may be disagreements and ambiguities as to what precisely the technical capacity of any artefact or system is, but holds to the view that some objective view of technical capacity is in principle available. In this perspective, technical capacity is viewed as inherent to the technology (artefact or system). For this reason this perspective will be referred to as *essentialist*: technical attributes derive from the internal characteristics of the technology. Moreover, these internal characteristics are (often) supposed to have resulted from the application of scientific method or from the linear extrapolation and/or development of previous technologies. This first perspective has been roundly criticized on several counts, most notably that it limits its discussion of 'the social' dimension to the effects of technological capacity.

The second, alternative approach is referred to as *anti-essentialist*. This encompasses a broad church of perspectives, including 'social shaping' (for example, MacKenzie, 1990), 'social construction of technology' (for example, Bijker et al., 1987; Bijker and Law, 1992), and what has been called 'designer technology' (cf. Grint and Woolgar, 1995b). These otherwise different approaches share the view that the nature, form and capacity of a technology are the upshot of various antecedent circumstances involved in its development (mainly taken to include design, manufacture and production). These circumstances are said to be 'built into' and/or 'embodied in' the final product; the resulting technology is 'congealed social relations' or 'society made durable'. Differences between anti-essentialists turn on the specific choice of antecedent circumstances – between, for example, 'social interests', the 'solutions sought by relevant social groups', and 'social structure and the distribution of power'. Although anti-essentialism is characterized by some heated internal disputes, all parties share the aim of specifying the effects of these circumstances upon technological capacity.

The anti-essentialist move has enormous policy implications for technology design, development and use, and this in turn has potentially important ramifications for securing gender equality amongst management. It is therefore important to note from the outset that three key features of the anti-essentialist approach threaten to compromise its radical potential. The first is the ambivalence associated with the idea of antecedent circumstances being 'built in'. The second is the difficulty in specifying the nature of these 'antecedent circumstances'. The third stems from the view that technologies, albeit those at the end of a cycle of embodying antecedent circumstances – the final, stabilized technological products – are still capable of having effects; that is effects which do not require interpretative action but speak for themselves. In the rest of this section these three features of anti-essentialist argument are shown to carry forward elements of the essentialism which they purport to criticize. Their occurrence in explicitly feminist approaches to the problem is considered later.

The first disadvantage of the metaphor of 'embodying' antecedent circumstances or having them 'built in' is that it implies the possibility that a technology can be neutral until such time as political or social values are ascribed or attributed to it. The problem here is that this view distinguishes between 'the object in itself', an objective and apolitical phenomenon, and the subsequent (?) acquisition of social and political veneer. The assumption is that objective accounts of a technology are what is left when the evaluative veneers are stripped away from the essential object. By contrast, the argument of the more thoroughgoing 'constitutive' variants of anti-essentialism is that it makes no sense to suppose that such an apolitical object could exist independent of evaluative veneers; it exists only in and through our descriptions and practices, and hence is never available in a raw, untainted state. This is not an ontological claim – that nothing exists outside of our construction of it – but rather an insistence on the thoroughness with which the technical is intertwined with the social. For example, if manufacturing technology has masculine characteristics built into it during the design or construction stage then, presumably, there was a point in time when the technology was gender-neutral; but when was this, and what does such technology look like? More significantly, who says it was neutral but is now masculine?

Essentialism remains evident in accounts of anti-essentialism which speak in terms of the technology having politics *attached* to it. Again the implication is that values, politics and the rest are, in principle, separable from the social relationships that generate them. The same problem occurs in some symbolic interactionist accounts of language, which, bizarrely, speak of items having meaning 'attached to them'. A more careful attempt to express the sentiments of thoroughgoing anti-essentialism might be to say that technology has politics (or whatever) *inscribed in it* in the very process of its construction, deployment and consumption. Yet even this variant carries essentialist overtones: what, we might ask, is the 'it' into which politics are being inscribed? In varying degrees, the same problem arises in other formulations: technology has been variously said 'to be affected by' 'social factors', or to have these 'social factors' 'built into' or 'embodied by' it.

A further problem with the embodiment metaphor is that its usage often presupposes the unproblematic character of what exactly is being built in. That is, attributes like interests and political values are assumed to be straightforwardly available to the analyst. The problem here is that this ignores the active interpretative work that goes into rendering motives as, say, social interests (Woolgar, 1981). In other words, the initial description and specification of antecedent circumstances, let alone their explication as causes of the design and shaping of technology, are part and parcel of the reading and interpretation of technologies. The same argument also applies to particular forms of equal opportunity policy: if they 'fail' does this mean that the failure was the result of antecedent patriarchal interests?

Some of the more sophisticated writing in this area recognizes the difficulty of treating features such as motive, interest, values and so on as objectively available *explanantes*. For example, van Zoonen comes close to this when she points out that 'gender can be thought of as a particular discourse ... a set of overlapping and often contradictory cultural descriptions and prescriptions ... not as a fixed property of individuals but as part of the ongoing disciplining process by which subjects are constituted' (1992: 20). The implication is that we should at least be extremely cautious in saying that technologies 'are gendered' precisely on account of the interpretative flexibility of the precept. Although van Zoonen begins to develop this, she still tends to reserve a realm of 'non-discursive elements' (1992: 26) and to talk of the way in which (in this case, new information and communication) technologies do not in themselves exclude women; instead, women are excluded by certain forms of discourse which she conceives of as 'surrounding' the technology. If, however, discourse constitutes the object then the implied division between discourse and object once again suggests the possibility of a discourse-free (neutral) technology.

A similar difficulty presents itself with regard to the aspect of anti-essentialist arguments which unproblematically accepts that technologies can have effects. Much anti-essentialist argument is pitched as a critique of technological determinism. However, it transpires that this is not a total denial of determinism, because the effects of technologies are alleged to be complex, its uses to be unpredictable, and, in particular, these effects do not stem from the inherent, that is unmediated and non-interpreted, technical characteristics of the technology in question. This form of anti-essentialism turns out to be an attempt to supplant technical determinism with social and political determinisms; it is the politics built into a technology which become the origin of 'effects'. The object of critique is *technological* determinism, not technological *determinism*.

This suggests that while anti-essentialist approaches help problematize the idea that we can ever have a neutral technology, they remain committed to a form of essentialism. This is particularly evident, for example, when a political-design argument of the kind offered by Winner (1985) concludes that political values are actually built into the artefact. The difficulty here is that a thoroughgoing critique of essentialism would insist that values (in this case 'politics') are imputed to an artefact in the course of their apprehension, description and use – which of course includes imputations at the hand of the historian of science and/or technology. Unfortunately, the political-design critique of essentialism ends up merely substituting one form of essentialism (that technologies are actually neutral) with another (that technologies are actually political).

Let us now examine the extent to which the same problems recur in some recent feminist arguments about technology and the role it plays in maintaining patriarchal dominance at work.

Feminism and technology

The tradition of associating technology and science – allegedly the twin arenas of reason and logic – with men goes back at least as far as the Enlightenment. This intellectual movement appeared, in its own terms at least, to throw light on all manner of irrationalities and unreasoning, but in terms of reflexive enlightenment on the role of patriarchy it appears to have been a miserable failure. Even if Voltaire worked with Madame du Châtelet, and Diderot with Sophie Holland, even if the French *salon* itself was the invention of the Marquise de Rambouillet in 1623 and was intended for women as well as men to facilitate intellectual exchange, the Enlightenment was never a vehicle for sexual equality (B. S. Anderson and Zinsser, 1990). Instead, women became associated with reflecting nature, and displaying emotion, with irrationality and subjectivity; men with their opposites: controlling and exploiting not reflecting nature, reason, logic and objectivity (McNeil, 1987; Harding, 1986). In revolutionary France a short-term consequence of the 'forced separation' between women and rationality was the banishing of women from the public institutions of power; a long-term consequence throughout the world has been the virtual monopolization of science and technology by men.

While many feminists have explicitly rejected this opposition between rationality and women, one variant has emerged, sometimes labelled eco-feminism, which celebrates rather than denigrates these allegedly innate differences. A development of this approach has been one which is consistent with the notion of political technology but uses this as a fundamentalist stepping stone to women's liberation from 'male' technology. Since, in this view, all technologies are carriers of their designers' intentions, it follows that many technologies are male (Cooley, 1968: 42–4) and this becomes manifest in the cultural attributes associated with working in, or studying, engineering (cf. Sorenson, 1992). As Hacker notes from her interviews with men from an engineering faculty: 'Status accrued to the masculine world of speed, sophistication, and abstraction rather than the feminine world of nature and people' (Hacker, 1989: 35–6). The consequence of this kind of reasoning is that women seeking to attain senior management positions are faced with either abandoning their 'true' selves and adopting masculine patterns of behaviour at work or securing promotion in areas that require managers to have feminine characteristics. It is the current wave of analyses that suggest that the most effective way to organize corporations is by attending to the emotional aspects that offer opportunities for this approach (see Fineman, 1993; Roper, 1994).

Military technology is often held to represent the most obvious differences between the ostensibly essential characters of men and women. There are various explanations for why military technology is considered as male, and why men are taken as inherently violent towards women and each other. For Easlea (1983) it stems from male 'womb envy'. His narrative of the nuclear bomb programme describes the scheme as flowing from the excitement of 'conception' through the laborious hours of labour up until the 'birth', manifest in the aptly named 'Little Boy' dropped on Hiroshima, and celebrated by the physicists at Los Alamos in a manner very much akin to that usual for the constructive success of birth rather than the destructive terror of death.

Nuclear technology is a useful example to illustrate some fundamental differences in approaches to technology. Whereas a traditional approach might concede that the design and deployment of nuclear weapons have 'political dimensions', it would probably balk at assumptions that nuclear technology *per se* was inherently masculine and thus, for (some) women at least, in need of replacement. Yet eco-feminism could point both to the immense power derived from nuclear sources and the prerequisite control over, and exploitation of, nature that this implied. Hence, what could be regarded as an inherently aggressive technology could not be harnessed for constructive purposes but must be interred and replaced by 'softer', renewable, green technologies such as wind and wave power. An alternative, but still essentialist, account nominates a particular form of political organization, rather than masculinity, as the essential feature of nuclear power. Thus Winner argues that: 'the atom bomb is an inherently political artifact. As long as it exists at all, its lethal properties demand that it be controlled by a centralized, rigidly hierarchical chain of command' (1985: 32). Here it is the politics of the bomb that have effects upon society.

Whether these effects are necessarily masculine or hierarchically non-gendered is, for our purposes, largely beside the point. It may well be that the controllers of the bomb provide accounts of its technical capacity which are used to persuade the public at large that a 'rigidly hierarchical chain of command' is essential. However, this does not entitle one to claim that the technology, in and through itself, demands such an organizational form or that such a form is masculine in structure. If some women's organizations themselves develop 'a rigidly hierarchical chain of command', does this mean they are doing so because they too are coerced by a political technology or by a masculine technology? In either case this poses problems in trying to explain some counter-examples. For instance, some religious orders of Christian nuns are both female and hierarchical. Of course, one might then want to consider the patriarchal culture of Christianity – but this is a cultural argument, not one grounded in the capacities and effects of technologies.

A further difficulty with the essentialist framework of eco-feminism, and one that also problematizes many of the psychoanalytic accounts, is that they tend to ground their arguments in notions of masculinity and femininity which are simultaneously inherent and permanent. Thus, whatever forms of action are deployed by men and women are ultimately derived from the 'natural' nature of each sex. But as Wajcman argues:

> The first thing that must be said is that the values being ascribed to women originate in the historical subordination of women. ... It is important to see how women came to value nurturance and how nurturance, associated with motherhood, came to be culturally defined as feminine within male-dominated culture ... Secondly, the idea of 'nature' is itself culturally constructed. Conceptions of the 'natural' have changed radically through-out human history. (1991: 9)

The implications of this account are particularly significant for those seeking to develop what might be called feminist technologies. If what counts as feminine and masculine are cultural attributes, subject to challenge and change, then replacing 'masculine' technologies with 'feminine' technologies leads to the question of what precisely is to count as 'feminine technology' (and who decides). Are all feminists the same? Unless they are, changes to the technology will not resolve the problem of asymmetric control over it. Would one expect the deployment and consumption of technologies in offices without men to be perfectly equal between their female members? Again, this does not mean that any 'residual' inequalities would undermine the quest to construct a culture in which technology was not interpreted and deployed by men against women, but it does imply that essentialist accounts of women – and men – remain deeply problematic.

Two further examples will suffice to illustrate this point. According to M. Roberts (1979), the replacement of the light, single-handed sickle by the heavy, double-handed scythe was, along with steam-powered machinery, crucial in the decline of women's agricultural employment during the industrial revolution. Since the new technology (the scythe) was more efficient, but required strength and skill beyond the capacity of women, the technology was crucial in the assertion of a male monopoly over crop cutting – one of the most highly paid jobs. Was the technology designed with this in mind? Or, whatever the designers' intention, was the objective effect of the technology to masculinize crop cutting? Unfortunately the intentions of the designer seem to be lost in time; which means, of course, that no historian has (yet) done the constructivist work to (re)constitute these intentions. (See Stanley (1992) for some artefacts designed by women that have been 'rediscovered'.) But whatever they were, we might want to remain sceptical of such determinist accounts on at least two counts. First, if the new technology did require greater strength and skill one might expect to see fewer women rather than none at all after its introduction – assuming that although most women are physically weaker than men, some women are stronger than some men (that strength is an attribute which can be enhanced through practices which are themselves gendered is not explored here). Secondly, as late as 1921 there were male-only farm gangs which still retained sickles cutting crops (*Guardian*, 20 May 1991). What does this imply? That the 'inherently' male scythe was also too heavy for men? Or that only a female sickle would have allowed women to remain as crop cutters? Clearly, neither of these alternatives makes sense of the persistence of the sickle in male-only agricultural gangs. We are thus led to seek explanations which, for example, concentrate on the patriarchal culture, including legal restraints on female labour, within which such technologies existed. The battle for access to relatively lucrative farming jobs was won not as a direct result of a specifically male technology but through the successful deployment of accounts of the technology that purported to 'prove' its necessarily male requirements, and through the recruitment of allies, such as the law banning women from gang labour. The readoption of the sickle did not facilitate the return of women to crop cutting; if the essentialist models of technology were correct, then it should have done.

The second, and similar, example relates to the British Post Office in the 1930s. There were, at the time, no urban postwomen or any full-time postwomen anywhere. They were not recruited as full-timers or in urban areas, officially because they could not physically carry the normal load. However, women were employed as part-time rural deliverers (with the same carrying requirements!), not because of the atypically strong physique of rural women, nor even because of the atypically weak physique of rural men, but because, as one manager admitted: 'no man can be obtained to perform the work' (Post Office, 1930: 6033). In terms of technology, it seems, even the British Post Office was subject to the rigours of relativism.

The process of displacing women at work through new technology has, of course, a very long history and not one that will be covered here (McNeil, 1987; Wajcman, 1991; Ehrenreich and English, 1979; Green et al., 1993). However, one of the crucial arguments often deployed to account for the predominance of men within the hierarchy of the medical profession, for example – besides the issue of technology – is the relative longevity of the occupation itself: through time men have managed to increase their control over medicine and displace the earlier influence of 'wise women' in an incremental way. This is especially significant where technology is introduced by men and used to oust women – obstetric forceps being perhaps the best-documented case (see Faulkner and Arnold, 1985). There are several accounts of the relationships between gender and new technology in the form of word processors, and these tend to highlight the confirmation or even exacerbation of existing inequalities (Barker and Downing, 1980; J. Webster, 1990). But what happens where a new technology is not introduced to an existing occupation but allegedly becomes the basis for a new occupation – in this case computing? This will form part of the argument in the next section.

Pink computers

Between essentialist and anti-essentialist perspectives there is clearly a multitude of overlapping positions. The difficulty seems to be in sustaining a (post-essentialist) position which remains deeply critical of all kinds of essentialist notion, whether they relate to humans or to non-humans: whether men and women have inherently and objectively different natures and interests or whether technology has inherent and objective capacities. That there are feminist approaches which are compatible with both essentialism and anti-essentialism is a manifestation of the flexible nature of feminism as much as anything. However, in the debate about patriarchy, the crucial point is not to reject the policy implications of these diverse accounts but to remain sceptical of the theoretical premises from which policies may flow.

A perspective which asserted that the problem for women seeking advancement through the management hierarchy was that (almost) all forms of technology were essentially masculine, for instance, implies a requirement for a feminine technology. But since what counts as masculine and feminine is culturally and historically variable, it is not clear what such an alternative would look like. The counter to this tends to focus on a technology which does indeed appear invariant in space and time; military technology, or just weapons, for example, have always been seen as 'masculine'. Yet knives, for instance, have been used for a whole variety of purposes other than wounding or killing others and there is considerable evidence that women would – if 'masculine regulations', or at least a powerful masculine culture, would allow them – become involved in all forms of military endeavour from the infantry through to flying combat aircraft in war (Dixon, 1979; Shields, 1988; Moskos, 1990; Wheelwright, 1992). For the post-essentialist, what counts as a feminine technology lies in the interpretation, not in the technology itself, since our apprehension of what the technology *is* requires that very interpretative effort.

This is not to say that technology constructed by women and consensually defined as feminine would be irrelevant to the undermining of patriarchy. If the significance of technology lies in the interpretation not the technology, then a radically feminist interpretation may well have some influence in the policy arena. For example, one of the apparent blocks to women's promotion through the managerial hierarchy is their relative lack of computer skills. A response might be to construct a computer, destined for use in schools, defined as 'girl-friendly' to dissuade boys from attempting to monopolize it and provide greater opportunities for girls to acquire high levels of computer literacy. In the long run this, in turn, might provide cohorts of computer-literate women who no longer faced the barrier of technological ignorance as a reason for their exclusion from senior management positions. (Since there appear, in my experience at least, to be very few male executives who are computer literate I am not convinced that this is a persuasive reason, but it is regularly trotted out none the less).

Let us play the devil's advocate a little more and paint this girl-friendly computer pink. The point is that potential changes in use now appear to result from a different apprehension of the computer's gender, rather than from an intrinsically 'female computer'. Does painting something pink make the technology feminine or our apprehension of its 'appropriate' gender one associated with femininity? The essentialist approach, notwithstanding the problem of identifying masculinity and femininity as stable entities when they appear not to be, would be undermined if the official (girl-friendly) interpretation of the computer was challenged by boys whose counter-interpretation invested the computer with neutral, androgynous or masculine traits. If the technology is *essentially* one thing, how can it be challenged? And, *if* it is, what kind of official response would satisfy the (male) critics? Other than descending into a 'yes it is – no it isn't' exchange, the essentialist position does not leave much room for manoeuvre. Moreover, by asserting that such technologies are essentially feminine – and by implication that most of the others are masculine – that leaves most technology under 'legitimate' male control.

The post-essentialist approach, on the other hand (or the approach in the pink *and* the blue corner, just to continue the chromatic analogy), is not to cede legitimacy to male control over non-pink computers by default but to suggest that, where male control exists, the legitimacy claims are themselves up for renegotiation – if an alliance of sufficiently powerful forces can be constructed. This, of course, means that pink computers are not inherently feminine. In sum, it *does* matter what the initial theoretical line is, because the essentialist position takes so much of the current technology as essentially masculine and therefore beyond the remit of women. For essentialists the colour of the computer is crucial; for post-essentialists what counts is which colours are constructed as masculine and feminine and how this contingent association can be utilized, decried or changed.

The anti-essentialist liberal feminist approach might not be concerned with computer colours, since the problem is deemed to lie not in the technology but in the unequal opportunities which deter girls and women from engaging with computers. As Kreinberg and Stage recount, with regard to US examples: 'The biggest barriers to women taking advantage of the computer revolution are the myths and stereotypes about technology that are well established in children's minds at a very early age ... Changes must take place in schools and outside of schools so that women will have equal access to computer technology' (1983: 28). Thus, we are more likely to see support for female pupils and students expressed in a variety of ways: advertising campaigns, more resources, stronger targeting of female pupils and students, 'awareness' campaigns and, perhaps, some provision for girl- or women-only computer and IT courses. Since this form of approach does not attribute the technology with any particular gender or gender-related capabilities, the constructivist might have some theoretical empathy with it, but liberal models do tend to assume that the technology is neutral, that is beyond the interpretative construction of the user. In effect, for the liberal, technology cannot be the problem and it is far more likely that the problem lies in women's 'failure' to realize their own potential (see Cockburn (1991) and Kvande and Rasmussen (1986) on women's alleged 'failure' in organizations). It may or may not be coincidental that the great majority of such liberal policies appear, at least so far, to have been abject failures. It is precisely because this perspective refuses to countenance the possibility that what we take to be the same technology is apprehended in radically different ways by different people that it will, in all probability, continue to fail. If the problem is that we see technology differently then no amount of lens cleaning will help – we need to recognize that people are using different lenses rather than assume that some are wearing smudged glasses.

Just how non-essentialist and liberal is such a perspective? If the essentialist model is one where the 'essence' of a phenomenon explains its behaviour or action, then although the liberal model rejects the idea that technology is distorted through its male origins it nevertheless implies that all humans, regardless of sex, have an essence. Admittedly, in the case of women, this essence is distorted through the gendered inequalities that persist, but once equal opportunities are deployed then the true and equal essence of men and women will prevail. In effect both liberal feminist and eco-feminist positions have at their heart a similar essentialist position.

Deus ex machina or machina ex dea?

The term *deus ex machina* is drawn from the world of theatre (appropriately enough, an arena replete with rhetoric, performance, persuasive accounts, irony and the rest) and describes a mechanical device from which, when it was drawn up over or on the stage, an actress or actor in the role of a goddess or god was deposited, usually to unravel a complicated plot (see Grint and Woolgar (1995b) for a longer review of this). The symbolic nature of a divine spirit being encased within a machine represents a typical response by many people to technology itself; indeed, the Enlightenment was, and modernism is, very much a movement bound tightly to the idea of freedom through reason, a reason often manifest as technology.

For the most part anti-essentialism takes issue with the identity of the god (or whatever entity) in the machine, rather than questioning the very idea that there is 'something' 'in there' in the first place. Anti-essentialists are busy trying to replace the god of technical rationality with the god of social and political interests; or, in the case of (some) feminists, with the god of gender bias. But theirs is still fundamentally a religious endeavour: this god rather than that one. By contrast, post-essentialism asks what it would take to challenge the existence of (any) god. It aspires to reject the essentialist notion of gods or goddesses in machines. The appearance of a deity within the machinery has to be understood as more akin to a mirror of human hopes and fears than to anything else.

In many ways, post-essentialism is another human hope rather than a definitive solution: it is a position to which one aspires rather than one that has been attained. One of the main reasons for the difficulty is that we are, of course, prisoners of the conventions of language and representation which display, reaffirm and sustain the basic premises of essentialism: that entities of all kinds, but most visibly and consequentially technical artefacts and technological systems, possess characteristics and capacities, and are capable of 'effects'. This seems to be a fundamental property of the objectivist language game in which we are all embroiled. It follows that a radical move away from essentialism, attempted but not achieved by many anti-essentialists, requires nothing short of a major reworking of the categories and conventions of conventional language use (cf. Haraway, 1991). Attempts to expose 'the actual' politics, social interests, gender biases etc. are liberating and inspiring, and certainly they are an improvement on traditionalist treatments of the topic. But in the end they are merely moves within the same essentialist language game. The especially dangerous temptation is to get wound up in disputes about whether one or another category of antecedent circumstances is the more appropriate essence of the machine. The problem, then, with most forms of anti-essentialism including anti-essentialist feminism, is that they are insufficiently anti-essentialist. Anti-essentialism fails to transcend essentialism in the way that post-essentialism aspires to. Anti-essentialists seem unable or unwilling to take the (difficult) step towards post-essentialism, which will turn their limited insinuations of antecedent circumstances into a radical critique of technology.

One reason is that post-essentialism (and in the context of disputes for the political and moral high ground, post-just about everything else) is regarded as simply beyond the pale. It is viewed as an extreme form of relativism which represents a distraction from the urgent demands of political action. The point is that the failings identified in constructivism arise not because it goes epistemologically 'over the top', but precisely because it equivocates in its efforts to escape essentialism.

Fox Keller (1988) and other anti-essentialists, like Kling (1992) and Winner (1993), consider that such 'excessive' relativism implies a rejection of the possibility of establishing 'the truth' about technology or science or anything else. They might claim that, in a discussion about bicycle tyres (Pinch and Bijker, 1989), this is all well and good: such debates can throw critical light on historical processes with little fear of moral or ethical contention. But when it comes to an issue like patriarchy, they would say, relativism is the font of moral compromise. Kirkup and Smith Keller (1992) put the point forcefully:

> epistemological relativism ... suggests that there are as many truths as individual people and that no single truth has any claim to be better than any other ... As a position it runs counter not only to the aims of science, but to those of feminism of the 1970s and '80s. Feminism as a theory and a political movement claims that there are 'facts' and 'realities' about the position of women, such as rape, domestic violence and unequal pay, that are a key to understanding sexual oppression, and that these have been hidden or distorted ... science and feminism have similar agendas in that they are both concerned to remedy distortion and move closer towards a more accurate description of how things are. (1992: 10)

There are three issues here. First is whether knowledge reflects or constructs the truth – and this book is premised firmly on the latter. Second is whether the denial of a single reflective and objective truth hides the 'realities' of women's position. The irony here is that constructivists are precisely concerned to support alternative truth claims rather than necessarily siding with prevailing ones. What constructivists might add to the debate here would be a critical analysis of patriarchal claims to 'truth' – without automatically supporting the claims of feminists to be in possession of the alternative but truly 'real' truth. After all, do all feminists claim to support the same interpretation of patriarchy? If not, then, under a realist approach, we are still left with having to assert that some feminists are in possession of the truth and others not. If, as has frequently happened, those who take such an approach are accused of siding with the powerful in such disputes, then presumably they would be guilty of siding with the powerful feminists, against the weak feminists so that we are still no nearer 'the truth'. The third issue, the related assertion that constructivism surrounds itself with contending claims to truth between which it has no means of discriminating is, however, misinformed. The constructivist does not assert that all claims have equal status but, instead, asks which claims attract the most significant support and why is this so?

Take the example of sexual harassment (by men of women) as a means by which male managers retain control over the men's club. Kirkup and Smith Keller's essentialist view is that feminism, like 'science', is (and should be) intent on uncovering 'the truth' about issues like sexual harassment, a truth allegedly hidden from view by patriarchal distortion. This approach implies that research can 'discover' the truth and that this discovery will lead, eventually at least, to mechanisms which prevent it. The charge against constructivism is that its denial of objective truth either allows its adherents to sit on the fence and procrastinate about truth claims while women are sexually harassed or, worse, actually sanctions sexual harassment by accepting the proposition that 'the truth' is that form of discourse which is the one most successfully deployed at the time. The latter charge is simply wrong: assessing the strength of a truth claim through an analysis of its social construction is not the equivalent of supporting that claim.

The former charge is more complex. Constructivism does leave one bereft of the certainties that might propel a political fanatic or religious fundamentalist; for these people the truth is self-evident and the line of action follows directly from such truth. For the constructivist there may, of course, be a pragmatic legitimation of action – 'Doubts about truth claims are fine for the university seminar but too dangerous for the real world', is the typical response here. Does this mean there is a clear limit to the application of Kant's injunction *sapere aude* (dare to know)? Acquiescence to the politics of the 'real world', to which we are enjoined by critics of relativism, implies not just a pragmatic boundary but an epistemological, and ultimately political, flaw. Certainly Kling (1992) and Winner (1993) have attacked constructivists for being politically naive and implicitly conservative.

Elam (1994) develops one form of liberal defence on behalf of (rather than in support of) relativism, using Rorty's (1989) distinction between a liberal 'ironicist' and a liberal 'metaphysician'. The ironicist accepts truth as contingent and refuses to privilege her or his own position over that of others, since this privileging is both dubious and potentially humiliating for those who believe otherwise. Liberal metaphysicians, and we can include Kling and Winner here, strive to coerce 'ironicists' into taking sides on moral issues, and castigate them for refusing to do so. According to Elam, ironicists argue that taking sides involves inflicting cruelty on the 'other' side for refusing to accede to one's own opinion. In Elam's words: 'because we can only ever know *differently* and never *better* than anyone else, we are never justified in thrusting our knowledge upon others' (1994: 104, emphasis in the original). Elam concludes with a liberal (though ultimately sceptical) defence of the ironicist's 'freedom to speak' and a positive evaluation of its utility in the face of those 'metaphysicians' who claim to have seen the truth and who demand that the rest of us follow suit (or risk, at best, the charge of not being politically correct). However, Elam, like Kirkup and Smith Keller (1992), still persists in assuming that constructivism remains a neutral – or perhaps uncommitted and hence untrustworthy – voyeur at the scene of a crime. In Orwellian terms: because constructivists remain sceptical of truth claims, all truth claims are equal. For anti-constructivists the result is that constructivists, albeit by default, allow the strong to remain strong and the weak to suffer: in this context, for men to remain in control. Yet, as suggested above, the constructivist approach does not necessarily adhere to the early and naive prescripts of *Animal Farm* – that all truths (animals) are equal – but rather to the more sceptical later prescript – that some truths (animals) are more equal than others. Anyway, why should constructivists not engage in political debate and action? The recognition of contingency in truth claims does not necessarily lead to self-inflicted inaction but merely to (more) reflexive action.

An ironicist's strategy in the seminar room may be fine, but what happens when the ironicist's potential target is not a student who needs encouraging but a male manager accused of sexually harassing a female manager? Is this the point where constructivists' scepticism buttresses the violence of the strong against the weak? That a woman's claim to have been harassed by a man can be considered as a construction of the truth is not the equivalent of relegating such claims to the land of fiction: a construction is not a lie; it is the way we construct narratives not the way we deliberately set out to deceive. The point here is why the claims of such women tend to be overridden in a society steeped in patriarchal values. The recognition that the truth is socially constructed facilitates rather than debilitates those who are relatively weak in society. The issue is not that constructivists undertake a self-denying ordinance to keep out of political or social controversies but that their engagement is grounded in a different appreciation of the construction of the world. Thus, in this example, women who claim to have been sexually harassed can utilize, and be supported by, constructivist decon-structions of patriarchal power in the office. For instance, the recog-nition of sexual harassment against women as something which society should not accept is not something that is undermined by the argument that society and its morality are socially constructed; it merely means that the sanction against sexual harassment derives from some form of social agreement and not from either the instructions of a god or the distillation of moral behaviour through a scientific assessment of human nature. Of course, this also means that morality is contingent in time and space – as indeed cultural historians and anthropologists are constantly reminding us. In effect, then, constructivism does not debar its adherents from supporting sexually harassed women against sexually harassing men, but it does provide a different kind of resource and it does require a reflexive monitoring of language and practice that realists or fundamentalists ignore.

Is the contingency of this approach valuable to such women? That is, what can constructivists offer that non-constructivists cannot? First, they can provide a recognition that the ability of male managers to harass female managers sexually does not depend upon distorting 'the truth', hiding reality from their colleagues or society. Endless accounts of work have suggested that women are regularly harassed by men but this does not appear to have inhibited men from continuing to harass women. If the reality which prevails in law courts is patriarchal and not objective, and if the quest for objective reality is of limited utility, then the strategy should be one in which the counter-claim to the truth is sculpted to appeal to the jury and where the patriarchal concept of truth is deconstructed so that doubt falls upon the harasser's story and not the victim's. Indeed, this is precisely what already happens in many court cases: the jury is frequently given two very different versions of the truth and asked to decide which one is most believable. In effect, the judicial system is premised upon conflicting truth claims, but this does not mean that patriarchy always wins – though it might explain why men frequently avoid conviction for alleged attacks upon women. Do we ever really know precisely what happened in any particular trial, or do we simply have to side with the defence or the prosecution and assume that one account is the most likely – the most persuasive construction of the truth? That several people have recently been released from prison in the UK, and had their convictions quashed, suggests that even persuasive constructions of the truth are contingent.

In sum, recognizing the contingent nature of the 'truth' need not immobilize the constructivist, but it may deter her or him from undertaking self-righteous action in pursuit of something which realists would claim is the truth. Thus, it is more likely to encourage scepticism than fanaticism and more likely to encourage liberalism than fascism or communism. Its adherents are more likely to remain unimpressed by claims that women are indeed witches and should be burnt at the stake, and less likely to be found in the ranks of the faithful, engaged in a holy war for the truth against all unbelievers. It is not the kind of philosophy to start revolutions in pursuit of Utopia, but it is the kind which remains unconvinced that burning people is the best way to save their souls, or that there is only one road to heaven and those not on it are going the wrong way and, for their own benefit, should be cleansed of their errors.

In pointing out the essentialist elements of much anti-essentialism, the argument has attempted to demonstrate the latter's inconsistency (thanks to Marianne de Laet for inspiring this section). In many respects, however, the same charge could be made about this argument: in order to specify the faults of anti-essentialism one must specify its 'essential' features; the articulation of the failings entailed in reliance upon the realist language game has itself been couched within the terms of that game. What is the consequence of this observation? One interpretation is that it simply casts doubt on the force of the criticism. Adopting a post-essentialist mode seems to entail doing away with or at least taking issue with the critical attitude. But the other important corollary of essentialism is that it is seen as providing a necessary condition for political import. In other words, criticism can be taken as a token of the 'political' motivations of its perpetrators, whereas non-criticism is all too easily identified with a lack of politics. This raises an important issue, for it makes us realize that realist conventions not only confine us to parameters of essentialist argument, but also commit us to a particular form of politics. The question is, then, whether, and to what extent, an exploration of alternative forms of post-essentialism can define an alternative form of politically relevant enquiry.

Conclusion

Where does this leave our machined deity? Is it a god or a goddess? Does it matter anyway? It has been suggested, against both essentialism and anti-essentialism, that the gender of a technology does not lie encased in the fabric of the material. It is instead the temporary, contingent upshot of ongoing interpretation by designers, sellers and users. The politics and values of technology, in this perspective, result from the gaze of the human; they do not lie in the gauze of the machine. This does not mean that the machine is neutral. Since what it is, what its capacities are and what it represents are social constructions not objective reflections, the machine always appears cooked and never raw. Descriptions of, and practices with, technology – the methods by which we come to know technology – necessarily embody social and political values, but these do not lie within the hard creases or soft folds of the machine. Thus where a goddess or devil appears in machine form it is us that construct this form. The 'truth' of the nuclear bomb appears to combine two diametrically opposite 'truths': it is inescapably a political device, even a masculine machine, destined first to terrorize and then to obliterate the entire human race – it is the god of war; or it is a neutral amalgam of chemicals and metals destined to eliminate the threat of world war – the deity designed to protect the human species. What the thing actually is, even what its exact capabilities and effects are, is not something that any kind of detached, objective or realist analysis seems capable of constructing. What it is depends on who is describing it.

It is not that every account of it is equal; self-evidently the eco-feminist account is not powerful enough to persuade political leaders to abandon the technology completely. But this is precisely why post-essentialism can provide resources for those seeking to change the world rather than just account for it. If Foucault is right that truth and power are intimately intertwined, those seeking to change the world might try strategies to recruit powerful allies rather than assuming that the quest for revealing 'the truth' will, in and through itself, lead to dramatic changes in levels and forms of social inequality. If the deity in the machine is male, if technology in a patriarchal society is essentially masculine, then no amount of reiteration of this point will alter 'reality' – would men really let the key to the men's club slip so easily from their grasp? On the other hand, if the gendered significance of a technology lies in the interpretative framework within which it is constructed, then there is a possibility of deconstructing and subsequently reconstructing the technology. As Prometheus found to his cost, even male gods with magical technologies to empower men can find themselves powerless. But whether the deity in the machine is a god or a goddess or just an actress or actor depends crucially on the active construction managed by the audience, rather than the management of wood, wire and flesh on the stage.

9

Fatalism, Freewill and Control: An Index of Possibilities

Introduction

If, as the previous chapter suggested, there is little that is determined in the world of gender and technology, does this imply that managers are ultimately free to choose any form of action? This chapter concerns the extent to which we are all, indeed, managers of our own fate. Fatalism and freewill are traditionally regarded as quintessentially problematic and irredeemably locked together as mutually irreconcilable opposites. Rather like oppositional magnets, freewill depends upon and yet contradicts fatalism. Fatalism, the assumption that action is predetermined either by the situational conditions or by some transcendental force, makes alternatives unrealizable. Freewill, the assumption that action is free from constraint, is often the repository of liberal pretensions, and something which many people might like to believe in, but such voluntaristic assumptions seem to make unrealizable claims about achieving alternatives – they are alleged to underestimate the force of structural impediments to voluntary action. Typically, fatalism and freewill sit at either end of a continuum that describes the varieties of forms of action. Yet, however much fatalism in particular is decried and derided, it remains an essential element of explanation: from the Greek and Norse fates, via religious philosophies of predestination like Calvinism, through to the notorious 'trench fatalism' of the First World War, and the animist origins of the perennial 'touch wood' declaration against fate, fatalism has remained popular. At the other extreme, the freedom to think otherwise has not just spawned a plethora of 'utopian' novels but ushered in many social and political experiments from which some have benefited and many have suffered.

This chapter does not concern itself with the 'validity' or veracity of either fatalism or freewill but is rather concerned to consider the significance of forms of fatalism and freedom for management control. The chapter is divided into three sections. The first part sets out an index of possible modes of belief about action and argues that fatalism can be usefully divided into three forms, premised upon the temporal divisions of present and future. It argues that certain forms of fatalism are enabling rather than disabling, but others much less so. The fourth form of belief, freewill, paradoxically denies the legitimacy of all the forms of fatalism, since, except in special circumstances, people are free to act in ways other than that required by those allegedly in control of them. The implication of this is that there are always alternative forms of action available to us but we may choose not to undertake these, either because we do not believe the alternative to be available or because we persuade ourselves, or are persuaded by others, that there is, indeed, no alternative.

The second part of the chapter uses the model as a template and expands it by considering it against what is commonly regarded as the most extreme form of human behaviour: the management of war. This form of 'managed violence' is deliberately chosen to illustrate the significance attributed to, and limits of, fatalism as an explanation of human action and inaction in extreme circumstances.

The third section of the chapter then applies the enriched model to the world of management and work and suggests that, again with some minor exceptions, all forms of managerial control require the complicity – if not the articulated support – of those who are being controlled. In most managerial circumstances this appears to be obvious: if employees do not want to comply with managerial control they are legally free to seek work elsewhere. Yet it is a commonplace that people explain their actions by reference to the absence of choice: 'What could I do? I had no option.' By taking some extreme examples, where it does indeed appear that subordinates do not have any choice at all, I want to argue that this is seldom the case, and this has ramifications for those situations that are apparently much less coercive than the extreme ones I shall consider: in effect, if soldiers at the front line are free to choose whether to obey the commands of their officers then civilian employees, in what many would regard as a qualitatively freer situation, are, *a fortiori*, not compelled to accept managerial control. Managerial control is therefore more concerned with *enrolling* subordinates into an active role within their own disciplinary systems than it is with *controlling* them from outside by an externally imposed disciplinary system. In other words, there is no logically discrete boundary between managers and workers which is called 'the disciplinary system' and which is wholly separate from and alien to the workers; instead workers are actively involved in their own subordination.

Fatalism and freedom: theory and origins

Traditionally, fatalism is taken to be the opposite of freewill: it implies a total determination of events. What we do is already prescribed for us and we can only execute these commands but never contradict them. The most popular form of fatalism is probably astrology. By establishing our precise time of birth, and relating this to the configuration of the planets, astrologists claim to be able to predict our future, or at least warn us of potential problems and opportunities that will come our way. Providing we accept our fate, reconfigure our actions to fit into the required pattern of events, and hence submit to external authority, everything will be fine. The conservative implications of this form of behaviour should be clear, as Adorno argued:

> It offers the advantage of veiling all deeper-lying causes of distress and thus promoting acceptance of the given. Moreover, by strengthening the sense of fatality, dependence and obedience, it paralyses the will to change objective conditions in any respect and relegates all worries to a private plane promising a cure-all by the very same compliance which prevents a change of conditions. (Adorno, 1974, quoted in Held, 1980: 99)

Although many will also be familiar with the role of fate in Greek and Norse mythology, it is probably to Max Weber that most sociologically inclined readers will turn originally for an account of fate. Weber, of course, developed his view of the Protestant ethic and the spirit of capitalism (1976) on the basis of Calvinist predestination: the assumption that each person was predestined from birth by God to rise to heaven or sink to hell. Again, the knowledge – or rather the hope – that one was predestined for heaven, and hence a member of the chosen few, the elect, did not necessarily ensure that every action was determined by God. Indeed, Weber argued that such a theology generated unparalleled psychological terror for Calvinists, since they could neither know whether they were amongst the elect nor do anything about it. This fatalistic essence might logically have been interpreted as implying that everyone might just as well do as she or he pleases (as some of the seventeenth-century Ranters believed), since nothing anyone could do would alter her or his ultimate destination. However, Calvin argued that his followers should all assume they were elected to go upwards and must act accordingly, that is, act as good Calvinists, avoiding worldly pleasures and keeping strictly to the faith. Weber's interpretation of this suggests that Calvinists should remain diligent in lawful callings, be ascetic, and use their time constructively (G. Marshall, 1982: 75). In effect, their contemporary actions were not determined by God but their eventual destination was.

We should be cautious, however, about the role of religion in inducing fatalism. Abercrombie et al.'s *The Dominant Ideology Thesis* (1980), for example, casts considerable doubt on the role of the church in prevailing upon the British and French peasantry to accept their lot, though there is little evidence of the same groups revolting *against* the church. Indeed, the absence of challenges to the church in the Middle Ages, and the suggestion that the majority of the population participated in church ceremonies, do not, in themselves, mean that the majority of the population were fervent admirers of Christian ethics, but rather that they were regular participants in Christian rituals: 'Where orthodoxy is unchallenged nothing more is required of most people than outward conformity, and orthodoxy is never less challenged than when the vast majority are illiterate, or almost so, and are incapable of either accepting or rejecting the doctrines which are orthodox' (Plamenatz, 1963: 345). Ritualism, here, is seen as reinforcing, rather than causing, fatalism.

More recently still, Durkheim has come back into view (Lockwood, 1982). His concept of fatalism is locked into his discussion of types of suicide: fatalistic suicide occurs when 'excessive regulation' or 'moral despotism' drives individuals to take their own lives. For example, a slave may kill herself because her life has become so miserable that death is not only preferable to life but an inevitable consequence of circumstances: an ineluctable action. Charles Ball, a black American slave in the nineteenth century, wrote in his autobiography of one such suicide by a runaway Congolese slave who hanged himself rather than face the twin fates of starvation or a return to the cruelties of his white master, a man who had whipped the slave so viciously that: 'The natural color of his skin had disappeared, and was succeeded by a streaked and speckled appearance of dusky white and pale flesh color, scarcely any of the original black remaining' (Ball, 1854, quoted in Lester, 1968: 96).

The relative absence of actual revolts by slaves (and there were many revolts, including those led by Spartacus against Rome, and by Toussaint-Louverture in San Domingo (James, 1938), plus several in the USA (Zinn, 1980) and in the West Indies (Bush, 1982)), does not, therefore, imply that slaves either supported the system, or were physically coerced by their owners and overseers to keep in line, and may suggest that many just regarded the system as inevitable – to the extent that revolt simply was not an issue to consider: they may have just believed that the material constraints were such that they were fated to live out their lives as slaves. I shall return to slavery later.

Fatalism can, of course, derive from physical as well as moral despotism; in Lester's (1968) terms, fatalism in slaves can be induced both by the whip and by taking the slave's independent identity away, including his or her name, to such an extent that slaves considered their condition normal and their existence necessarily locked into that of their owner. Physical despotism, then, is the direct personal oppression that we are probably more accustomed to hearing of in some prisons and concentration camps. In the haunting words of Primo Levi (1987), a survivor of Auschwitz, after several weeks of terror and starvation:

> I have stopped trying to understand for a long time now. As far as I am concerned, I am by now so tired of standing on my wounded foot, still untended, so hungry and frozen, that nothing can interest me anymore. This might easily be my last day and this room the gas chamber of which all speak, but what can I do about it? I might just as well lean against the wall, close my eyes and wait. (1987: 54)

Moral or social despotism can occur when conditions appear unattributable to anyone, and therefore unalterable by anyone; a predicament captured in Wright Mills's (1970) discussion of the way 'personal troubles' are frequently dislocated from their root cause: social problems. This is most frequently reproduced in terms of people's rationalizations of practices and predicaments that might seem avoidable to others: 'What can you do?', 'It's inevitable', 'It's just the way it is' are just some of the ways this fatalist view is articulated.

The power of the 'leader' or a system of control, therefore, can be enhanced by developing a system which the subordinates interpret as inevitable: leadership, here, becomes a consequence of ineluctable fate. Whether the system which is being led is regarded as 'just' too, is a separate issue. To quote Marx's words again, 'the dull compulsion of economic relations' (1970: 737) is often sufficient to undermine hope for an alternative or better life.

But the social order can also be attacked by the very same fatalism. Marx's entire edifice of revolution, particularly the interpretation developed by Kautsky, was premised upon a fatalistic assumption that history was on the side of the working classes and that the German Social Democrats had only to wait for the revolutionary moment to mature. In Kautsky's words: 'Our task is not to organize the revolution, but to organize ourselves *for* the revolution; it is not to *make* the revolution, but *to take advantage of it'* (quoted in Salvadori, 1979: 21, my emphasis). That moment, if it ever came, is no longer with us, but the fatalism of communist visionaries seems, in some places, to have been replaced by the fatalism of globalist visionaries. Just as Marcuse (1964) considered capitalism to have reduced the critical faculties of its consumers to a fatalistic 'one-dimensional thought', so too, one could argue, nation states themselves appear to have been reduced to a fatalistic acquiescence in the face of an apparently unstoppable globalization of the world economy (Redwood, 1993). Where once politicians were elected to execute different policies and construct different societies they now seem to be reduced to accepting that unemployment, financial insecurity and deindustrialization are the responsibility of globalization – that is, of no one. Since none of the major traditional political parties in the West appears to have a viable alternative to global domination of national economies (indeed, most of them are doing the opposite by removing all barriers to global trade), it is little wonder that politicians are held in such contempt by their voters, who appear to be turning to political extremes of all forms. In effect, fatalism can act as both a mechanism for inducing quiescence and a device to stimulate revolt. As Margaret Thatcher found to her cost, when there was 'no alternative' it was time to find one.

This perception of the dual nature of fatalism, as problem and solution, is hardly novel. Despite the musings of various recent and contemporary sociologists, much of our original knowledge about fatalism derives not from twentieth-century sociology but from the work of Boethius, which was adopted by Chaucer as an important element in his *Knight's Tale* and *Troilus and Criseyde*. Written in the sixth century AD, and subsequently translated from the Latin original by Alfred the Great, Chaucer and Queen Elizabeth I (and a crucial part of all scholars' education throughout the Middle Ages), *The Consolation of Philosophy* tells the story of Boethius's own imprisonment and his account of the human condition whilst awaiting his execution. Boethius is wracked with self-pity and confusion over the inequities of a world allegedly controlled by an omnipotent God. In conversation with his visitor, the Lady Philosophy, Boethius is reconciled to the problems that he faces, particularly the absence of earthly pleasures, by subordinating matter to mind. Since, according to Lady Philosophy, material pleasures are transient and insignificant in the context of human life, Boethius is persuaded that his conditions are insignificant. The power of the mind over matter, and the corollary that one can free oneself from material fate by constructive thought, make up one of the two essential elements of the Boethian position.

But how, asked Boethius, can everything be predestined by God and yet people have the freewill necessary to choose between good and evil? If God knows what we will do then how can we be ultimately responsible for our actions? Lady Philosophy answers that God is indeed all-seeing: God knows what choices we will make. However, this knowledge does not determine our choices. On the contrary, we are completely free to make whatever choices we like (and are therefore responsible for these choices), but this does not stop God from seeing in advance what we will choose. Thus the ideas of fatalism and freewill are reconciled in the knowledge that what we do is forewritten by a being who sees, but does not determine, what will happen in the future (Brewer, 1984).

This sense of freedom coupled with fatalism, the absence of immediate constraint allied to the knowledge that what one does is already predicted, joined with the idea that the material situation within which one finds oneself does not determine one's thoughts or actions, I call 'Boethian fatalism'.

Fatalism, therefore, embodies at least two variants rooted in time: on the one hand, one can be fatalistic about the future in the sense of it being predestined: fated. Since this does not inhibit any contemporary action this is the form I consider as Boethian fatalism. On the other hand, one can be fatalistic about the present situation in the sense of there being no choice about the action to take – the absence of alternatives or choice – but this need not be locked into any form of predestined future. This latter form I call 'situational fatalism'. The two connect where individuals believe themselves to have no choice: what will be will be *and* they are coerced by circumstances into taking one form of action. This double form I call 'total fatalism'. The fourth form of action is the opposite of any sort of fatalism: it consists of complete freewill: any action is possible and anything may happen. A corollary of this is that individuals are totally responsible for all their actions. They are, in Sartre's (1948: 33) words, 'condemned to be free', alone in the world without God and without other authority: this form of existential free thought or assumption I call 'freewill'.

The various possibilities are represented in figure 2, though it should be remembered that the precise meaning and significance of fatalism and freedom will depend very much upon the interpretation of the individual concerned. As Fromm (1960: 146) argues about fatalism: 'For a soldier it may mean the will or whim of his superior ... for the small business man the economic laws are his fate ... fate may be rationalized philosophically as "natural law" or as "destiny of man", religiously as the "will of the Lord" (or) ethically as "duty".'

It is worth speculating on the significance of Boethian fatalism for the

PRESENT

		Unfree	Free
	Unfree	Total fatalism	Boethian fatalism
FUTURE			
	Free	Situational fatalism	Freewill

Figure 2 *Fatalism and freedom: an index of possibilities*

development of leadership. Could it be that the 'great' leaders are not those whose thoughts lie untrammelled by fate but those that sit in the top right quadrant: those who believe themselves to be predestined for greatness, so that this very fatalism allows them the freedom to choose actions that other, lesser, mortals would avoid? Fatalism under these circumstances is not the debilitating and enervating philosophy that leads to uncreative and fatal (in the terminal sense of the word) inaction or acquiescence (the kind of action likely under either of the other fatalist states). On the other hand, the Sartrean soul is potentially creative but perhaps not emboldened with the sure knowledge that it is right. Of course, many people might fit into the Boethian fatalist mould, believing themselves destined for glory; but many will also fail. The point is that this form of belief structure might be a necessary but not sufficient precondition for 'great leadership'. This still leaves the followers to construct the leader, but we should avoid assuming that the leader plays no active role in the construction of his or her own image. In short, to argue that leaders are active constructors of leadership does not mean that leadership is an inherent or objective phenomenon. On the contrary, it may well be that 'great' leaders are those who fit into the Boethian fatalist mould but who also go out of their way to generate the image of themselves that they consider to be the most valuable; whether it is perceived as such by their followers, of course, is a separate issue (see chapter 6).

In the next section I want to add some flesh to the bones of the model by assessing its utility in an extreme situation: war.

The management of war: a fatal profession

Total fatalism

An illustration of total fatalism in this context might be taken from the First World War, where, in trench warfare, the peer pressure and military discipline system could imply to troops that they must go over the top and that the fates would determine whether they survived. In the French army during the First World War the term *le cafard* came to represent this total fatalism for the many *poilus* (ordinary soldiers). As one such soldier described the feeling just before an attack:

> the sergeant-major comes round to take our parents' addresses: 'You know why, you never know what's going to happen.' I don't know whether it was the effect of such disturbing phrases or the cold mist which still hung over the countryside, but I felt overwhelmed by a peculiar melancholy; a sadness in which men and things and thoughts all looked grey. I have never felt anything like it. I learned later that it was a *poilus* speciality and was called '*le cafard*' ... it is born of the feeling that we are being crushed by events that are inimical but which lack any special distinction. (Quoted in Audoin-Rouzeau, 1992: 54–5).

As Audoin-Rouzeau himself summarizes it, *le cafard* is 'the nightmare of one's own death and, dominating everything, this feeling of being crushed, the uselessness of any resistance' (1992: 56).

It was this kind of helplessness that stimulated both the status of victim amongst the troops and a vehement condemnation of those in command who were not in the firing line. As a French trench newspaper proclaimed in 1917: 'The rank stupidity of the army and the vastness of the sea are the only two things which can give an idea of infinity' (quoted in Audoin-Rouzeau, 1992: 60).

In the British lines, an instance of (temporarily erroneous) total fatalism is provided by Private Burke in his description of the Battle of Bullecourt in May 1917, in which both the future and the present are predetermined: 'Whilst we were waiting out time to go over, the wounded were coming down in their dozens, and we were under the severest bombardment I have ever known Fritz to send over. We knew it was certain death for all of us – [but] orders are orders in the army and we had to obey them, (M. Brown, 1993: 139). In fact, it was not certain death for Private Burke then, though he was killed five months later.

Exactly four hundred years earlier, in 1517, the Aztec king

Moctezuma also fell victim to a total fatalism, in which the landing of Cortés was prefigured by the prophecy that Quetzalcoatl, a disgraced Aztec god, would return to wreak vengeance. Quetzalcoatl's predicted appearance, as a white-skinned, bearded man on a strange ship and in a particular year in the Aztec time cycle, convinced Moctezuma that Cortés was indeed Quetzalcoatl, and Moctezuma's subsequent actions appear to have been driven by his perception of this terrible fate (Luecke, 1994).

Boethian fatalism

The forms of fatalism are decoupled where it is believed that the ultimate destiny of any individual is already written for her or him but, paradoxically, this implies too that any form of action (or inaction) is viable: she or he may refuse to go over the top despite the imminent threat of summary execution by her or his own side, but may justify this on the basis of fate. Boethian fatalism, then, can release people from day-to-day fears in precisely the way that Boethius managed to free himself from the immediate deprivations of imprisonment. As Lieutenant John Staniforth wrote: 'I'm a great believer in my star. If I were going to be killed I'd have been killed long ago. Walking about the trenches all day long hand-in-hand with death, you can't help [but] become a fatalist (quoted in M. Brown, 1993: 93). The experience of R. H. Tawney (a leading economic historian of the post-war era) on the first day of the Somme was very similar: 'I hadn't gone ten yards before I felt a load fall from me. I knew it was alright ... I knew I was in no danger. I knew I shouldn't be hurt – knew it positively' (quoted in Winter, 1979: 180).

Such a philosophy became inscribed into popular culture through the translation of the French saying: 'ça ne fait rien' into the English 'San Fairy Ann' (ibid.: 95). North Vietnamese soldiers later seem to have had similar thoughts; as Ninh (1993: 12) recalls in his novel of the war:

Soldiers of that year, 1974, sang:

> Oh this is war without end,
> war without end.
> Tomorrow or today,
> Today or tomorrow.
> Tell me my fate,
> when will I die ...

The French in the First World War appeared equally fatalistic, in so far as they knew they would die, but that it was not the hail of bullets that would inevitably cut them to shreds; on the contrary, it was the single shot that should be feared because only one had your name on it: 'A stray bullet: it was wasted, but you must not trust it! You don't know where it is coming from, but it knows where it is going' (*Le 120 court*, 15 November 1917, quoted in Audoin-Rouzeau, 1992: 76). Even more macabre were the assumptions that death stalked the living even before the battle, marking out its victims with a kiss, not of love, but of death:

> Then all at once I saw, besides the straw,
> A ghostly being, who on battle mornings
> I thought to see bend over some of us.
> He passed on, watching men and wild
> With lightning flashes from mad eyes,
> At times he kissed the sleepers on the mouth!
>
> (*Le 120 court*, 10 June 1916,
> quoted in Audoin-Rouzeau, 1992: 76)

Note here the assumption that those who did not receive the kiss of death were destined to survive the next battle, irrespective of the amount of lead the enemy would hurl at them: they were, in effect, fated to fight – and die – another day. The fatalistic idea that death would only occur if the bullet had your name on it seems to have been very common. For Ernest Martin, paradoxically, the Flanders mud *might* save you:

> Many a fellow owes his life to the mud 'killing' the effect of shells; and they were frequent and fearful. For an explanation of fear, imprisoned in a muddy post, with no hope whatever of escape, and being peppered with 5.9 high explosives, was *it* to the full. It was almost like being tied to the railway lines waiting for the express. The approach of a 5.9 was just like an oncoming train, you yourself shrivelling up to the size of an ant – waiting. If it – the shell – bore your name and number it was all up, that was the only way, to grin and bear it; but many a one went under with the strain, and no wonder. (Martin, 1990: 15, emphasis in the original)

Some, though, were less convinced about their fated bullet and more concerned about the ones that read: 'to whom it may concern'. Or, as S.H. Raggett noted from a colleague: 'I was most struck by the bullets that missed me' (quoted by M. Brown, 1993: 94).

Situational fatalism

The forms of fatalism, present and future, material and prophetic, are also decoupled where the individual believes him or herself to have no choice but to go over the top given the pressure and discipline, but that, once over, there is no reason to assume that his or her chances of surviving are presaged. This is an example of situational but not Boethian fatalism, and is nicely captured by the words of Frank Sumpter, one of the five remaining 'Old Contemptibles' at the time of writing (January, 1994), speaking about 'going over the top':

> You knew the next minute *might* be your last but you didn't walk in fear ... You exchanged your addresses of your wives or mothers or whatever with your mates in case you got hit ... When the time came along the whistle blew and over you'd go, and of course the officers were behind. They weren't in front, waving a sword or anything like that, like some people think, they saw that everybody got over, that was their job. You never questioned anything in the army ... you'd got to obey orders ... there's nothing you can do about it, and you're in terrible trouble if you don't anyway. (Sumpter, quoted in *It Will All be Over by Christmas*, BBC2, 21 December 1993)

This particular account of fate, and the absence of freedom, is probably the most popular. It explains the action of 'going over the top' as the result of an absence of choice, thanks to the military discipline. Under these constraints soldiers are represented as 'lambs to the slaughter' (Ellis, 1993: 124). In sum, their freedom to act beyond the limits set by the immediate situation is nil. When the chances of surviving by refusing to go over the top and suffering the consequences at the hands of one's own execution squad are probably lower than the chances of surviving by doing as one is told (Babington, 1985), there is no choice; or is there?

Freewill

The fourth form of action is the opposite of any form of fatalism and suggests that there is always an alternative open to people: it consists of freewill. A corollary of this is that individuals are totally responsible for all their actions. They are, in Sartre's (1948: 33) words, 'condemned to be free', alone in the world without God and without other authority.

Yet in the First World War many soldiers on both sides seemed to have trusted in God for their protection. That many on opposite sides trusted in the same God to bring them victory suggests not so much a problem of logic as a manifestation of faith. Moreover, much of the faith was deemed to be significant in that faith could *alter* fate. As Tom Allen, Second Lieutenant in the Irish Guards (I.G.) and censor of the troops' mail, wrote home in 1915: 'there cannot be many villages in Ireland where prayers are not being said for the I.G. One man writing was quite convinced that "prayers turns bullets"' (quoted in M. Brown, 1993: 91).

So far it would seem that there are clear cases where either the material circumstances or the belief structure of those involved, or both, ensure that control can be secured. But are there any examples that we can draw on to suggest that freewill is an essential element of even the most coercive of environments? After all, Boethius managed to transcend his material confinements, so can soldiers? Well, there appears to be a major difference: Boethius's freedom rested wholly within his imagination – he was, in fact, imprisoned and thus not really involved in enacting freewill. He could not, for instance, imagine his way out of prison. So is freewill in similar circumstances merely a self-delusion, manufactured to stave off reality rather than change it? To claim that people are always free to do otherwise we need to provide cases where under apparently irresistible force people did otherwise. Again, I am not claiming that we have freewill under *all* circumstances: to be bound hand and foot to a chair and thrown over a cliff does not provide you with much chance of enacting freewill. But outside these forms of physical coercion I want to see how far we can push the limits of the coercion argument. In the military scenario we need to see whether soldiers are indeed free to do anything other than 'go over the top' when the whistle blows. Three examples will suffice.

First, on Christmas day in 1914 soldiers from both the German and Allied sides got out of their trenches and fraternized with 'the enemy', often for several hours. The truce between the French 74th Infantry Regiment and the Germans opposite resembled '"a village fair", with the convivial exchange of items from Christmas packages sent from home – food, tobacco, beer, wine, etc.' (L. V. Smith, 1994: 91). This particular truce was eventually broken up when the commanding officer – but notably not the NCOs or junior officers – ordered the artillery to fire some shells high into the air, but not onto German lines. Even then one of the French soldiers had temporarily gone over to the German side and was subsequently returned by the Germans across no man's land rather the worse for drink. Equally significant is the account of Frank Sumpter, the 'Old Contemptible' whose situational fatalism was summarized above in terms of his claim that 'you'd got to obey orders ... there's nothing you can do about it, and you're in terrible trouble if you don't anyway'. Yet Frank's account of the Christmas Truce in his sector suggests that there was something you could do about it and, furthermore, you were not necessarily in 'terrible trouble' if you did do something about it:

> The Germans started it [The Christmas Truce] ... they were singing 'Happy Noel Tommy.' We said 'Happy Christmas Fritz', and one of our men got up on top of the trench and signalled to the Germans to come forward to the barbed wire. And our platoon commander said 'get down from there, get down'. And we said, 'It's Christmas'. And they [the Germans] invited us over, and we got up to the barbed wire. (Sumpter, quoted in *It Will All be Over by Christmas*, BBC2 21 December 1993)

Thus, a man for whom there is no freedom suddenly finds some when he – or rather they (an important aspect of the issue) – decides to deny the authority normally given to superordinates.

The second example of the limits of fatalism concerns a related phenomenon: the issue of 'tacit truces'. Ashworth (1980) argues that, despite the attempts of the high commands on both sides, all the troops engaged in a system of tacit truces, a 'live-and-let-live' system which minimized hostilities and allowed 'normal' life to continue, at least outside major offences.

The third example is perhaps the most significant and concerns the way the outcome of battles was configured through the negotiated practices that L. V. Smith (1994) calls 'proportionality'. In a marvellously detailed account of one particular French infantry division, Smith shows how the balance between obedience and disobedience, between acceptance and mutiny, was one that was permanently played out on the battlefields of France. There were no cases where the casualty rate reached 100 per cent – and yet the orders to take or defend a particular position 'at all costs' certainly required such sacrifices. As Jean Norton Cru (1929) claims: 'If the orders had always been obeyed, to the letter, the entire French army would have been massacred before August 1915' (quoted in L. V. Smith, 1994: 14). Indeed, the participation by the 5th Infantry Division in both the 1917 mutinies and the 1918 successful attacks suggest that whether troops engage in war, mutiny or peaceful coexistence is a contingent issue and not something determined by the coercive nature of circumstances. In short, the power of superordinates over subordinates is something to be achieved in and through the relationship between the bodies, not something which inheres within the superordinate; or, to put it another way, leaders do not 'have' power, because power is not a possession, it is a relationship. *If* subordinates do what is required of them by their superordinates then the superordinate becomes powerful as a *consequence* of the subordinate action.

Even if subordinate action is required for the superordinate to become powerful, there are two subsequent issues to raise. First, is this not merely a circular argument, or at least a virtuous circle? Whatever starts off the subordinate action, its effect is to buttress the assumption that, indeed, superordinates are powerful, and hence subsequent subordinate action occurs *because* of the power of superordinates. The issue is perhaps most clearly seen when we consider how the virtuous circle might stop turning. If the superordinates do indeed have power then subordinate action should continue – despite any resistance – providing the superordinate retains power. But how can the fall from grace of leaders like Thatcher be explained if leadership remains configured as a possession and not a relationship? (See chapter 6).

Second, the shift from power as a cause of others' action to power as a consequence of others' action also generates the issue of motivation. Irrespective of whether subordinates do or don't do as they are required to, *why* do they act one way or the other? Latour (1986) suggests that this motivational scheme necessarily involves an element of translation: if subordinates act, they do so for their own reasons, which may have nothing to do with the assumptions of the superordinate. For example, soldiers may go over the top not through a desire to fulfil their patriotic duty, or because they are afraid of the disciplinary consequences of not going over the top, but because not to do so would appear cowardly to their peers, or because they wish to commit suicide, or for any number of other reasons. The point of this is twofold: first, motivational systems of control, as we shall shortly see, are often premised on extraordinarily simplistic and naive accounts of human motivation. For example, if the motivational assumptions of managers are that money motivates, and the subordinates do indeed settle down to work, this does not mean that they are driven by money. Second, exactly what it is that subordinates do may well depend upon why they appear to accept the orders of a superordinate – they may appear to work hard because they are driven by money, but they may actually be working hard because it is one way of managing their time. Either way, the underlying point, and the critical conclusion from authority systems in the trenches, is that subordinates' execution of superordinate requirements is likely to be premised upon some degree of active compliance. In effect, it is only in a very small number of cases that superordinates can get their subordinates to do things wholly against the will of the subordinate. As the French military authorities discovered in 1917, when this assumption is negated and attempts are made to coerce subordinates into extreme action completely against their will, it is by no means a foregone conclusion that soldiers will continue to obey – still less that civilians will obey the orders of a manager (for naval mutinies see Gutteridge, 1992). As Giddens (1979: 149) asserts, 'all power relations, or relations of autonomy and dependence, are reciprocal.'

Managing fate

In the third part of this chapter I want to consider how this relationship between fatalism and freewill affects the way managers seek to attain and retain control over employees. At one extreme, in the total fatalism quarter, we can consider slavery. Since the slave is usually bound to his or her owner for life, since the coercive mechanisms for controlling slaves often include both corporal and capital punishments, and since one of the ways that slaves appear to be induced to acquiesce to their condition is precisely the kind of fatalist belief structure that we have considered at length above, I would argue that slavery constitutes the equivalent of total fatalism. Yet, again, we should remain aware that fatalism of all forms rests upon an interpretative framework that is contingent – slaves can and did revolt, slaves can and did resist. Thus the management of slaves is, in principle, just an extreme variant of management and not a qualitatively different form of control. For example, the historical records of slave plantations in the West Indies suggest that resistance by slaves, at various levels and in various forms, was widespread, as slaves struggled to deny their owners total control over them and owners struggled to deny that their power rested ultimately upon the slaves acting as slaves were allegedly supposed to. We also know from several sources that the open revolt of slaves was both a practical possibility and one that was sometimes enacted and occasionally successful. Bush's review of slave resistance in the British Caribbean argues that: 'Slaves, both male and female, exasperated their masters in countless ways – shirking work, damaging crops, dissembling, feigning illness' (1982: 17). Even suicide was a method of resistance, in so far as it was regarded by some slave populations as a way of returning home, a route to freedom (ibid.). As the slave records of the king's plantations in the West Indies reveal, everyday resistance was a common occurrence, with: 'shamming sick', 'excessive laziness', 'disorderly conduct', 'disobedience' and 'quarrelling' frequently mentioned complaints (ibid.). In one plantation: 'in the six month period from January to June 1827, 34 slaves (out of a total of 171 from the plantation as a whole) were punished, of whom 21 were women. The women, moreover, tended to be more persistent offenders than the men and several of them were punished three times and one woman four times during the said period' (Bush, 1982: 19,20). Similarly, even concentration camp prisoners find ways of resisting. Levi recounts the 'lesson' he learned from Steinlauf, another prisoner in Auschwitz, who insisted on washing everyday – even though he had no soap:

> Steinlauf sees me and greets me, and without preamble asks me severely why I do not wash. Why should I wash? Would I be better off than I am? ... Would I live a day, an hour longer? I would probably live a shorter time, because to wash is an effort, a waste of energy and warmth ... The more I think about it, the more washing one's face in our condition seems a stupid feat, even frivolous: a mechanical habit ... We will all die ... [but] precisely because the Lager [camp] was a great machine to reduce us to beasts, we must not become beasts ... We are slaves, deprived of every right, exposed to every insult, condemned to certain death, but we still possess one power, and we must defend it with all our strength for it is the last – the power to refuse our consent. So we must certainly wash our faces without soap in dirty water and dry ourselves on our jackets. We must polish our shoes, not because the regulation states it, but for dignity and propriety. We must walk erect, without dragging our feet, not in homage to Prussian discipline but to remain alive, not to begin to die. (Levi, 1982: 46–7)

But the two most relevant quarters in the model are those occupied by situational and Boethian fatalism. In the former case it is the circumstances of the present, whether material or non-material, which coerce the individual into obedience, but these circumstances have a temporal or spatial limit. Thus, for example, under Fordist conditions of production, employees may consider themselves to be coerced by the system of overseers or supervisors that regularly patrol the assembly line, haranguing slackers and sacking the haranguers. Or employees may feel themselves to be coerced more by the technology of the assembly line itself, with a machine-imposed speed and requirement that cannot be bucked. Yet even where this assumption is common, the accounts of those involved in such work often suggest a contrary reading of events. Cavendish (1985), for instance, notes how the assembly line – itself synchronized by a flashing red light – appears to control the actions of the women operatives, yet, 'The light was controlled by management who laid down the speed for each set' (1985: 107). Here, technical determinism becomes the causal factor behind fatalistic acquiescence (see Grint and Woolgar (1995b) for an extended review of technical determinism). However, the fatalistic acquiescence to managerial authority is only temporary – at the end of the shift the employees regain their freedom until the next shift starts again. Thus they are merely 'day slaves' for whom work is, in the words of a war-time munitions worker, 'merely the blank patch between one brief evening and the next' (Mass Observation, 1943: 43). Yet the contemporary shifts towards systems of management control informed by human resource management approaches appear to free such 'day slaves' from servitude by extending the degree of freedom and responsibility well beyond that associated with Fordist styles of situational fatalism towards Boethian fatalism, manifest, for example, in post-Fordism.

One can read the development of management philosophies at work over time in juxtaposition to the development of management philosophies in the treatment of mental illness over time. Foucault (1967) notes how the end of the eighteenth century and the beginning of the nineteenth century witnessed the rise of institutions like Tuke's 'Retreat' at York and Pinel's 'liberation' of the insane from Bicetre, a Parisian asylum. These appeared to preface the shift away from the regressive incarceration of the unknown towards the progressive, humanitarian care of the known. In response to Couthon's jibe that it would be mad to unchain the 'beasts' of Bicetre, Pinel asserts: 'Citizens, I am convinced that these madmen are so intractable only because they have been deprived of air and liberty' (quoted in Foucault, 1967: 241). But Foucault's point is that the exterior and physical chains that bind 'the mad' are not removed to allow the patient to recuperate through liberation; rather, they are replaced by interior and moral chains that are anything but liberatory. In this sense one form of control is replaced by another, but it is not self-evident that the latter is more 'humane' than the former. The enforcement of Quaker religion upon an inmate of the Retreat at York, therefore, placed 'the insane individual within a moral element where he [would] be in debate with himself and his surroundings; to constitute for him a milieu where, far from being protected, he [would] be kept in a perpetual state of anxiety, ceaselessly threatened by Law and Transgression' (Foucault, 1967: 243). This substitution of control methods, rather than liberation from control – what Foucault calls replacing the 'free terror of madness' with the 'stifling anguish of responsibility' – was, then, a move to internalize the chains of control. The second aspect of this which is significant is the role of the insane in self-policing and, by extrapolation, the positive role that all individuals play in their own disciplining. In effect, even the most coercive systems of control are premised upon a degree of 'voluntary' compliance on the part of the individual at the receiving end: even those about to be executed rarely resist their executioners, and if they regularly did then 'executions', *qua* deliberate, public, formal, controlled and judicial acts of death, could not take place; only if the victim plays the role of the victim can the executioner play the equivalent.

The shift in the 'treatment' of mental illness can also be reconstructed in the philosophies underlying management, from the equivalent nineteenth-century assumptions about the recalcitrant nature of 'free' labour (as opposed to the conventional chaining of slave labour) to the contemporary movements to develop approaches to labour where responsibility for the actions of workers is reconstituted away from the manager or supervisor towards the individual employee her- or himself. There are obvious differences, one of the most prominent being the construction of team-based responsibilities.

One can use the model of fatalism and freedom developed earlier to sketch out the way management theories of control can be read along the same axes. For instance, Fordism as a system of management control rests, in principle, upon the employee giving up her or his right to autonomous action in exchange for a specific amount of money and other rewards. Under Fordism the individual remains free outside the factory gates but inside them voluntarily accepts the status of a day wage-slave. The Fordist controls system is primarily external and operates upon the body of the individual employee. Employees are not required to think on behalf of the company; on the contrary, following Taylor, thinking is strictly outlawed, since managers think and employees merely execute the orders of managers or the 'requirements' of the machinery. However, personal commitment and loyalty to the company are not part of the exchange process; employees are expected to leave their brains in a bucket by the factory entrance and become precisely what they used to be called in Britain in the nineteenth century – merely 'hands'. The corollary of this system of external constraint is that once outside the factory their lives are their own; factory owners have no rights to police the moral rectitude of their employees, and a largely unbridgeable gap is created between life inside and outside the factory gates. Of course the two arenas are heavily influenced by, and indeed dependent upon, each other; but employees are not expected to develop identities in and through the company (though their occupations, as opposed to their employing companies, may nevertheless play a critical role in this).

This form of fatalism is not new; indeed, the fatalism of the British working class is legendary. However resistant to the managers, most trade unionists seem to have been resigned to their 'fate'. As Allen Clarke (a nineteenth-century English socialist) described the Bolton workers at the turn of the century: 'They believe they are bound to work; they do not see that work is but a means to life ... they think that the masters build factories and workshops not to make a living for themselves by trading but in order to find the people employment' (quoted in Joyce, 1991: 126). Joyce writes this of the nineteenth-century industrial culture: 'a fatalism evident alike in patterns of belief and in some manifestations of a "culture of control" surely cannot but have contributed to the ideas that prevailing social hierarchies were well nigh immovable and, indeed, pre-ordained and "natural"' (1991: 163).

Much later, in the Britain of the 1950s and 1960s, the same concern for the maintenance of cultural boundaries seemed to prevail. The working class thus split between 'rough' and 'respectable' and morality was heavily ritualized, primarily through the distinct lives of men and women, lived out in public and private respectively. But it was also lived out at work between 'us' and 'them', between workers and managers. However, despite the divisions, what united the working class seems to have been a fatalism. As Hoggart asserted:

> Working people feel that they cannot do much about the main elements in their situation, feel it not with despair, or disapproval or resentment but simply as a fact of life, they adopt attitudes towards that situation which allows them to have a liveable life under its shadow ... The attitudes remove the main elements in the situation to the realm of natural law; the given and the raw, the almost implacable, material form from which a living has to be carved. (1957, quoted in Joyce, 1991: 159)

Although this view seems to have been predominant in the nineteenth and early to mid-twentieth centuries in Britain, Goldthorpe et al.'s *Affluent Worker* (1969: 116–56) suggested that the wealthier members of the working class, while not adopting middle-class values of individual advancement in career and status terms, were certainly less fatalistic about their material prosperity than previous working-class generations. But, again, 'the revolution of rising expectations' was considered in a fatalistic way, as an inherently collective but limited advancement within a society that was inevitably or naturally class based; not something individuals could do much about. Social order, then, need not rest on either consensus or coercion but just on fatalism, because resistance seems pointless when the social order is ineluctable (see Held, 1987, for a discussion of different forms of 'legitimacy').

The fatalistic response on the part of the workers is, of course, mirrored by the equivalent fatalistic acceptance on the part of management that control is their essential responsibility. This reciprocity is precisely the form of argument that underlies Braverman's (1974) case that management under capitalism was inevitably an exploitive and alienating effect of the capitalist system. Under these conditions, management control and the deskilling of the workforce that accompanied it were both inevitable and inevitably successful.

However, once we shift the zone of freedom from the future, beyond work, to the present, inside work, a different scenario unfolds. Here, just as Foucault's insane creatures become creatures of internal rather than external chains, so too the contemporary developments in management control systems have shifted along the same axis towards self-policing, an issue at the heart of the move towards human resource management. For example, those fortunate enough to retain employment over the last twenty-five years may have noticed the accretion of 'responsibilities' due to the 'corporation' on behalf of the corporate employee. In the brave new world of human resource management, where employees are empowered to take ever more responsibility, they are expected to be much more dedicated and committed to the corporation with whom they 'share' a culture, a vision, a mission and 'a way of life' (see Storey, 1992; Guest, 1990; Beaumont, 1993; Towers, 1992; Blyton and Turnbull, 1992). Such corporate zealots used to be restricted to the ranks of senior managers whose reward package was suitably generous. However, the recent growth of corporate systems is firmly rooted in overt loyalty systems, and employees are expected to bring their brains into work and leave their private lives in a bucket at the door. Here, the disciplinary system is overtly internalistic: corporate warriors are expected to develop at all levels and to devote themselves to the corporation, to be Boethian in their acquiescence to their ultimate and inevitable fate as corporate warriors – but they are nevertheless free to act responsibly to facilitate this fate.

Moreover, devotion to a corporate ideal is much easier when other ideals have been shown to be flawed or simply outdated: loyalty to a national ideal is difficult when the national government appears to be at the mercy of global economic trends and when many transnational corporate practices make it virtually impossible to know where products and services come from; loyalty to radical political ideals is suspect in an age when extremes of left and right have tarnished histories; loyalty to trade union principles remains but perhaps not in the idealistic sense that there may once have been. In short, the gradual erosion of alternative ideologies and oppositional institutions to the corporation has provided few counter-cultural locations of loyalty, and consequently fertilized the fatalistic soil of the global corporation and human resource management.

Conclusion

This chapter has considered the nature of fatalism and freewill in the context of managing the business of war and the war of business. I began by considering the popularity of fatalistic belief and its contrast with humanistic assumptions about freewill and personal responsibility for one's actions. By splitting the apparent forms of fatalism along time axes, present and future, I developed a model of fatalism that distinguished between a situational fatalism, construed as deriving from the contemporary material constraints, and a Boethian fatalism, in which the ineluctable eventual fate of an individual did not determine his or her current actions. Indeed, such prophetic assumptions often seemed to free individuals from the constraints that others saw as necessarily coercive and determining. The third form of fatalism, total fatalism, combines both situational and Boethian and provides no room for the freedom of action that marks out the fourth possibility. I then fleshed out this model in the fields of Flanders where luck, fate and chance seem to have played more than their 'fair' share in guiding some safely through battle while others fell at the first step. The final section applied this model to a range of managerial approaches to control that seem to have moved, after the total fatalism of slavery, from primarily external to essentially internal methods of control, that is from situational to Boethian fatalism. This has probably been aided by the decline of alternative bases of loyalty, so that loyalty to the corporation now appears a fate that many employees and managers have taken on board, at least for the present.

Beyond the differential approaches to control, though, a critical issue here is the nature of compliance to that control. While traditional explanations of troop behaviour in the First World War regarded their fate as a sad and heteronomous act of the slaughter of innocents, the theoretical concerns raised by Foucault (1988), Latour (1986) and Giddens (1979) in their different ways suggest that heteronomous coercion is not an adequate account. While there undoubtedly was enormous pressure on soldiers to act in alignment with the orders of their superordinate officers, there are sufficient examples of resistance to question the heteronomous nature of such action. Rather, it appears that such soldiers were actively involved in decisions of their own making. This suggests that accounts of managerial control in arguably less coercive systems, such as free wage labour, are even less likely to be rooted in systems where the subordinates have no control of, or responsibility for, their own actions. In short, because we are all 'condemned to be free' we are all actively involved in the fabrication of our own restraints. In sum, management is not just something which some people do to, for or against others, but something which requires some degree of compliance from all of us: we are fated to be free to manage ourselves.

10

Reflections

Summary reflections

In this final chapter I want not to attempt to summarize all the essential elements of each preceding chapter, but rather to spend a little time reflecting upon the overarching themes and the limitations of the approach used.

In this first section I discuss one particular aspect of management that I take as representative of the substantive area discussed in each chapter and, in good competitive tradition, I will discuss them in reverse order and spend more time on the final elements. The last three sections go beyond the individual chapters to expand slightly on the role of politics, rationality and paradox, and I conclude by reconsidering whether historical forces corral contemporary managers into what they do and why they do what they do – in sum, the way the past creates the present. However, I also want to use the last theme to consider the role of the present in the construction of the past (Chapman et al., 1989, quoted in Case, 1994). This reversal of historical 'effect' has crucial implications for any reading of management, past and present, including this one.

The idea that the present constructs the past and not vice versa is particularly influential when we reconsider the role of fatalism in the development of management. We need not slip into the mud of Flanders to recognize the way people appear to be rendered powerless in circumstances of their own making. There must be many managers whose present position is experienced as one of fatalistic acquiescence but the responsibility for which lies in their own making. As a simple example, each salary rise appears to rescue managers from their current financial problems, but instead it serves to keep their level of indebtedness whilst improving their standard of living. In effect, managers – like everyone else – seem to develop levels of consumption that rise with each salary increase, so that each rise merely adds another bar to the treadmill of obligation that coerces managers into yet further obligations. Yesterday's luxuries soon become today's necessities and so the cycle of consumption and obligation continues. As Bauman (1991) asserts, social stability is probably as much to do with the seduction of consumption experienced by the 'haves' as the coercion of the 'have nots', though it may be that both are experienced fatalistically as heteronomous actions, produced externally by others or by 'the system', not reproduced internally by the self.

The fatalistic element of technology is another issue that may resonate powerfully for many: driven by the assembly line, made redundant by robots, or threatened with erasure by the technology of death. Yet one of the issues raised in chapter 8 suggests that we might consider technology and gender as resources to be deployed in the acquisition of positions rather than as coercive mechanisms whose power operates directly, and in an unmediated fashion, upon people. If the resource-based approach is adopted then technology loses not only its determinate quality but also its determinate effect: what the machine does is as ambiguous as what its 'effects' are, because both are dependent upon persuasive renderings. Once again, the implication of this is to suggest that powerful networks and their interpretative deployment of technologies *may* form the basis for advancing gender equality at work – though they are also the basis for the retention or even strengthening of gender inequalities.

Another aspect of the technology–gender relationship is the form of boundary that is constructed around or between humans and non-humans, and chapter 7 extended this debate by examining the significance of boundary control in the debate on the management of culture. There are, perhaps, two issues that need to be retained in this area. First, cultures may not be just the 'body of ideas' beloved of most current accounts of 'corporate culture' but may actually involve a host of practices, technologies and traditions as well. Second, and following from this, it may be that one of the reasons that corporate-culture change programmes seem destined to fail or, at best, to generate limited success is precisely this assumption: that the imposition of an all-encompassing boundary around the entire workforce, based upon the body of ideas emanating from the boardroom, will suffice to displace the weft and warp of heterogeneous cultures that ordinarily make up any organization. There clearly are organizations where total unity appears to prevail, but these also tend to be total institutions of the kind best described by Goffman (1961), such as armies, prisons, asylums and political and religious cults. In other words, under certain conditions, you probably could change a corporation's culture to the extent outlined by some consultants – but would that be an efficient way to construct a dynamic and flexible organization? I have my doubts.

Yet many attempts to enforce radical organizational change seem to rely upon some form of charismatic leadership to drive the change through, though I suggested in chapter 6 that we might take a sceptical step back from the mystical world of the leader to step instead into the shoes of the followers. That is, since leadership appears to be a skill that is attributed by followers to leaders after an act has occurred,it may be worth reconsidering it as the alchemy of followership not the science of leadership. This does not mean that the potential leader is helpless to act – indeed many of the world's 'great leaders', including Alexander the Great, Julius Caesar, Nelson and Napoleon (Grabsky, 1993), were prominent writers, or employers of writers, of their own history. This, of course, does not ensure lasting historical fame; but it helps if the story of your life and great feats is written by you rather than your enemy.

Another significant part of leadership is the ability to get others to do things, since most leaders spend most of their time giving orders rather than executing them themselves. In chapter 5 I considered the significance of this for the management of change, particularly radical organizational change. Here, not only did there appear to be a reversal of traditional perspectives – from power as a cause of others' action to power as a consequence of it – but also a concern that the legitimation of change rested rather more on the contemporaneous nature of orthodoxy than most of us care to imagine. Thus managing change was critically premised on the construction of arguments that manifested themselves as 'common sense' until, of course, common sense changed. Reengineering's success, then, hinges on the way its supporters characterize it as simultaneously novel yet traditional, radical yet conservative, and futuristic yet rooted in the past. It is managing these paradoxes that reengineers do best of all.

'Mismanaging the paradoxes of appraisals' might have been the title of chapter 4, in which the practical fetish of assessors for squeezing those being assessed into preconstructed categories leads to all kinds of misshapen managers. That managers' characters and competences are constructed by these approaches, rather than discovered by them, might be considered as a demonstration of both the theoretical strength and the practical weakness of the constructivist approach. Managers probably are more complex than any appraisal system pretends – but how can we cope with infinity? The response suggested in this chapter was to use the plurality of perspectives rather than suffer from them, by adopting upward or even 360° multiple appraisals. This, however, calls for a major commitment by all to accept the political ramifications of such a scheme, including some potential embarrassment at board level. But then management is, above everything else, a political phenomenon.

The politics of management: from Mayo to Machiavelli

Let me begin this second part of the reflective journey back at a starting point, this time, in the early fifteenth century. After the Battle of Agincourt in 1415, at least in Shakespeare's version of *Henry V*, the Duke of Burgundy rails against the effects of war and beseeches the kings of both France and England to look upon the battle as an opportunity for peace to prevail, to drive out the savagery of war with the abundance of peace; he longs for the lush garden of France to recover and for the rusting 'coulter' (part of a plough) to be put back to work – to tear up the weeds of war by the roots, to 'deracinate such savagery'.

This uprooting relates not only to the organizational form – whether it be flattened hierarchies or teams or whatever – but also to the displacement of 'normal' management practices. In effect, the very act of deracination is designed to cut off the oxygen from managers' conventional, Machiavellian (war-like) activities and to facilitate an entirely novel form of management practice under peaceful conditions. The desire for a sudden outbreak of peace at work was probably first described from management's perspective in the twentieth century by Mayo (1933). That his involvement at the famous Hawthorne experiments was quite possibly minimal and distorting (see Gillespie, 1991) is not significant here, but what is important is the assumption that, through a particular form of management, the conflicts of previous generations of employers and employees could be removed and channelled into constructive (that is productive) developments. In short, Machiavelli was essentially wrong: peace and unity could prevail at work – providing the roots of conflict were torn up and destroyed.

The problem is, to continue the horticultural metaphor, that politics at work is not an annual plant that can be killed off permanently by shearing the roots; rather it is a hardy perennial that just keeps coming back no matter what. But what was the original paradise like before the weeds of conflict grew?

From the beginnings of industrial capitalism in the late eighteenth century in England, and certainly after Adam Smith's *Wealth of Nations*, published in 1776, management tasks and causal explanations have been locked into models of rational behaviour, ultimately embedded in the operations of the market: managers do what they do because the imperatives of the market require that it be done. Those managers who do not manage in this way follow the fate of the dodo – their inability to adapt to a changing environment ensures their extinction. As I mentioned at the beginning of this book, according to Hales (1986), managers achieve this by leading, liaising, monitoring, allocating resources, maintaining production, maintaining peace, innovating, planning and controlling. In other words, managers manage the organization for the benefit of all or for the benefit of the shareholders or for the benefit of stakeholders. Whichever beneficiaries spring to the fore there are often two groups singularly downplayed: workers and the managers themselves. Paradise only exists in so far as these groups are essentially non-political, having no interests of their own beyond those aligned with the interests of the firm.

Although most texts acknowledge the probability of conflict between managers and workers, the assumption that much of management itself is concerned with the 'politics of management' rather than the 'rationality of management' is less popular, but hardly novel in the literature either. From Dalton's (1959) *Men who Manage* and Jay's (1967) *Management and Machiavelli*, where political goals were deemed to be critical, through Child's (1972) notion of organizations being run by a 'dominant coalition' of senior executives, to R. Lee and Lawrence's (1985) concerns for the power of social networks, and on to Hannaway's (1989) account of the duality of management, where working for the company and for oneself are the twin aims (and need not coincide), there have been arguments that management is as much a political process as a rational one. Indeed, we only need to glance through the pages of Machiavelli's *Prince* (1975) to know that the pursuit of power has never been far from the minds of leaders of organizations. From a critical perspective, of course, management as a political activity – in the sense of being exploitive – has a history almost as long; from Marx (1970) to Braverman (1974) and the Labour Process approaches, and from Bendix (1956) to Baldamus (1961), management's rational action has been configured, or rationalized (Gowler and Legge, 1983), as action in the interests of capitalists or managers but not of all. In effect, management is a political activity in terms of either the politics of competing groups or the politics of personal ascendancy through the corporate ladder (see Stewart's (1994) useful review). As Robinson's (1994) account of his MBA education suggests, this latter politicking starts early.

In effect, therefore, management practice appears to be deeply rooted in a political approach to life where individual preferences, interests and desires often prevail over those that are aligned with the requirements of the organization. The world of management is not so much a place of Mayoite rationality as a Machiavellian jungle. To appeal to the rational interests of all in securing a peaceful domain – as the Duke of Burgundy did after the Battle of Agincourt – is to fight the war to end all wars, again and again.

Managing rationality

You may recall that this journey began with a theoretical sojourn, followed by an historical scene setting, in which the significance of traditions, culture and customs played a part in the development of contemporary management as much as did any 'rational' responses to existing material conditions. The limitations of relying upon rationality as a satisfactory explanation of managerial behaviour can be examined in any number of areas, but they are perhaps most clearly manifest where the resolution of a paradox appears to defy a rational explanation. For example, the manager of a retail outlet may have a 'shortage' problem in so far as a certain amount of the shop's goods 'disappear' every month. One explanation and resolution of this problem would be to install cameras in the shop to detect the apparent thieves. But suppose those responsible turn out to be staff rather than customers? The manager may 'rationally' respond by sacking those detected and hiring new staff – though the problem may remain. On the other hand, the manager may decide to ignore the pilfering on the grounds that it is good for staff morale, which Mars (1994) describes as one manager's tactic. In this case the staff appeared to take great satisfaction – and a few goods – from their rightful owner while, unbeknown to them, their rightful owner managed to avoid incurring increased wage costs that would have far outstripped the costs associated with the theft. Yet does not the manager act in a rational way here, while the staff are actually acting 'irrationally'? Perhaps, but we should remember that one of the reasons for criminal activity appears to be the 'thrill' of lawbreaking rather than any rational attempt to secure material resources that could not lawfully be acquired. Thus, the notion of rationality, when premised upon some allegedly objective notion of acquisition, appears unable to explain such forms of behaviour.

Let us take this paradox a little further. In this next shop we know that the staff are not involved in pilfering but our manager cannot afford the cameras that may help us catch the guilty party. Suppose we decide to spend the weekend stock taking and employ an outside contractor to check the stock for us. The report provided by the stock taker suggests that even more material seems to have gone missing over the weekend of the check. The rational conclusion: the stock checker has turned into a stock taker. But when we confront the checker with this the response is equally rational: 'Would I steal stock when the only person who could have taken it was me?' Thus we have two rational interpretations of the event which imply opposite conclusions. In effect, the rationality is imposed by the interpreter; it does not lie within the actions or the material forces that pre-exist the interpretation.

The hold which this imperialistic notion of rationality appears to have over conventional approaches to management is also evident, for example, in the way consumer magazines develop their arguments on the basis of 'scientific' approaches to consumer products. For example, as Aldridge (1994) has so clearly demonstrated, when the consumer magazine *Which?* assessed jeans their analysis consisted of subjecting various pairs of jeans to tests to evaluate the strength of the materials. But this can only be an appropriate test for strength, not for what consumers necessarily want from jeans. Undoubtedly there are some jeans wearers who do want the strongest pair available, but it is just as likely that the majority are more concerned with the image that the jeans embody rather than whether they will still be wearing them twenty years from the date of purchase. Since image, style, and the degree of fashionability of any item are notoriously difficult to assess – that is subjective – the utility of the 'rational' approach persuades the examiners to examine that which can be evaluated 'rationally' – even if this approach is almost completely irrelevant. The lesson of this tale is surely that managers (here of a clothing company) would be well advised to heed the health warning that ought to be on the side of the rational approach: 'Beware, this may not be what you want.' So, is there, then, a pattern to the development of management that a constructivist account can provide in a disinterested way?

Paradox and pattern: From *Find Wally* to the *Magic Eye*

Those readers who occasionally find themselves searching for presents in book shops may have some experience with the *Find Wally* books, in which the cartoon character Wally is hidden amongst the hundreds of similar characters drawn on the page. Many readers will also have come across the *Magic Eye* or 'autostereogram' posters, which readers are encouraged to 'stare through' in order for the hidden pattern to emerge from the apparent jumble of forms on the page. These alternative forms of representation appear, at least at first sight, to go some way to demonstrate a major difference in the conventional and the constructivist approaches to management. The conventional assumption is that the pattern of management action, for which a rational explanation can be developed, lies waiting to be discovered: if you search hard enough through the data the reality will appear in the same way as Wally will if you search carefully enough. But the *Magic Eye* pictures require the reader to perform the patterning action, and indeed many readers 'fail' to see the pattern, some even disputing its reality. This latter approach appears close to the constructivist one in the sense that the reader is the one responsible for imposing rather than exposing the pattern of management action. However, the *Magic Eye* autostereograms, at least in theory, do contain the hidden code, which merely requires more active decoding by the reader than conventional pictures do, and in this sense the *Magic Eye* approach is not a strictly accurate representation of the constructivist one. Perhaps we should turn back to the consumers of *Where's Wally* for inspiration. When children act in particular ways we tend to place their behaviour in certain categories: good, naughty, bored, devious and so on. But the point is: where do these categories – or patterns – come from? Is the behaviour objectively devious or do we impute deviousness to it in order to explain it? If so, then a similar activity may well occur with regard to management: perhaps it is we who impose patterns on managers rather than discover the patterns that they are following. But if this is the case then we should also be aware of the implications this has for asserting that management is about politics and not rationality. Reflexively speaking, this means that the point of this chapter – and indeed the rest of the book – should also be subject to the same critical scrutiny: is this me imposing the pattern rather than me revealing it?

Hence, to conclude the journey where it began, and to bring us back to the metaphorical Thames that Conrad's *Heart of Darkness* begins with, we might usefully reconsider how our present concerns prevail upon us to look upon the past in different ways, to such an extent that the past does, indeed, appear to be rewritten by each generation. Currently, for instance, there appears to be a growing interest in the forms and levels of environmental pollution by previous generations; yet previous generations of scholars appeared less concerned with this than with comparing different forms of industrialization so that the 'lessons' of the past could aid the industrializing nations of the present. The point is not that each generation fabricates (that is lies about) the past for its own interests, but that the past is essentially an ambiguous creature that we cannot know in its entirety and must therefore choose to understand in one of a potentially unlimited number of ways.

Finally, let me just reiterate that this does not mean that any interpretation is as valid as any other: clearly some interpretations of management carry more weight than others; but what is of especial interest is *why*, given the constructed nature of each account, some are more equal than others. As Napoleon and the other pigs of *Animal Farm* recognized early on in their revolution (and they knew their Bacon), 'Nam et ipsa scientia potestas est'.

Bibliography

Abeggelen, J.C. 1958: *The Japanese Factory: Aspects of its Social Organization.* Glencoe, Ill.: Free Press.

Abercrombie, N., Hill, S. and Turner, B. 1980: *The Dominant Ideology Thesis.* London: Allen & Unwin.

Ackrill, M. 1988: 'Britain's Managers and the British Economy', *Oxford Review of Economic Policy*, no. 4, pp. 59–73.

Ackroyd, S. and Crowdy, P.A. 1990: 'Can Culture be Managed? Working with "Raw" Material: The Case of the English Slaughtermen', *Personnel Review*, vol. 19, no. 5, pp. 3–13.

Adair, J. 1992: 'Great Leaders: Nelson', in Syrett, M. and Hogg, C. (eds), *Frontiers of Leadership.* Oxford: Blackwell.

Adorno, T. 1974: 'The Stars Down to Earth: The *Los Angeles Times* Astrology Column', *Telos*, no. 19, pp. 20–47.

Adorno, T.W., Frenkel-Brunswick, E., Levinson, D.J. and Nevitt Stanford, R. 1950: *The Authoritarian Personality.* New York: Harper.

Ahlström, G. 1993: 'Technical Education, Engineering and Industrial Growth: Sweden in the Nineteenth and Early Twentieth Centuries', in Fox, R. and Guagnini, A. (eds), 1993: *Education, Technology and Industrial Performance in Europe, 1850–1939.* Cambridge: Cambridge University Press.

Aitkenhead, M. and Liff, S. 1990: 'The Effectiveness of Equal Opportunity Policies', in Firth-Cozens, J. and West, M. (eds), *Women at Work: Psychological and Organizational Perspectives.* Milton Keynes: Open University Press.

Alcorn, D.S. 1992: 'Dynamic Followership: Empowerment at Work', *Management Quarterly*, Spring, pp. 9–13.

Aldridge, A. 1994: 'The Construction of Rational Consumption in *Which?* Magazine: The More Blobs the Better?', *Sociology*, vol. 28, no. 4, pp. 899–912.

Anderson, B. 1983: *Imagined Communities*. London: Verso.

Anderson, B.S. and Zinsser, J.P. 1990: *A History of their Own: Women in Europe from Prehistory to the Present*. Harmondsworth: Penguin.

Anderson, G.C. and Barrett, J.G. 1987: 'Characteristics of Effective Appraisal Interviews', *Personnel Review*, vol. 16, no. 4, pp. 18–25.

Anderson, P. 1964: 'The Origins of the Present Crisis', *New Left Review*, no. 23, pp. 26–53.

Applebaum, H. 1992: *The Concept of Work: Ancient, Medieval and Modern*. New York: State University of New York Press.

Aristotle. 1981: *Politics*. Harmondsworth: Penguin.

Armstrong, p. 1984: 'Competition Between the Organizational Professions and the Evolution of Management Control', in Thompson, K. (ed.), *Work, Employment and Unemployment*. Milton Keynes: Open University Press.

Ashmore, M., Edwards, D. and Potter, J. 1993: 'Death and Furniture: An Analysis of Bottom Line Arguments Against Relativism'. Mimeo, Department of Social Sciences, Loughborough University.

Ashworth, T. 1980: *Trench Warfare 1914–1918: The Live and Let Live System*. New York: Holmes & Meier.

Atkinson, P. 1990: *The Ethnographic Imagination*. London: Routledge.

Audoin-Rouzeau, S. 1992: *Men at War 1914–1918*. Oxford: Berg.

Babington, A. 1985: *For the Sake of Example: Capital Courts Martial, 1914–18*. London: Paladin.

Badham, R. undated: 'Production Islands and Utopian Design: Reasserting the Cultural Dimension'. Mimeo, Department of Management, University of Wollongong.

Badham, R. and Mathews, J. 1989: 'The New Production Systems Debate', *Labour and Industry*, vol. 2, no. 2, pp. 194–246.

Bailey, F.G. 1992: 'Understanding Leadership: A Question of Virtue', in Syrett, M. and Hogg, C. (eds), *Frontiers of Leadership*. Oxford: Blackwell.

Baldamus, W. 1961: *Efficiency and Effort*. London: Tavistock.

Ball, C. 1854: *A Narrative of the Life and Adventures of Charles Ball, A Black Man*. Pittsburgh: John T. Shryock.

Barker, J. and Downing, H. 1980: 'Word Processing and the Transformation of Patriarchal Relations of Control in the Office', *Capital and Class*, vol. 10, pp. 64–99.

Barnett, C. 1986: *The Audit of War*. London: Macmillan.

Barney, J.B. 1986: 'Organizational Culture: Can it be a Source of Sustained Competitive Advantage?', *Academy of Management Review*, vol. 11, no. 3, pp. 656–65.

Bartelett, C.A. and Ghoshal, S. 1990: 'The Multinational Organization as an Interorganizational Network', *Academy of Management Review*, vol. 15, no. 4, pp. 603–25.

Barthes, R. 1973: *Mythologies*. London: Paladin.

Barthes, R. 1990: *S/Z*. Oxford: Blackwell.

Bartov, O. 1991: *Hitler's Army: Soldiers, Nazis, and the War in the Third Reich.* New York: Oxford University Press.

Bass, B.M. 1981: *Handbook of Leadership.* New York: Free Press.

Bass, B.M. and Stogdill, R.M. 1990: *Handbook of Leadership.* New York: Free Press.

Batstone, E. 1979: 'Systems of Accommodation, Domination and Industrial Enterprise', in Burns, T. (ed.), *Work and Power.* London: Sage.

Batstone, E., Boraston, I. and Frenkel, S. (eds) 1978: *The Social Organization of Strikes.* Oxford: Blackwell.

Baudrillard, J. 1988: *Selected Writings* (ed.) Poster, M. Cambridge: Polity Press.

Bauman, Z. 1991: *Modernity and Ambivalence.* Cambridge: Polity Press.

Baumol, W.J. 1959: *Business Behaviour: Value and Growth.* New York: Macmillan.

BBC2, 1993: *It Will All Be Over By Christmas.* 21 December.

Beaumont, P.B. 1993: *Human Resource Management: Key Concepts and Skills.* London: Sage.

Beetham, D. 1987: *Bureaucracy.* Milton Keynes: Open University Press.

Belluh, R. 1985: *Habits of the Heart.* Berkeley, Cal.: California University Press.

Bendix, R. 1956: *Work and Authority in Industry.* New York: John Wiley.

Bennis, W.G. and Nanus, B. 1985: *Leaders: The Strategies for Taking Charge.* New York: Harper and Row.

Bercovitch, S. 1993: *The Rites of Assent: Transformations in the Symbolic Construction of America.* London: Routledge.

Berg, A.J. 1991: 'He, She and I.T. - Designing the Technological House of the Future', IFIM Paper no. 12/91. Trondheim: Institute for Social Research in Industry, Trondheim.

Berle, A.A. and Means, G.C. 1932: *The Modern Corporation and Private Property.* New York: Macmillan.

Berggren, C. 1989: 'New Product Concepts in Final Assembly; The Swedish Experience', in Wood, S. (ed.), *The Transformation of Work?.* London: Unwin Hyman.

Berggren, C. 1992: *The Volvo Experience: Alternatives to Lean Production.* London: Macmillan.

Bertalanffy, L. 1950: 'An outline of General System Theory', *British Journal of Philosophical Science*, vol. 1, pp. 134–65.

Bijker, W.E. and Law, J. (eds), 1992: *Shaping Technology/Building Society.* Cambridge, Mass.: MIT Press.

Bijker, W.E., Hughes, T. and Pinch, T.J. (eds), 1987: *The Social Construction of Technological Systems.* Cambridge, Mass.: MIT Press.

Black, J.S. and Mendenhall, M. 1993: 'Resolving Conflicts with the Japanese: Mission Impossible?', *Sloan Management Review*, vol.34, no. 3, pp. 49–59.

Bland, A.E., Brown, P.A. and Tawney, R.H. (eds), 1933: *English Economic History: Select Documents.* London: Bell & Sons.

Bloch, E. 1986: *The Principle of Hope.* London: Blackwell.

Bloor, D. 1991: *Knowledge and Social Enquiry*. Cambridge, Mass.: MIT Press.

Blyton, p. and Turnbull, p. (eds) 1992: *Reassessing Human Resource Management*. London: Sage.

Booth, W.J. 1993: *Households: On the Moral Architecture of the Economy*. Ithaca, N.Y.: Cornell University Press.

Boswell, D. 1992: 'Health, the Self and Social Interaction', in Bocock, R. and Thompson, K. (eds), *Social and Cultural Forms of Modernity*. Cambridge: Polity Press.

Bourdieu, p. and Passeron, J. 1977: *Reproduction in Education, Society and Culture*. London: Sage.

Brannen, p. 1983: *Authority and Participation in Industry*. London: Batsford.

Braudel, F. 1973: *Capitalism and Material Life*. London: Weidenfeld and Nicolson.

Braverman, H. 1974: *Labor and Monopoly Capital*. New York: Monthly Review Press.

Brewer, E. 1984: *Studying Chaucer*. London: Longman.

Brown, J.A.C. 1964: *Social Psychology of Industry*. Harmondsworth: Penguin.

Brown, M. 1993: *The Imperial War Museum Book of the Western Front*. London: Sidgwick and Jackson.

Bryman, A. 1988: *Quantity and Quality in Social Research*. London: Unwin Hyman.

Buchanan, D.A. and Huczynski, A.A. 1985: *Organizational Behaviour: An Introductory Text*. London: Prentice Hall International.

Buckingham, L. 1992: 'Swashbucklers Put to the Sword', *Guardian*, 12 December.

Buhalo, I.H. 1991: 'Performance Appraisals Become Democratic', *Personnel*, vol. 68, no. 5, May, p. 23.

Buhler, P. 1993: 'Managing in the 90s', *Supervision*, March, pp. 17–19.

Burch, P.H. Jr. 1972: *The Managerial Revolution Reassessed*. Lexington, Mass.: Lexington Books.

Burke, R.J., Weitzel, W. and Weir, T. 1978: 'Characteristics of Effective Employee Performance Review and Development Interviews', *Personnel Psychology*, vol. 31, no. 3, pp. 903–18.

Burnham. J. 1962: *The Managerial Revolution*. London: Macmillan.

Burns, J.M. 1978: *Leadership*. New York: Harper and Row.

Burns, T. (ed.) 1979: *Work and Power*. London: Sage.

Burrell, G. 1988: 'Modernism, Postmodernism and Organizational Analysis: the Contribution of Michel Foucault', *Organization Studies*, vol. 9, no. 2, pp. 221–35.

Burrell, G. 1994: 'Modernism, Postmodernism and Organizational Analysis: the Contribution of Jürgen Habermas', *Organization Studies*, vol. 15, no. 1, pp. 1–19.

Burrell, G. and Morgan, G. 1979: *Sociological Paradigms and Organizational Analysis*. London: Heinemann.

Bush, B. 1982: 'Defiance or Submission? The Role of the Slave Woman in Slave Resistance in the British Caribbean', *Immigrants and Minorities*, vol. 1, no. 1, pp. 16–38.

Business Intelligence, 1994: *Re-engineering: The Critical Success Factors*. London: Business Intelligence/Financial Times.

Butler, S. 1970: *Erewhon*. Harmondsworth: Penguin (originally 1872).

Cafasso, R. 1993: 'Re-engineering: Just the First Step', *Computer World*, 19 April, p. 94.

Cain, P.J. and Hopkins, A.G. 1993a: *British Imperialism: Innovation and Expansion 1688-1914*. Harlow: Longman.

Cain, P.J. and Hopkins, A.G. 1993b: *British Imperialism: Crisis and Deconstruction 1914-1990*. Harlow: Longman.

Callon, M. 1986: 'Some Elements of a Sociology of Translation: Domestication of the Scallops and the Fishermen of St Brieuc Bay', in Law, J. (ed.), *Power, Action and Belief: A New Sociology of Knowledge?*. London: Routledge and Kegan Paul.

Cannadine, D. 1992: *The Decline and Fall of the British Aristocracy*. London: Picador.

Cannadine, D. 1994: 'The Context, Performance and Meaning of Ritual: The British Monarchy and the "Invention of Tradition"', in Hobsbawm, E. and Ranger, T. (eds), *The Invention of Tradition*. Cambridge: Canto. ·

Carlson, S. 1951: *Executive Behaviour: A Study of the Workload and Working Methods of Managing Directors*. Stockholm: Strombergs.

Carlton, I. and Sloman, M. 1992: 'Performance Appraisal in Practice', *Human Resource Management Journal*, vol. 2, no. 3, pp. 80–94.

Case, P. 1994: 'Virtually the End of History: A Critique of Business Process Re-Engineering'. Paper presented at the 12th International Standing Conference on Organizational Symbolism, 'Organizing the Past', Calgary, Alberta, July.

Caulkin, S. 1993: 'Leaner, Faster, Cheaper', *Observer*, 3 October.

Cavalli, L. 1987: 'Charisma and Twentieth Century Politics', in Whimster, S. and Lash, S. (eds), *Max Weber, Rationality and Modernity*. London: Allen & Unwin.

Cavendish, R. 1985: 'Women on the Line', in Littler, C.R. (ed.), *The Experience of Work*. Aldershot: Gower.

Chandler, A.D. 1977: *The Visible Hand: The Managerial Revolution in American Business*. Cambridge, Mass.: Harvard University Press.

Chandler, A.D. 1992: 'Managerial Enterprise and Competitive Capabilities', *Business History*, vol. 34, no. 1, pp. 11–41.

Chandler, A.D. 1990: *Scale and Scope: The Dynamics of Industrial Capitalism*. Cambridge, Mass.: The Belknap Press.

Chapman, M., McDonald, M. and Tonkin, E. 1989: 'Introduction', in Tonkin, E., McDonald, M. and Chapman, M. (eds), *History and Ethnicity*. London: Routledge.

Child, J. 1969: *British Management Thought*. Allen & Unwin.

Child, J. 1972: 'Organizational Structure, Environment and Performance', *Sociology*, vol. 6, no. 1, pp. 1–22.

Child, J., Fores, M., Glover, I. and Lawrence, P. 1983: 'A Price to Pay?', *Sociology*, vol. 17, no. 1, pp. 63–78.

Church, R. 1993: 'The Family Firm in Industrial Capitalism: International Perspectives on Hypotheses and History', *Business History*, vol. 35, no. 4, pp. 17–43.

Clegg, S. 1990: *Modern Organizations*. London: Sage.

Coarse, R.H. 1953: 'The Nature of the Firm', in Boulding, K.E. and Stigler, G.J. (eds), *Readings in Price Theory*. Chicago: University of Chicago Press.

Coates, D. 1992: *UK Economic Decline: A Review of the Literature*. Leeds Centre for Industrial Policy and Performance, University of Leeds.

Cockburn, C. 1983: *Brothers: Male Dominance and Technological Change*. London: Pluto Press.

Cockburn, C. 1985: *Machinery of Dominance: Women, Men and Technical Know-how*. London: Pluto Press.

Cockburn, C. 1991: *In the Way of Women*. London: Macmillan.

Cockburn, C. and Ormrod, S. 1993: *Gender and Technology in the Making*. London: Sage.

Coe, T. 1992: *The Key to the Men's Club: Opening the Door to Women in Management*. London: Institute of Management.

Cole, R.E. 1992: 'Work and Leisure in Japan', *California Management Review*, Spring, pp. 52–63.

Coleman, D.C. 1987: 'Failings and Achievings: Some British Businesses, 1910–80', *Business History*, vol. 29, pp. 1–2.

Colley, L. 1994: *Britons: Forging the Nation 1707–1837*. London: Pimlico.

Collins, H. 1992: *Labour Law: Management Decisions and Workers' Rights*. London: Butterworth.

Conger, J.A. 1993: 'The Brave New World of Leadership Training', *Organizational Dynamics*, Winter, pp. 46–58.

Constable, J. and McCormick, R. 1987: *The Making of British Management*. London: CBI/BIM.

Cook, H. 1993: *Samurai*. London: Blandford Press.

Cooley, M. 1968: *Architect or Bee?*. Slough: Langley Technical Services.

Cooper, R. 1989: 'Modernism, Postmodernism and Organizational Analysis: the Contribution of Jacques Derrida', *Organization Studies*, vol. 10, no. 4, pp. 479–502.

Cooper, R. and Burrell, G. 1988: 'Modernism, Postmodernism and Organizational Analysis: An Introduction', *Organization Studies*, vol. 9, pp. 91–112.

Cowe, R. 1992: 'Curse of the Business Idols', *Guardian*, 27 November.

Crafts, N. 1989: 'Revealed Comparative Advantages in Marketing 1899–1950', *Journal of European Economic History*, no. 18, pp. 126–37.

Crittenden, J. 1987: *Beyond Individualism: Reconstituting the Liberal Self*. New York: Oxford University Press.

Crozier, M. 1964: *The Bureaucratic Phenomenon*. London: Tavistock.

Cru, J.N. 1929: *Témoins: Essai d'analyse et de critique des souvenirs de combatants édités en français de 1915 à 1928*. Paris: Les Entincelles.

Crump, L. 1989: 'Japanese Managers - Western Workers: Cross-cultural Training and Development Issues', *Journal of Management Development*, vol. 8, no. 4, pp. 48–55.

Cyert, R.M. and March, J.G. 1963: *A Behavioural Theory of the Firm*. Englewood Cliffs, N.J.: Prentice Hall.

Czarniawska-Joerges, B. and Wolff, R. 1991: 'Leaders, Managers, Entrepreneurs On and Off the Organizational Stage', *Organization Studies*, vol. 12, no. 4, pp. 529–46.

Dahl, R.A. 1956: *A Preface to Democratic Theory*. Chicago: Chicago University Press.

Dahl, R.A. 1985: *A Preface to Economic Democracy*. Cambridge: Polity Press.

Dallas, G. and Gill, D. 1985: *The Unknown Army: Mutinies in the British Army in World War 1*. London: Verso.

Dalton, M. 1959: *Men who Manage*. New York: McGraw-Hill.

Daunton, M. 1989: '"Gentlemanly Capitalism" and British Industry, 1820–1914', *Past and Present*, no. 122, pp. 119–58.

Davidson, M. and Cooper, C. 1992: *Shattering the Glass Ceiling*. London: Paul Chapman.

Day, G. 1993: 'New Directions for Corporations', *European Management Journal*, vol. 11, No. 2, pp. 229–37.

Deal, T. and Kennedy, A.E. 1982: *Corporate Cultures*. Reading, Mass.: Addison-Wesley.

Dennis, N., Henriques, F. and Slaughter, C. 1956: *Coal is Our Life*. London: Eyre and Spottiswoode.

Denison, D.R. 1990: *Corporate Culture and Organizational Effectiveness*. London: John Wiley.

Derrida, J. 1976: *Of Grammatology*. Baltimore, Md.: Johns Hopkins University Press.

Derrida, J. 1978: *Writing and Difference*. London: Routledge.

Dintenfass, M. 1992: *The Decline of Industrial Britain 1870–1980*. London: Routledge.

Dixon, N.F. 1979: *On the Psychology of Military Incompetence*. London: Futura.

Donovan, A. 1993: 'Education, Industry and the American University', in Fox, R. and Guagnini, A. (eds), *Education, Technology and Industrial Performance in Europe, 1850–1939*. Cambridge: Cambridge University Press.

Donovan Commission, 1968: *Report of the Royal Commission on Trade Unions and Employer's Associations*. London: HMSO.

Dore, R. 1973: *British Factory, Japanese Factory: The Origins of National Diversity in Industrial Relations*. London: Allen & Unwin.

Dore, R. 1994: 'Equality–efficiency Trade-offs: Japanese Perceptions and

Choices', in Aoki, M. and Dore, R. (eds), *The Japanese Firm*. Oxford: Clarendon Press.

Dorfman, J. 1961: *Thorstein Veblen and his America*. New York: Augustus M. Kelley.

Douglas, M. 1966: *Purity and Danger*. London: Routledge and Kegan Paul.

Douglas, M. and Douglas, J. 1989: 'Institutions of the Third Kind: British and Swedish Labour Markets Compared', *Journal of General Management*, vol. 14, no. 4, pp. 34–52.

Drummond, D. 1989: '"Specifically Designed?" Employers' Labour Strategies and Worker Responses in British Railway Workshops, 1838–1914', *Business History*, vol. XXXI, no. 2, pp. 8–29.

Durkheim, E. 1952: *Suicide: A Study in Sociology*. London: Routledge and Kegan Paul.

Durkheim, E. 1961: *The Elementary Forms of the Religious Life*. New York: Collier Books.

Easlea, B. 1983: *Fathering the Unthinkable: Masculinity, Scientists and the Nuclear Arms Race*. London: Pluto Press.

Eco, U. 1981: *The Role of the Reader: Explorations in the Semiotics of Texts*. London: Hutchinson.

Edwards, M.R. 1989: 'Making Performance Appraisals Meaningful and Fair', *Business*, July–September, pp. 17–25.

Ehrenreich, B. and English, D. 1979: *For Her Own Good*. London: Pluto Press.

Elam, M. 1994: 'Anti Anticonstructivism, or Laying the Fears of a Langdon Winner to Rest', *Science Technology and Human Values*, vol. 19, no. 1, pp. 101–6.

Elbaum, B. 1989: 'Why Apprenticeship Persisted in Britain but not in the United States', *Journal of Economic History*, vol. XLIX, no. 2, pp. 337–49.

Ellis, J. 1993: *The Social History of the Machine Gun*. London: Pimlico.

Ellwood, W. 1993: 'Multinationals and the Subversion of Sovereignty', *New Internationalist*, no. 246, August, pp. 4–7.

Employment Policy Institute, 1993: *A Case for Work Sharing?*. London: EPI.

ESRC (Economic and Social Research Council) 1994: *Building Partnerships: Enhancing the Quality of Management Research*. Swindon: ESRC.

Evans, W.A, Hau, K.C. and Sculli, D. 1989: 'A Cross Cultural Comparison of Management Styles', *Journal of Management Development*, vol. 8, no. 3, pp. 3–14.

Faulkner, W. and Arnold, E. (eds) 1985: *Smothered by Invention*. London: Pluto Press.

Fayol, G.H. 1949: *General and Industrial Management*. London: Pitman.

Fidler, J. 1981: *The British Business Elite*. London: Routledge and Kegan Paul.

Fiedler, F.E. 1967: *A Theory of Leadership Effectiveness*. New York: McGraw-Hill.

Fiedler, F.E. 1978: 'The Contingency Model and the Dynamics of the Leadership Process', in Berkowitz, L. (ed.), *Advances in Experimental Social Psychology*. New York: Academic Press.

Fiedler, F.E. and Garcia, J.E. 1987: *New Approaches to Leadership: Cognitive Resources and Organizational Development*. New York: John Wiley.

Fineman, S. 1993: *Emotion in Organizations*. London: Sage.

Finley, M.I. 1963: *The Ancient Greeks*. Harmondsworth: Penguin.

Finniston, M. 1980: *Engineering Our Future, Report of the Committee of Enquiry into the Engineering Profession*. London: HMSO.

Flower, J. 1991: 'The Art and Craft of Followership', *Healthcare Forum Journal*, no. 56, January, pp. 56–60.

Flower, J .1992: 'Differences Make a Difference', *Healthcare Forum Journal*, no. 62, September, pp. 62–9.

Follett, M.P. 1949: 'The Essentials of Leadership', in Urwick, L. (ed.), *Freedom and Co-ordination*. London: Management Publications Trust.

Fortado, B. 1992: 'Subordinate Views in Supervisory Conflict Situations: Peering into the Subcultural Chasm', *Human Relations*, vol. 45, no. 11, pp. 1141–67.

Foucault, M. 1967: *Madness and Civilization: A History of Insanity in the Age of Reason*. London: Tavistock.

Foucault, M. 1979: *Discipline and Punish*. Harmondsworth: Penguin.

Foucault, M. 1980: *Power–Knowledge*. Brighton: Harvester.

Foucault, M. 1988: 'The Ethic of Care for the Self as a Practice of Freedom', in Bernauer, J. and Rasmussen, D. (eds), *The Final Foucault*. Cambridge, Mass.: MIT Press.

Fox, A. 1974: *Beyond Contract*. London: Faber.

Fox, A. 1985: *History and Heritage: The Social Origins of the British Industrial Relations System*. London: Allen & Unwin.

Fox, N.J. 1993: *Postmodernism, Sociology and Health*. Buckingham: Open University Press.

Fox, R. and Guagnini, A. (eds) 1993: *Education, Technology and Industrial Performance in Europe, 1850–1939*. Cambridge: Cambridge University Press.

Fox Keller, E. 1988: 'Feminist Perspectives on Science Studies', *Science, Technology & Human Values*, vol. 13, pp. 235–49.

Friedman, A. 1977: *Industry and Labour*. London: Macmillan.

Frisby, D. 1984: *Georg Simmel*. London: Tavistock.

Fromm, E. 1960: *The Fear of Freedom*. London: Routledge.

Fukuyama, F. 1992: *The End of History and the Last Man*. London: Hamish Hamilton.

Galin, A. 1989: 'The Relevance of Leadership Variables of Performance Appraisal', *Personnel Review*, vol. 18, no. 1, pp. 35–40.

Gammage, R.C. 1976: *A History of the Chartist Movement*. London: Merlin Press.

Gatrell, V.A.C. 1971: 'The Commercial Class in Manchester *c*.1820–1857', PhD dissertation, Cambridge University.

Gay, P. 1973: *The Enlightenment: An Interpretation*. Vols 1 & 2. London: Wildwood House.

Gay, P. du, and Salaman, G. 1992: 'The Cult[ure] of the Customer', *Journal of Management Studies*, vol. 29, no. 5, pp. 615–33.

Geary, J.F. 1992: 'Pay, Control and Commitment: Linking Appraisal and Reward', *Human Resource Management Journal*, vol. 2, no. 4, pp. 36–54.

Geertz, C. 1973: *The Interpretation of Culture*. London: Hutchinson.

Gellerman, S.W. and Hodgson, W.G. 1988: 'Cyanimid's New Take on Performance Appraisal', *Harvard Business Review*, vol. 64, no. 4, pp. 85–90.

Gergen, K.J. 1992: 'Organization Theory in the Postmodern Era', in Reed, M. and Hughes, M. (eds), *Rethinking Organization: New Directions in Organization Theory and Analysis*. London: Sage.

Giddens, A. 1979: *Central Problems in Social Theory*. London: Macmillan.

Giddens, A. 1990: *The Consequences of Modernity*. Cambridge: Polity Press.

Gilbert, G.R. and Hyde, A.C. 1988: 'Followership and the Federal Worker', *Public Administration Review*, November/December, pp. 962–8.

Gilbert, M. 1986: *The Holocaust: The Jewish Tragedy*. London: Guild Publishing.

Gill, D. 1977: *Appraising Performance: Present Trends and the Next Decade*. London: Institute of Personnel Management.

Gill, D., Ungerson, B. and Thakur, M. 1973: *Performance Appraisal in Perspective*. London: Institute of Personnel Management.

Gillespie, R. 1991: *Manufacturing Knowledge: A History of the Hawthorne Experiments*. Cambridge: Cambridge University Press.

Gimpel, J. 1992: *The Medieval Machine*. London: Pimlico.

Gleick, J. 1987: *Chaos: Making a new Science*. London: Cardinal.

Glover, I.A. 1992: '"But Westward, Look, the Land is Bright"? Reflections on What is to be Learnt From British Management Education and Practice', *Journal of Strategic Change*, vol. 1, pp. 319–31.

Goffman, E. 1961: *Asylums*. Harmondsworth: Penguin.

Goldthorpe, J.H., Lockwood, D., Bechhofer, F. and Platt, J. 1969: *The Affluent Worker in the Class Structure*. Cambridge: Cambridge University Press.

Goold, M. and Luchs, K. 1993: 'Why Diversify? Four Decades of Management Thinking', *Executive*, vol. 7, no. 3, pp. 7–25.

Gordon, G.C. and DiTomaso, N. 1992: 'Predicting Corporate Performance from Organizational Culture', *Journal of Management Studies*, vol. 29, no. 6, pp. 783–98.

Gospel, H. 1989: 'Product Markets, Labour Markets and Industrial Relations: The Case of Flour Milling', *Business History*, vol. XXXI, no. 2, pp. 84–97.

Gospel, H. 1992: *Markets, Firms and the Management of Modern Labour in Britain*. Cambridge: Cambridge University Press.

Gowler, D. and Legge, K. 1983: 'The Meaning of Management and the Management of Meaning', in Earl, M.J. (ed.), *Perspectives on Management: A Multidisciplinary Analysis*. Oxford: Oxford University Press.

Grabsky, P. 1993: *The Great Commanders*. London: Boxtree.

Gray, R. 1987: 'The Languages of Factory Reform in Britain, 1830–1860', in Joyce, P. (ed.), *The Historical Meanings of Work*. Cambridge: Cambridge University Press.

Green, E., Owen, J. and Pain, D. (eds) 1993: *Gendered by Design?*. London: Taylor and Francis.

Gregersen, H. and Sailer, L. 1993: 'Chaos Theory and its Implications for Social Science Research', *Human Relations*, vol. 46, no. 7, pp. 777–802.

Grint, K. 1988: 'Women and Equality', *Sociology*, vol. 22, no. 1, pp. 87–108.

Grint, K. 1991: *The Sociology of Work*. Cambridge: Polity Press.

Grint, K. 1993a: 'What's Wrong with Performance Appraisals', *Human Resource Management Journal*, vol. 3, no. 3, pp. 61–77.

Grint, K. 1993b: 'Japanisation? Some Early Lessons From the British Post Office', *Industrial Relations Journal*, vol. 24, no.1, pp. 14–27.

Grint, K. 1994: 'Reengineering History', *Organization*, vol. 1, no. 1, pp. 179–202.

Grint, K. and Choi, J.C. 1993: 'Whither the Embrangled East? Trust and Informality in Eastern Europe'. Templeton College Management Research Paper. Oxford: Templeton College.

Grint, K. and Gill, R. (eds) 1995: *The Gender–Technology Relation*. London: Taylor and Francis.

Grint, K. and Hogan, E. 1994a: 'Utopian Management'. Templeton College. Management Research Paper. Oxford: Templeton College.

Grint, K. & Hogan, E. 1994b: 'Fatalism and Utopia: Constructing an Index of Possibilities'. Templeton College Management Research Paper. Oxford: Templeton College.

Grint, K. and Woolgar, S. 1992: 'Computers, Guns and Roses: What's Social about being Shot?', *Science, Technology and Human Values*, vol. 17, no. 3, pp. 366–80.

Grint, K. and Woolgar, S. 1995a: 'On some Failure of Nerve in Constructivist and Feminist Analyses of Technology', in Grint, K. and Gill, R. (eds), *The Gender–Technology Relation*. London: Taylor and Francis.

Grint, K. and Woolgar, S. 1995b: *Deus ex Machina: Technology, Constructivism and Beyond*. Cambridge: Polity Press.

Guagnini, A. 1993: 'Worlds Apart: Academic Instruction and Professional Qualifications in the Training of Mechanical Engineers in England, 1850–1914', in Fox, R. and Guagnini, A. (eds), *Education, Technology and Industrial Performance in Europe, 1850–1939*. Cambridge: Cambridge University Press.

Guest, D. 1990: 'Human Resource Management and the American Dream', *Journal of Management Studies*, vol. 27, no. 4, pp. 377–97.

Guilford, J.P. 1954: *Psychometric Methods*. New York: McGraw-Hill.

Gutteridge, L.F. 1992: *Mutiny: A History of Naval Insurrection*. Shepperton: Ian Allen.

Habermas, J. 1971: *Towards a Rational Society*. London: Heinemann.

Hacker, S. 1989: *Pleasure, Power and Technology*. London: Unwin.

Hales, C.P. 1986: 'What Do Managers Do? A Critical Review of the Evidence', *Journal of Management Studies*, vol. 23, no. 1, pp. 88–115.

Hall, G., Rosenthal, J. and Wade, J. 1993: 'How to Make Reengineering *Really* Work', *Harvard Business Review*, November/December, pp. 119–31.

Hall, S. 1992: 'The Question of Cultural Identity', in Hall, S., Held, D. and McGrew, T. (eds), *Modernity and its Futures*. Cambridge: Polity Press.

Hamilton, P. 1992: 'The Enlightenment and the Birth of Social Science', in Hall, S. and Gieben, B. (eds), *Formations of Modernity*. Cambridge: Polity Press.

Hammer, M. 1990: 'Reengineering Work: Don't Automate, Obliterate', *Harvard Business Review*, July–August, pp. 104–12.

Hammer, M. and Champy, J. 1993a: 'Reengineering the Corporation', *Insights Quarterly*, Summer, pp. 3–19.

Hammer, M. and Champy, J. 1993b: *Reengineering the Corporation: A Manifesto for Business Revolution*. London: Nicholas Brealey.

Hampden-Turner, C. and Trompenaars, F. 1994: *The Seven Cultures of Capitalism*. London: Piatkus.

Handy, C. 1985: *Understanding Organizations*. Harmondsworth: Penguin.

Hannaway, J. 1989: *Managers Managing*. New York: Oxford University Press.

Hantrais, L. and Walters, P. 1994: 'Making It In and Making Out: Women in Professional Occupations in Britain and France', *Gender, Work and Organization*, vol. 1, no. 1, pp. 23–32.

Haralambos, M. and Holborn, M. 1991: *Sociology: Themes and Perspectives*. London: Collins Educational.

Haraway, D.J. 1991: *Simians, Cyborgs and Women: The Reinvention of Women*. London: Free Association Books.

Harding, S. (ed.) 1986: *Perspectives on Gender and Science*. Brighton: Falmer.

Hardy, D. 1979: *Alternative Communities in Nineteenth Century England*. London: Longman.

Harkins, S. and Szymanski, K. 1987: 'Social Loafing and Social Facilitation', in Hendrick, C. (ed.), *Group Processes and Intergroup Relations*. Newbury Park, Cal.: Sage.

Harkins, S. and Szymanski, K. 1989: 'Social Loafing and Group Evaluation', *Journal of Personality and Social Psychology*, vol. 56, pp. 934–41.

Harrison, D.B. and Pratt, M.D. 1993: 'A Methodology for Reengineering Businesses', *Planning Review*, March–April, pp. 6–11.

Hartley, J. and Hawkes, T. 1977: *Popular Culture and High Culture: History and Theory*. Milton Keynes: Open University Press.

Harvey, B. 1993: *Living and Dying in England 1100–1540: The Monastic Experience*. Oxford: Clarendon Press.

Harvey, C. and Press, J. 1989: 'Overseas Investment and the Professional Advance of British Metal Mining Engineers, 1851–1914', *Economic History Review*, vol. XLII, no. 1, pp. 64–86.

Harvey, D. 1989: *The Condition of Postmodernity*. Oxford: Blackwell.

Hassard, J. 1993: *Sociology and Organization Theory: Positivism, Paradigms and Postmodernity*. Cambridge: Cambridge University Press.

Hassard, J. 1994: 'Postmodern Organizational Analysis: Towards a Conceptual Framework', *Journal of Management Studies*, vol. 31, no. 3, pp. 303–24.

Hassard, J. and Parker, M. 1993: *Postmodernism and Organizations*. London: Sage.

Hassard, J. and Pym, D. 1990: *The Theory and Philosophy of Organizations*. London: Routledge.

Hawthorn, G. 1976: *Enlightenment and Despair: A History of Sociology*. Cambridge: Cambridge University Press.

Haynes, M. 1988: 'Employers and Trade Unions, 1824–1850', in Rule, J. (ed.), *British Trade Unionism 1750–1850*. Harlow: Longman.

Held, D. 1980: *Introduction to Critical Theory*. London: Hutchinson.

Held, D. 1987: *Models of Democracy*. Cambridge: Polity Press.

Held, D. 1989: *Political Theory and the Modern State*. Cambridge: Polity Press.

Heller, F. 1979: *What do the British Want from Participation and Industrial Democracy?* London: Anglo-German Foundation.

Heller, R. 1993: 'Leading Edge', *Observer*, 28 March.

Helmers, S. 1991: 'Anthropological Contributions to Organizational Culture'. Paper presented at the conference on the Anthropology of Organizations, University College, Swansea, April.

Hendry, J. 1993: *Wrapping Culture: Politeness, Presentation, and Power in Japan and Other Societies*. Oxford: Oxford University Press.

Hersey, P. and Blanchard, K.H. 1982: *Management of Organizational Behaviour*. Englewood Cliffs, N.J.: Prentice Hall.

Hirschauer, S. and Mol, A. 1993: 'Beyond Embrace: Multiple Sexes at Multiple Sites'. Paper presented to the conference on European Theoretical Perspectives on New Technology: Feminism, Constructivism and Utility, CRICT, Brunel University, 16–17 September.

Hirszowicz, M. 1981: *Industrial Sociology*. Oxford: Martin Robertson.

Hobbes, T. 1968: *Leviathan*. Harmondsworth: Penguin.

Hobsbawm, E.J. 1962: *The Age of Revolutions*. New York: Mentor Books.

Hobsbawm, E.J. and Rudé, G. 1969: *Captain Swing*. London: Lawrence and Wishart.

Hofstede, G. 1980: *Culture's Consequences*. Beverly Hills, Cal.: Sage.

Hofstede, G. 1991: *Cultures and Organizations: Software of the Mind*. London: McGraw-Hill.

Hofstede, G. 1993. 'Cultural Constraints in Management Theories', *Academy of Management Executive*, vol. 7, no. 1, pp. 81–94.

Hogan, G. and Goodson, J. 1990: 'The Key to Expatriate Success', *Training and Development Journal*, January, pp. 50–2.

Hoggart, R. 1959: *The Uses of Literacy*. London: Chatto and Windus.

Holmes, R. 1987: *Firing Line*. Harmondsworth: Penguin.

Honeyman, K. 1982: *Origins of Enterprise: Business Leadership in the Industrial Revolution*. New York: Manchester University Press.

Hopkins, E. 1979: *A Social History of the English Working Classes*. London: Edward Arnold.

Human Relations 1994: Special edition, vol. 47, no. 6.

Hunter, J.E. 1989: *The Emergence of Modern Japan*. London: Longman.

Hunter, L.C. and Thomson, A.W.J. 1976: 'British Labour in the Twentieth Century'. Paper presented at the 4th World Congress of the International Industrial Relations Association, Geneva.

Inagami, T. 1983: 'Labor–Management Communication at the Workshop Level', *Japanese Industrial Relations*, series 11, pp. 15–18.

Jabes, J. 1982: 'Individual Decision Making', in McGrew, A.G. and Wilson, M.J. (eds), *Decision Making: Approaches and Analysis*. Manchester: Manchester University Press.

James, C.L.R. 1938: *The Black Jacobins: Toussaint-Louverture and the San Domingo Revolution*. London: Secker and Warburg

Janis, I.L. 1972: *Victims of Group Think*. Boston: Houghton Mifflin.

Janson, R. 1992/3: 'How Reengineering Transforms Organizations to Satisfy Customers', *National Productivity Review*, Winter, pp. 45–53.

Jaques, E. 1951: *The Changing Culture of a Factory*. London: Tavistock.

Jay, A. 1967: *Management and Machiavelli*. New York: Benton Books.

Jenks, C. 1993: *Culture*. London: Routledge.

Jeremy, D.J. 1990: 'The Hundred Largest Employers in the United Kingdom, in Manufacturing and Non-Manufacturing Industries, in 1907, 1935 and 1955', *Business History*, vol. 33, no. 1, pp. 93–111.

Jones, D. 1975: *Chartism and the Chartists*. London: Allen Lane.

Jones, G. and Rose, M.B. 1993: 'Family Capitalism', *Business History*, vol. 35, no. 4, pp. 1–16.

Jones, J.V. 1989: *Rebecca's Children: A Study of Rural Society, Crime and Protest*. Oxford: Oxford University Press.

Joyce, P. 1980: *Work, Society and Politics*. London: Methuen.

Joyce, P. 1991: *Visions of the People*. Cambridge: Cambridge University Press.

Kamin, L. 1977: *The Science and Politics of IQ*. Harmondsworth: Penguin.

Kane, J.S. and Lawler, E.E. III. 1979: 'Performance Appraisal Effectiveness: Its Assessment and Determination', *Research in Organizational Behaviour*, no. 1, pp. 425–78.

Karier, C.J. 1976a: 'Business Values and the Educational State', in Dale, R., Esland, G. and MacDonald, M. (eds), *Schooling and Capitalism*. London: Routledge and Kegan Paul.

Karier, C.J. 1976b: 'Testing for Order and Control in the Corporate Liberal State', in Dale, R. et al. (eds), *Schooling and Capitalism*. London: Routledge and Kegan Paul.

Kawai, T. 1992: 'Generating Innovation through Strategic Action Planning', *Long Range Planning*, June, pp. 36–42.

Kaye, J. 1993: *Foundations of Corporate Success*. Oxford: Oxford University Press.

Keeble, S.P. 1992: *The Ability to Manage: A Study of British Management, 1890–1990*. Manchester: Manchester University Press.

Keegan, J. 1976: *The Face of Battle*. Harmondsworth: Penguin.

Keegan, J .1987: *The Mask of Command*. London: Jonathan Cape.

Keegan, J. 1991: 'The Imperative of Example', in Syrett, M. and Hogg, C. (eds), *Frontiers of Leadership*. Oxford: Blackwell.

Keegan, J. 1993: *A History of Warfare*. London: Hutchinson.

Kelley, R. E. 1988: 'In Praise of Followers', *Harvard Business Review*, vol. 88, no. 6, pp. 142–48.

Kelly, J. 1982: *Scientific Management, Job Redesign and Work Performance*. London: Academic Press.

Kelly, R.M. 1991: *The Gendered Economy: Work, Careers and Success*. London: Sage.

Kertzer, D. 1988: *Ritual, Politics and Power*. New Haven, Conn.: Yale University Press.

Kessler, I. 1994: 'Performance Related Pay: Contrasting Approaches', *Industrial Relations Journal*, vol. 25, no. 2, pp. 122–35.

Kessler, I. and Purcell, J. 1992: 'Performance Related Pay: Objectives and Application', *Human Resource Management Journal*, vol. 2, no. 3, Spring, pp. 16–33.

Kiechel, W. III. 1989: 'When Subordinates Evaluate the Boss', *Fortune*, 19 June, pp. 201–2.

Kieser, A. 1989: 'Organizational, Institutional and Societal Evolution: Medieval Craft Guilds and the Genesis of Formal Organizations', *Administrative Science Quarterly*, no. 34, pp. 540–64.

Kilman, R.H., Saxton, M.J. and Serpa, R. (eds), 1985: *Gaining Control of the Corporate Culture*. San Francisco: Jossey-Bass.

Kirchner, W.K. and Reisberg, D.J. 1962: 'Differences between Better and Less Effective Supervisors in Appraisal of Subordinates', *Personnel Psychology*, no. 15, pp. 295–302.

Kirkpatrick, D.L. 1992: 'The Power of Empowerment', *Training and Development*, September, pp. 29–31.

Kirkup, G. and Smith Keller, L. 1992: 'The Nature of Science and Technology', in Kirkup, G. and Smith Keller, L. (eds), *Inventing Women: Science, Technology and Gender*. Cambridge: Polity Press.

Klein, H.J., Snell, S.A. and Wexley, K.N. 1987: 'Systems Model of the Performance Appraisal Interview Process', *Industrial Relations*, vol. 26, no. 3, pp. 267–80.

Kling, R. 1992: 'Audiences, Narratives and Human Values in Social Studies of Technology', *Science, Technology and Human Values*, vol. 17, no. 3, pp. 349–65.

Kolind, L. 1994: 'Thinking the Unthinkable', *Focus on Change Management*, no. 3, pp. 4–7.

König, W. 1993: 'Technical Education and Industrial Performance in Germany: A Triumph of Heterogeneity', in Fox, R. and Guagnini, A. (eds), *Education, Technology and Industrial Performance in Europe, 1850–1939*. Cambridge: Cambridge University Press.

Kotter, J. 1982: *The General Managers*. New York: Free Press.

Knights, D. and Willmott, H. 1992: 'Conceptualizing Leadership Processes: A Study of Senior Managers in a Financial Services Company', *Journal of Management Studies*, vol. 29, no. 6, pp. 761–82.

Kouzes, J.M. and Posner, B. 1990: 'The Credibility Factor', *Business Credit*, July, pp. 24–8.

Kreinberg, N. and Stage, E.K. 1983: 'EQUALS in Computer Technology', in Zimmerman, J. (ed.), *The Technological Woman: Interfacing with Tomorrow*. New York: Praeger.

Kroeber, A.L. and Kluckhohn, C. 1963: *Culture: A Critical Review of Concepts and Definitions*. New York: Vintage Books.

Kuhn, T.S. 1970: *The Structure of Scientific Revolutions*. Chicago: Chicago University Press.

Kvande, E. and Rasmussen, B. 1986: 'Who Lacks Courage – the Organizations or the Women?'. NOTAT Paper no. 5. Trondheim: Institute for Social Research in Industry, Trondheim.

Kynaston, D. 1976: *King Labour: The British Working Class 1850–1914*. London: Allen & Unwin.

Laet, M. de. 1993: Discussant's remarks at the workshop on European Theoretical Perspectives on New Technology: Feminism, Constructivism and Utility, CRICT, Brunel University, 16–17 September 1993.

Lam, A. 1992: *Women and Japanese Management: Discrimination and Reform*. London: Routledge.

Landes, D. 1986: 'What Do Bosses Really Do?', *Journal of Economic History*, vol. 46, no. 3, pp. 585–623.

Langford, P. 1989: *A Polite and Commercial People: England, 1727–1783*. Oxford: Oxford University Press.

Lash, S. and Urry, J. 1987: *The End of Organized Capitalism*. Cambridge: Polity Press.

Latour, B. 1986: 'The Powers of Association', in Law, J. (ed.), *Power, Action and Belief: A New Sociology of Knowledge?*. London: Routledge and Kegan Paul.

Latour, B. 1987: *Science in Action: How to Follow Scientists and Engineers through Society*. Milton Keynes: Open University Press.

Latour, B. 1988: 'The Prince for Machines as well as for Machinations', in Elliott, B. (ed.), *Technology and Social Process*. Edinburgh: Edinburgh University Press.

Latour, B. 1993: *We Have Never Been Modern*. Hemel Hempstead: Harvester Wheatsheaf.

Law, J. (ed.), 1986: *Power, Action and Belief*. London: Routledge and Kegan Paul.

Law, J. (ed.), 1991: *A Sociology of Monsters: Essays on Power, Technology and Domination*. London: Routledge.

Lazonick, W. 1993: *Business Organization and the Myth of the Market Economy*. Cambridge: Cambridge University Press.

Lee, C. 1991: 'Followership: the Essence of Leadership', *Training*, January, pp. 27–35.

Lee, C.H. 1990: 'Corporate Behaviour in Theory and History, I: The Evolution of Theory', *Business History*, vol. XXXI, pp. 17–31.

Lee, R. and Lawrence, P. 1985: *Organizational Behaviour: Politics at Work*. London: Hutchinson.

Lenin, V.I. 1971: *State and Revolution*. New York: International Publishers.

Lester, J. 1968: *To Be a Slave*. London: Penguin.

Levi, P. 1987: *If This is a Man*. London: Abacus.

Levinson, H. 1987: 'How They Rate the Boss', *Across the Board*, vol. 24, no. 6, pp. 53–7.

Levi-Strauss, C. 1966: *The Savage Mind*. London: Weidenfeld and Nicolson.

Levitas, R. 1990: *The Concept of Utopia*. Hertford: Simon and Schuster.

Lewchuck, W. 1986: 'The Motor Vehicle Industry', in Elbaum, B. and Lazonick, W. (eds), *The Decline of the British Economy*. Oxford: Clarendon Press.

Lewis, G.R. 1924: *The Stanneries: A Study of the English Tin Miner*. Cambridge, Mass.: Harvard University Press.

Lieberson, S. and O'Connor, J.F. 1972: 'Leadership and Organizational Performance', *American Sociological Review*, vol. 37, pp. 117–30.

Liebenstein, H. 1966: 'Allocative Efficiency Versus X-Inefficiency', *American Economic Review*, vol. 56, pp. 392–415.

Ligus, R.G. 1993: 'Methods to Help Reengineer Your Company for Improved Agility', *Industrial Engineering*, January, pp. 58–9.

Likert, R. 1961: *New Patterns of Management*. New York: McGraw-Hill.

Lilley, S.J. and Platt, G.M. 1994: 'Correspondents' Images of Martin Luther King, Jr: An Interpretive Theory of Movement Leadership', in Sarbin, T.R. and Kitsuse, J.I. (eds), *Constructing the Social*. London: Sage.

Lindblom, C. 1959: 'The Science of Muddling Through', *Public Administration Review*, vol. 19, pp. 79–99.

Lockwood, D. 1982: 'Fatalism: Durkheim's Hidden Theory of Order', in Giddens, A. and Mackenzie, G. (eds), *Social Class and the Division of Labour*. Cambridge: Cambridge University Press.

Long, P. 1986: *Performance Appraisal Revisited*. London: Institute of Personnel Management.

Longenecker, C.O. and Gioia, D.A. 1988: 'Neglected at the Top: Executives

Talk About Executive Appraisal', *Sloan Management Review*, vol. 29, no. 2, pp. 41–8.

Longenecker, C.O. and Gioia, D.A. 1991: 'SMR Forum: Ten Myths of Managing Managers', *Sloan Management Review*, Fall, pp. 81–90.

Lorenz, E.H. 1992: 'Trust and the Flexible Firm: International Comparisons', *Industrial Relations*, vol. 31, no. 3, pp. 455–72.

Luecke, R.A. 1994: *Scuttle Your Ships Before Advancing*. Oxford: Oxford University Press.

Lundin, S.C. and Lancaster, L.G. 1990: 'Beyond Leadership: The Importance of Followership', *The Futurist*, May–June, pp. 18–22.

Lyotard, J.-F. 1984: *The Postmodern Condition*. Manchester: Manchester University Press.

McCabe, D.M. 1988: *Corporate Nonunion Complaint Procedures and Systems: A Strategic Human Resources Management Analysis*. New York: Praeger.

McCabe, D.M. and Lewin, D. 1992: 'Employee Voice: A Human Resource Management Perspective', *California Management Review*, Spring, pp. 112–23.

McCauley, C. 1989: 'The Nature of Social Influence in Groupthink: Compliance and Internalization', *Journal of Personality and Social Psychology*, no. 57, pp. 250–60.

McGregor, D. 1957: 'An Uneasy Look at Performance Appraisal', *Harvard Business Review*, May–June, pp. 89–94. (Reprinted *Training and Development Journal*, June, 1987, pp. 66–9.)

McGrew, A.G. and Wilson, M.J. 1982: *Decision Making: Approaches and Analysis*. Manchester: Manchester University Press.

McKenna, S. 1988: 'Japanization and Recent Developments in Britain', *Employee Relations*, vol. 10, no. 4, pp. 6–11.

McKinlay, A. and Zeitlin, J. 1989: 'The Meaning of Managerial Prerogative: Industrial Relations and the Organization of Work in British Engineering, 1880–1939', *Business History*, vol. XXXI, no. 2, pp. 32–47.

McLoughlin, J. 1992: *Up and Running: Women in Business*. London: Virago.

McNeil, M. (ed.) 1987: *Gender and Expertise*. London: Free Association Books.

Macfarlane, A. 1978: *The Origins of English Individualism*. Oxford: Oxford University Press.

Machiavelli, N. 1975: *The Prince*. Harmondsworth: Penguin.

MacKenzie, D. 1990: *Inventing Accuracy: A Historical Sociology of Missile Guidance*. Cambridge, Mass.: MIT Press.

Macpherson, C.B. 1966: *The Real World of Democracy*. Oxford: Oxford University Press.

Macpherson, C.B. 1977: *The Life and Times of Liberal Democracy*. Oxford: Oxford University Press.

Madison, J. 1966: *The Federalist Papers*. New York: Doubleday.

Maguire, T.M. and Kleiner, B.H. 1993: 'Formal and Informal Organizational

Barriers to Women and How to Overcome Them', *Equal Opportunities International*, vol. 12, no. 5, pp. 22–25.

Maier, N.R.F. 1952: *Principles of Human Relations*. New York: John Wiley.

Maier, N.R.F. 1958: *The Appraisal Interview*. New York: John Wiley.

Malcolmson, R.W. 1981: *Life and Labour in England*. London: Hutchinson.

Malinowski, B. 1921: 'The Primitive Economics of the Trobriand Islanders', *The Economic Journal*, March, pp. 1–16.

Mann, M. 1986: *The Sources of Social Power*. Vol. 1. Cambridge: Cambridge University Press.

Mannheim, K. 1960: *Ideology and Utopia*. London: Routledge and Kegan Paul.

Marcuse, H. 1964: *One Dimensional Man*. Boston, Mass.: Beacon Press.

Marglin, S. 1982: 'What do Bosses Do?', in Giddens, A. and Held, D. (eds), *Classes, Power and Conflict*. London: Macmillan.

Mars, G. 1994: *Cheats at Work*. London: Dartmouth.

Marshall, G. 1982: *In Search of the Spirit of Capitalism*. London: Hutchinson.

Marshall, R. 1993: *Storm from the East: From Genghis Khan to Khubilai Khan*. London: BBC.

Martin, E.H. 1990: *What Did You Do in the Great War, Dad? Recollections of 1914–18 taken from the Notebook of Ernest Harry Martin Sergt. 200708*. Oxford: Oxon Rowley Press.

Marx, K. 1968: *Selected Works in One Volume*. London: Lawrence and Wishart.

Marx, K. 1970: *Capital*. Vol. 1. Harmondsworth: Penguin.

Mass Observation. 1943: *War Factory*. London: Hutchinson.

Mathias, P. 1969: *The First Industrial Nation*. Cambridge: Cambridge University Press.

Mayo, E. 1933: *The Human Problems of an Industrial Civilization*. New York: Macmillan.

Meek, V.L. 1988: 'Organizational Culture, Origins and Weaknesses', *Organization Studies*, Vol. 9, no. 4, pp. 423–37.

Mellor, M., Hannah, J. and Stirling, J. 1988: *Worker Cooperatives in Theory and Practice*. Milton Keynes: Open University Press.

Mendelssohn, K. 1974: *The Riddle of the Pyramids*. London: Thames and Hudson.

Merton, R.K. 1957: *Social Theory and Social Structure*. New York: Free Press.

Metz, E.J. 1988: 'Designing Legally Defensible Performance Appraisal Systems', *Training and Development Journal*, July, pp. 47–51.

Mill, J.S. 1982: *On Liberty*. Harmondsworth: Penguin.

Miller, D. 1984: *Anarchism*. London: Dent.

Mills, A.J. and Tancred, P. (eds) 1992: *Gendering Organizational Analysis*. London: Sage.

Mintzberg, H. 1973: *The Nature of Managerial Work*. New York: Harper and Row.

Mitchell, J. and Parris, H. 1983: *The Politics and Government of Britain*. Milton Keynes: Open University Press.

Mmobuosi, I.B. 1991: 'Followership Behaviour: A Neglected Aspect of Leadership Studies', *Leadership and Organizational Development Journal*, vol. 12, no. 7, pp. 11–16.

Moore, B. Jr. 1966: *Social Origins of Dictatorship and Democracy*. Harmondsworth: Penguin.

Moore, R. 1974: *Pit-men, Preachers and Politics: The Effects of Methodism in a Durham Mining Community*. Cambridge: Cambridge University Press.

Morgan, G. 1986: *Images of Organization*. London: Sage.

Morris, D. and Brandon, J. 1993: *Re-engineering Your Business*. New York: McGraw-Hill.

Morris, W. 1962: *News From Nowhere*, in Briggs, A. (ed.), *William Morris: Selected Writings and Designs*. London: Penguin.

Morris, W. 1983: 'What We Have To Look For', *Guardian*, 18 July.

Morrison, A.M., White, R.P. and Van Velson, E. 1987: *Breaking the Glass Ceiling*. Wokingham: Addison-Wesley.

Morse, D. 1993: *High Victorian Culture*. London: Macmillan.

Morson, G.S. 1981: *The Boundaries of Genre: Dostoevsky's Diary of a Writer and the Traditions of Literary Utopia*. Austin, Tex.: Austin University Press.

Moskos, C. 1990: 'Army Women', *Atlantic Monthly*, August, pp. 81–93.

Mount, M.K. 1983: 'Comparison of Managerial and Employee Satisfaction with a Performance Appraisal System', *Personnel Psychology*, vol. 36, pp. 99–110.

Mount, M.K. 1984: 'Psychometric Properties of Subordinate Ratings of Managerial Performance', *Personnel Psychology*, vol. 37, pp. 687–702.

Mugford, S. and O'Malley, P. 1991: 'Heroin Policy and Deficit Models', *Crime, Law and Social Change*, vol. 15, no. 1, pp. 19–36.

Murphy, K.R. and Anhalt, R.L. 1992: 'Is Halo Error a Property of the Rater, Ratees, or the Specific Behaviours Observed?', *Journal of Applied Psychology*, vol. 77, no. 4, pp. 494–500.

Nibley, H. 1987: 'Management Vs. Leadership', *Executive Excellence*, vol. 4, no. 12, p. 9.

NIESR (National Institute of Economic and Social Research) 1994: *High Level Skills and Industrial Competitiveness*. London: NIESR.

Ninh, B. 1993: *The Sorrow of War*. London: Secker and Warburg.

Noble, D. 1983: 'Present Tense Technology', *Democracy*, Spring, pp. 8–27.

Norman, C.A. and Zawacki, R.A. 1991: 'Team Appraisals - Team Approach', *Personnel Journal*, September, pp. 101–4.

Norris, W.R. and Vecchio, R.P. 1992: 'Situational Leadership Theory: A Replication', *Group and Organization Management*, vol. 17, no. 3, pp. 31–42.

Nostrand, C.H. Van. 1993: *Gender-Responsible Leadership: Detecting Bias, Implementing Interventions*. London: Sage.

Nyland, C. 1987: 'Scientific Planning and Management', *Capital and Class*, no. 33, pp. 55–83.

Obeng, E. and Crainer, S. 1994: *Making Re-engineering Happen*. London: Pitman.

OECD. 1977: *The Development of Industrial Relations Systems: Some Implications of the Japanese Experience*. Paris: OECD.

Olson, M. 1982: *The Rise and Decline of Nations*. New Haven, Conn.: Yale University Press.

Ouchi, W. 1981: *Theory Z - How American Business can Meet the Japanese Challenge*. Reading, Mass.: Addison-Wesley.

Oxfordshire County Council. n.d.: 'Managing the Introduction of Appraisal in Schools'. Oxfordshire County Council publication.

Overholt, W.H. 1993: *China: The Next Economic Superpower*. London: Weidenfeld and Nicolson.

Padulo, R. 1994: 'Reengineering Management Learning'. Templeton College Management Research Paper. Oxford: Templeton College.

Pagnamenta, R. and Overy, R. 1984: *All Our Working Lives*. London: BBC.

Parkin, F. 1979: *Marxism and Class Theory: A Bourgeois Critique*. London: Tavistock.

Pascale, R.T. and Athos, A.G. 1982: *The Art of Japanese Management*. Harmondsworth: Penguin.

Pateman, C. 1970: *Participation and Democratic Theory*. Cambridge: Cambridge University Press.

Pateman, C. 1979: 'Hierarchical Organizations and Democratic Participation: The Problem of Sex'. Paper presented at the conference on 'Non-hierarchical Systems and Conditions for Democratic Participation, Dubrovnik, January.

Pauchant, T.C. 1991: 'Transferential Leadership: Towards a More Complex Understanding of Charisma in Organizations', *Organization Studies*, vol. 12, No. 4, pp. 507–27.

Pawson, D.J. 1992: *Leadership is Male*. London: Highland.

Payne, R. 1991: 'Taking Stock of Corporate Culture', *Personnel Management*, July, pp. 26–9.

Pears, I. 1993: 'The Gentleman and the Hero: Wellington and Napoleon in the Nineteenth Century', in Porter, R. (ed.), *Myths of the English*. Cambridge: Polity Press.

Perkin, H. 1972: *The Origins of Modern English Society 1780–1880*. London: Routledge.

Peter, L. (ed.) 1978: *Quotation for Our Time*. London: Souvenir Press.

Peter, L.J. and Hull, R. 1970: *The Peter Principle*. London: Pan.

Peters, T.J. 1993: *Management Revolution and Corporate Reinvention*. London: BBC.

Peters, T.J. and Waterman, R.H. 1982: *In Search of Excellence: Lessons from America's Best Run Companies*. New York: Harper and Row.

Pettigrew, A. 1973: *The Politics of Organizational Decision-making*. London: Tavistock.

Pfeffer, J. 1977: 'The Ambiguity of Leadership', *Academy of Management Review*, vol. 2, no. 1, pp. 104–12.

Pheysey, D.C. 1993: *Organizational Cultures: Types and Transformations*. London: Routledge.

Pick, D. 1993: *War Machine: The Rationalization of Slaughter in the Modern Age*. London: Yale University Press.

Pinch, T. and Bijker, W.E. 1989: 'The Social Construction of Facts and Artefacts: Or How the Sociology of Science and the Sociology of Technology Might Benefit Each Other', in Bijker, W.E., Hughes, T.P. and Pinch, T. (eds), *The Social Construction of Technological Systems*. Cambridge, Mass.: MIT Press.

Piore, M.J. and Sabel, C. 1984: *The Second Industrial Divide*. New York: Basic Books.

Pipes, R. 1994: *Russia Under the Bolshevik Regime*. London: Harvill.

Plamenatz, J. 1963: *Man and Society*. Vol. 2. London: Longman.

Poggi, G. 1978: *The Development of the Modern State*. London: Hutchinson.

Pollard, S. 1965: *The Genesis of Modern Management*. Harmondsworth: Penguin.

Pollard, S. 1989: *Britain's Prime and Britain's Decline: The British Economy, 1870–1914*. London: Edward Arnold.

Pollitt, C. 1986: 'Democracy and Bureaucracy', in Held, D. and Pollitt, C. (eds), *New Forms of Democracy*. Cambridge: Polity Press.

Ponting, C. 1994: *Churchill*. London: Sinclair-Stevenson.

Porter, B.L. and Parker, W.S. Jr. 1993: 'Culture Change', *Human Resource Management*, Spring and Summer, pp. 46–67.

Porter, R. 1990: *The Enlightenment*. London: Macmillan.

Post Office 1930: *Post Office Records*. London: Post Office.

Prais, S.J. 1981: *Productivity and Industrial Structure*. Cambridge: Cambridge University Press.

Purcell, K. 1990: 'Gender and the Experience of Employment', in Gallie, D. (ed.), *Employment in Britain*. Oxford: Blackwell.

Ramsay, H. 1983: 'Evolution or Cycle? Workers' Participation in the 1970s and 1980s', in Crouch, C. and Heller, F.A. (eds), *International Yearbook of Organizational Democracy*. Chichester: John Wiley.

Randall, A. 1990: 'New Languages or Old? Labour, Capital and Discourse in the Industrial Revolution', *Social History*, vol. 15, no. 2, pp. 195–216.

Randall, A. 1991: *Before the Luddites*. Cambridge: Cambridge University Press.

Randell, G. 1989: 'Employee Appraisal', in Sisson, K. (ed.), *Personnel Management in Britain*. Oxford: Blackwell.

Raven, J. 1989: 'British History and the Enterprise Culture', *Past and Present*, no. 123, pp. 178–204.

Redwood, J. 1993: *The Global Marketplace: Capitalism and its Future*. London: HarperCollins.

Reed, M. 1990: 'The Labour Process Perspective on Management Organization: A Critique and Reformulation', in Hassard, J. and Pym, D. (eds), *The Theory and Philosophy of Organizations*. London: Routledge.

Reed, M. and Anthony, P. 1992: 'Professionalizing Management and Managing Professionalization: British Management in the 1980s', *Journal of Management Studies*, vol. 25, no. 5, pp. 591–613.

Reed, M. and Hughes, M. (eds) 1992: *Rethinking Organization: New Directions in Organization Theory and Analysis*. London: Sage.

Reibstein, L. 1986: 'More Firms Use Peer Review Panels to Solve Employees' Grievances', The Wall Street Journal, 3 December.

Reich, R.B. 1992: *The Work of Nations*. London: Simon and Schuster.

Reich, W. 1972: *The Mass Psychology of Fascism*. London: Souvenir Press.

Reich, W. 1975: *Listen Little Man*. Harmondsworth: Penguin.

Ridley, T.M. 1992: 'Motivating and Rewarding Employees: Some Aspects of Theory and Practice'. ACAS Occasional Paper no. 51. London: ACAS.

Roberts, A. 1994: *Eminent Churchillians*. London: Weidenfeld and Nicolson.

Roberts, M. 1979: 'Sickles and Scythes', *History Workshop Journal*, no. 7, pp. 3–28.

Robertson Smith, W. 1956: *The Religion of the Semites*. New York: Harper and Row.

Robinson, P. 1994: *Snapshots from Hell (The Making of an MBA)*. London: Nicholas Brealey.

Roderick, G. and Stephens, M. (eds) 1981: *Where Did We Go Wrong? Industrial Performance, Education and the Economy in Victorian Britain*. Brighton: Falmer.

Roethlisberger, F.J. and Dickson, W.J. 1947: *Management and the Worker*. Cambridge, Mass.: Harvard University Press.

Rooth, T. 1993: *British Protectionism and the International Economy: Overseas Commercial Policy in the 1930s*. Oxford: Oxford University Press.

Roper, M. 1994: *Masculinity and the British Organization Man*. Oxford: Oxford University Press.

Rorty, R. 1989: *Contingency, Irony and Solidarity*. Cambridge: Cambridge University Press.

Rose, N. 1990: *Governing the Soul*. London: Routledge.

Rosener, J.B. 1990: 'Ways Women Lead', *Harvard Business Review*, November/December, pp. 119–33.

Rothschild, M. 1992: 'How to be a High IQ Company', *Forbes*, 7 December.

Rousseau, J.J. 1968: *The Social Contract*. Harmondsworth: Penguin.

Rowlinson, M. and Hassard, J. 1993: 'The Invention of Corporate Culture: A History of the Histories of Cadbury', *Human Relations*, vol. 46, no. 3, pp. 299–326.

Royal Society for the Arts. 1994: *Tomorrow's Company*. London: RSA.

Rubinstein, W.D. 1993: *Capitalism, Culture, and Decline in Britain 1750–1990*. London: Routledge.

Ruether, R.R. 1992: *Sexism and God-Talk*. London: SCM.

Russ, J. 1975: *The Female Man*. Boston, Mass.: Beacon Press.

Russel, J.S. and Goode, D.L. 1988: 'An Analysis of Managers' Reactions to their Own Performance Appraisal Feedback', *Journal of Applied Psychology*, vol. 73, no. 1, pp. 63–7.

Rustow, D.A. 1970: 'Transitions to Democracy: Towards a Dynamic Model', *Comparative Politics*, no. 2, pp. 337–63.

Sahagún, B. de, 1978: *The War of Conquest*. Salt Lake City: University of Utah Press.

Salaman, G. 1980a: 'Roles and Rules', in Salaman, G. and Thompson, K. (eds), *Control and Ideology in Organizations*. Milton Keynes: Open University Press.

Salaman, G. 1980b: 'Organizations as Constructors of Social Reality', in Salaman, G. and Thompson, K. (eds), *Control and Ideology in Organizations*. Milton Keynes: Open University Press.

Salaman, G. (ed) 1992: *Human Resource Strategies*. London: Sage.

Salamon, M. 1987: *Industrial Relations: Theory and Practice*. London: Prentice Hall.

Salvadori, M. 1979: *Karl Kautsky and the Socialist Revolution 1880–1938*. London: New Left Books.

Sanderson, M. 1972: *The Universities and British Industry, 1850–1970*. London: Routledge and Kegan Paul.

Sanderson, M. 1988: 'Technical Education and Economic Decline: 1890–1980s', *Oxford Review of Economic Policy*, no. 4, pp. 38–50.

Sanderson, M. 1993: *The Missing Stratum: Technical School Education in England 1900-1990*. London: Athlone Press.

Sartre, J.P. 1948: *Existentialism and Humanism*. London: Methuen.

Sathe, V. 1983: 'Implications of Corporate Culture: A Manager's Guide to Action', *Organizational Dynamics*, August, pp. 5–23.

Saussure, F. de 1974: *Course in General Linguistics*. London: Fontana.

Sayles, L. 1964: *Managerial Behaviour*. New York: McGraw-Hill.

Schein, E.H. 1983: 'The Role of the Founder in Creating Organizational Culture', *Organizational Dynamics*, vol. 12, no. 1, pp. 13–28.

Schumpeter, J.A. 1976: *Capitalism, Socialism and Democracy*. London: George Allen and Unwin.

Scott, J.P. 1979: *Corporations, Classes and Capitalism*. London: Hutchinson.

Searle, G.R. 1993: *Entrepreneurial Politics in Mid-Victorian Britain*. Oxford: Clarendon Press.

Searle-Chatterjee, M. 1979: 'The Polluted Identity of Work', in Wallman, S. (ed.), *Social Anthropology of Work*. London: Academic Press.

Sekaran, U. and Kassner, M. 1992: 'University Systems for the 21st Century', in Sekaran, U. and Leong, F. T. (eds), *Womanpower: Managing in Times of Demographic Turbulence*. London: Sage.

Sekaran, U. and Leong, F.T. (eds), 1992: *Womanpower: Managing in Times of Demographic Turbulence*. London: Sage.

Selznick, P. 1957: *Leadership in Administration*. New York: Harper and Row.

Sewell, G. and Wilkinson, B. 1992: 'Surveillance, Discipline and Just-in-time Process', *Sociology*, vol. 26, no. 2, pp. 271–89.

Shields, P.M. 1988: 'Sex Roles in the Military', in Moskos, C. and Wood, F.R. (eds), *The Military: More Than Just a Job?*. Oxford: Pergamon-Brassey.

Shils, E.A. and Janowitz, M. 1948: 'Cohesion and Disintegration: The Wermacht in World War II', *Public Opinion Quarterly*, no. 12, pp. 280–315.

Shiman, L.L. 1992: *Women and Leadership in 19th-Century England*. London: Macmillan.

Shklovsky, V. 1965: 'Art as Technique', in Lemon, L.T. and Reis, M.J. (eds), *Russian Formalist Criticism: Four Essays*. Lincoln, Nebr.: University of Nebraska Press.

Short, J.E. and Venkatraman, N. 1992: 'Beyond Business Process Redesign', *Sloan Management Review*, Fall, pp. 7–21.

Silverstone, R. and Hirsch, E. (eds) 1992: *Consuming Technologies*. London: Routledge.

Simon, H.A. 1947: *Administrative Behaviour*. New York: Macmillan.

Sinclair, R.C. 1988: 'Mood, Categorization Breadth and Performance Appraisal', *Organizational Behaviour and Human Decision Processes*, vol. 42, pp. 22–46.

Sirianni, C. 1982: *Workers' Control and Socialist Democracy: The Soviet Experience*. London: Verso.

Skinner, B.F. 1976: *Walden Two*. New York: Macmillan.

Smail, J. 1987: 'New Languages for Labour and Capital: The Transformation of Discourse in the Early Years of the Industrial Revolution', *Social History*, vol. 12, no. 1, pp. 49–71.

Smail, J. 1991: 'New Languages? Yes Indeed: A Reply to Adrian Randall', *Social History*, vol. 16, no. 2, pp. 217–22.

Smiles, S. 1958: *Self Help*. London: Murray. (First published in 1859).

Smircich, L. 1983: 'Concepts of Culture and Organizational Analysis', *Administrative Science Quarterly*, vol. 28, pp. 339–59.

Smith, A. 1974: *The Wealth of Nations*. Harmondsworth: Penguin.

Smith, L.V. 1994: *Between Mutiny and Obedience: The Case of the French Fifth Infantry Division During World War 1*. Princeton, N.J.: Princeton University Press.

Smith, R.J. 1983: *Japanese Society: Tradition, Self and the Social Order*. Cambridge: Cambridge University Press.

Smither, R.D. 1988: *The Psychology of Work and Human Performance*. New York: Harper and Row.

Sonenscher, M. 1989: *Work and Wages: Natural Law, Politics and the Eighteenth Century French Trades*. Cambridge: Cambridge University Press.

Sorensen, K.H. 1992: 'Towards a Feminized Technology? Gendered Values in the Construction of Technology', *Social Studies of Science*, no. 22, pp. 5–31.

Stahl, M.J. 1983: 'Achievement, Power and Managerial Motivation', *Personnel Psychology*, vol. 36, pp. 775–89.

Stalk, G. Jr. and Webber, A.M. 1993: 'Japan's Dark Side of Time', *Harvard Business Review*, July–August, pp. 93–102.

Stanley, A. 1992: *Mothers of Invention*. Newark, N.J.: Scarecrow Press.

Stanton, M., Hammer, M. and Power, B. 1993: 'Reengineering: Getting Everyone on Board', *I.T. Magazine*, April, pp. 22–7.

Steedman, H., Mason, G. and Wagner, K. 1991: 'Intermediate Skills in the Workplace: Deployment, Standards and Supply in Britain, France and Germany', *National Institute Economic Review*, no. 136, pp. 60–73.

Stewart, R. 1967: *Managers and their Jobs*. Maidenhead: McGraw-Hill.

Stewart, R. 1976: *Contrasts in Management*. Maidenhead: McGraw-Hill.

Stewart, R. 1982: *Choices for the Manager*. Maidenhead: McGraw-Hill.

Stewart, R. 1994: 'Managerial Behaviour'. Templeton College Management Research Paper. Oxford: Templeton College.

Stewart, R., Barsoux, J.L., Ganter, H., Kieser, A. and Walgenbach, P. 1994: *Managing in Britain and Germany*. Basingstoke: Macmillan.

Stogdill, R.M. 1974: *Handbook of Leadership*. New York: Free Press.

Storey, J. 1992: *Developments in the Management of Human Resources*. Oxford: Blackwell.

Stroul, N.A. 1987: 'Whither Performance Appraisal?', *Training and Development Journal*, November, pp. 70–4.

Summers, D. 1993: 'Perceptions of Leadership', *Financial Times*, 26 July.

Sutton, A. 1994: *Slavery in Brazil*. London: Anti-Slavery International.

Suvin, D. 1973: 'Defining the Literary Genre of Utopia', *Studies in Literary Imagination*, vol. 6, no. 2, pp. 121–44.

Suzuki , N. 1989: 'The Attributes of Japanese CEO's : Can They be Trained?', *Journal of Management Development*, vol. 8, no. 4, pp. 5–11.

Swan, W.S. 1991: *How to Do a Superior Performance Appraisal*. New York: John Wiley.

Szymanski, S. 1992: 'Executive Pay and Performance'. Research Seminar Paper presented at Templeton College, Oxford, 12 November.

Takezawa, S. and Whitehill, A.M. 1981: *Work Ways: Japan and America*. Tokyo: Japan Institute of Labour.

Tanaka, T. 1989: 'Developing Managers in the Hitachi Institute of Management Development', *Journal of Management Development*, vol. 8, no. 4, pp. 12–21.

Tanouye, E.T. 1990: 'What is Your Staff Afraid to Tell You?', *Working Woman*, April, pp. 35–8.

Taylor, A.J. 1972: *Laissez Faire and State Intervention in Nineteenth Century Britain*. London: Longman.

Therborn, G. 1977: 'The Rule of Capital and the Rise of Democracy', *New Left Review*, no. 103, pp. 3–41.

Thomas, M.L. 1993: 'Reengineering: The Frantic Discovery of the Obvious', *Information and Image Management*, January, p. 48.

Thompson, E.P. 1961: 'Review of Raymond Williams' *The Long Revolution'*, *New Left Review*, no. 9, pp. 24–33.

Thompson, E.P. 1977: *Whigs and Hunters: The Origin of the Black Act*. Harmondsworth: Penguin.

Thompson, F.M.L. 1990: 'Life after Death: How Successful Nineteenth Century Businessmen Disposed of their Fortunes', *Economic History Review*, vol. XLIII, pp. 40–61.

Thompson, P. and McHugh, D. 1990: *Work Organizations: A Critical Introduction*. London: Macmillan.

Thucydides. 1972: *The Peloponnesian War*. Harmondsworth: Penguin.

Tisdall, S. 1993: 'America Wrestles with its Identity', *Guardian*, 18 September.

Tisdall, S. 1994: 'The Alamo Falls to Revisionists', *Guardian*, 30 March.

Tomb, H. 1991: *Wicked Japanese*. London: Fontana.

Tönnies, F. 1955: *Community and Society: Gemeinschaft und Gesellschaft*. London: Routledge.

Towers, B. (ed.) 1992: *The Handbook of Human Resource Management*. Oxford: Blackwell.

Townley, B. 1990: 'A Discriminating Approach to Appraisal', *Personnel Management*, December, pp. 34–7.

Townley, B. 1991: 'Selection and Appraisal: Reconstituting "Social Relations"?', in Storey, J. (ed.), *New Perspectives on Human Resource Management*. London: Routledge.

Townsend, P.L. and Gebhardt, J.E. 1989: 'What the Military can Teach Business about Leadership', *Executive Excellence*, vol. 6, no. 2, pp. 11–12.

Training and Development 1991: 'Upside-down Performance Appraisal', *Training and Development*, July, pp. 15–22.

Traub, R. 1978: 'Lenin and Taylor: The Fate of "Scientific Management" in the Early Soviet Union', *Telos*, vol. 37, pp. 82–92.

Trist, E.L. and Bamforth, K.W. 1951: 'Some Social and Psychological Consequences of the Longwall Method of Coal Getting', *Human Relations*, vol. 4, no.1, pp. 3–38.

Trotsky, L. 1969: *The Permanent Revolution*. New York: Pathfinder Press.

Veblen, T. 1914: *The Instinct of Workmanship*. New York: Viking Press.

Veblen, T. 1953: *The Theory of the Leisure Class*. New York: Mentor Books.

Ventura, S. and Harvey, E. 1988: 'Peer Review: Trusting Employees', *Management Review*, January, pp. 48–51.

Wajcman, J. 1991: *Feminism Confronts Technology*. Cambridge: Polity Press.

Walby, S. 1986: *Patriarchy at Work*. Cambridge: Polity Press.

Wall, T.D. and Licheron, J.A. 1977: *Workers' Participation*. New York: McGraw-Hill.

Wallerstein, I. 1983: *Historical Capitalism*. London: Verso.

Warner, M. 1994: 'Home: Our Famous Island Race'. Reith Lecture. BBC, 2 March.

Watson, S. 1993: *The Place for Universities in Management Education*. Research Paper in Management Studies, 13. Cambridge: Cambridge University Press.

Weber, M. 1976: *The Protestant Ethic and the Spirit of Capitalism*. London: George Allen and Unwin.

Weber, M. 1978: *Economy and Society*. London: University of California Press.

Webster, F. and Robins, K. 1993: 'I'll be Watching You', *Sociology*, vol. 27, no. 3. pp. 243–52.

Webster, J. 1990: *Office Automation: The Labour Process and Women's Work in Britain*. London: Harvester Wheatsheaf.

Weick, K.E. 1987: 'Organizational Culture as a Source of High Reliability', *California Management Review*, vol. XXIX, no. 2, pp. 112–27.

Wexley, K.N. and Yukl, G.A. 1977: *Organizational Behaviour and Personnel Psychology*. Homewood, IU: Richard D. Irwin.

Wheelwright, J. 1992: 'A Brother in Arms, a Sister in Peace: Contemporary Issues of Gender and Military Technology', in Kirkup, G. and Smith Keller, L. (eds), *Inventing Women*. Cambridge: Polity Press.

Whisler, T.L. and Harper, S.F. (eds.) 1962: *Performance Appraisal: Research and Appraisal*. New York: Holt, Rinehart & Winston.

White, B., Cox, C. and Cooper, C. 1992: *Women's Career Development: A Study of High Flyers*. Oxford: Blackwell.

White, R. and Lippitt, R. 1960: *Autocracy and Democracy*. New York: Harper and Row.

Whitehill, A.M. 1991: *Japanese Management: Tradition and Transition*. London: Routledge.

Whitley, R. 1989: 'On the Nature of Managerial Tasks and Skills', *Journal of Management Studies*, vol. 26, no. 3, pp. 209–24.

Whyte, W.F. 1955: *Street Corner Society*. Chicago: Chicago University Press.

Wiener, M.J. 1981: *English Culture and the Decline of the Industrial Spirit*. Cambridge: Cambridge University Press.

Wilkinson, A., Marchington, M., Goodman, J. and Ackers, P. 1992: 'Total Quality Management and Employee Involvement', *Human Resources Management Journal*, vol. 2, no. 4, pp. 1–20.

Williams, R. 1958: *Culture and Society*, 1780–1950. Harmondsworth: Penguin.

Williamson, O.E. 1975: *The Economic Institutions of Capitalism*. New York: Free Press.

Willis, P. 1977: *Learning to Labour*. Aldershot: Gower.

Willmott, H. 1984: 'Images and Ideals of Managerial Work', *Journal of Management Studies*, no. 24, pp. 249–70.

Willmott, H. 1993: 'Strength is Ignorance; Slavery is Freedom: Managing Culture in Modern Organizations', *Journal of Management Studies*, vol. 30, no. 4, pp. 515–52.

Willner, A.K. 1984: *The Spellbinders: Charismatic Political Leadership*. New Haven, Conn.: Yale University Press.

Wills, G. 1992: *Lincoln at Gettysburg*. London: Simon and Schuster.

Winner, L. 1985: 'Do Artefacts Have Politics?', in Mackenzie, D. and Wajcman,

J. (eds), *The Social Shaping of Technology*. Milton Keynes: Open University Press.

Winner, L. 1993: 'Upon Opening the Black Box and Finding it Empty: Social Constructivism and the Philosophy of Technology', *Science Technology and Human Values*, vol. 18, no. 3, pp. 362–78.

Winter, D. 1979: *Death's Men: Soldiers of the Great War*. Harmondsworth: Penguin.

Winterson, J. 1990: *Sexing the Cherry*. London: Vintage.

Woods, P.F. 1913: *The Influence of Monarchs*. New York: Macmillan.

Woolgar, S. 1981: 'Interests and Explanation in the Social Study of Science', *Social Studies of Science*, no. 11, pp. 365–94.

Woolgar, S. 1988a: *Science: The Very Idea*. London: Routledge.

Woolgar, S. (ed.) 1988b: *Knowledge and Reflexivity: New Frontiers in the Sociology of Knowledge*. London: Sage.

Woolgar, S. 1991: 'Configuring the User: The Case of Usability Trials'. CRICT Discussion Paper no. 21, Brunel University.

Woolgar, S. 1992: 'Who/What is This For? - Utility and Value as Textual Accomplishments'. Paper presented to 4S/EASST conference, Gothenburg, 12–15 August.

Woolgar, S. 1993: 'What's at Stake in the Sociology of Technology?', *Science Technology and Human Values*, vol. 18, no. 4, pp. 523–9.

Woolgar, S. 1994: 'Rethinking Agency: New Moves in Science and Technology Studies', *Mexican Journal of Behavior Analysis*.

Wright, A.W. 1979: *G.D.H. Cole and Socialist Democracy*. Oxford: Clarendon Press.

Wright, T. 1867: *Some Habits and Customs of the Working Classes by a Journeyman Engineer*. London: Tinsley Brothers. (Republished 1967 by Augustus M. Kelly Publishers.)

Wright Mills, C.W. 1970: *The Sociological Imagination*. Harmondsworth: Penguin.

Yoshino, K. 1993: 'Corporate Culture in Teradyne Inc.'. MSc. dissertation, Oxford University.

Yu, C. and Wilkinson, B. 1989: 'Pay and Appraisal in Japanese Companies in Britain'. Japanese Management Research Unit Working Paper, 8. Cardiff Business School.

Yukl, G. 1989: 'Managerial Leadership: A Review of Theory and Research', *Journal of Management*, vol. 15, no. 2, pp. 251–89.

Zedeck, S., Imparato, N., Krausz, M. and Oleno, T. 1974: 'Development of Behaviourally Anchored Rating Scales as a Function of Organizational Level', *Journal of Applied Psychology*, vol. 59, no. 2, pp. 355–70.

Zimmerman, D. 1973: 'The Practicalities of Rule Use', in Salaman, G. and Thompson, K.(eds), *People and Organizations*. London: Longman.

Zinn, H. 1980: *A People's History of the United States*. London: Longman.

Zoonen, L. van 1992: 'Feminist Theory and Information Technology', *Media, Culture and Society*, vol. 14, no. 1, pp. 9–30.

Zuboff, S. 1989: *In the Age of the Smart Machine: The Future of Work and Power*. London: Heinemann.

Index